RESTful .NET

Other Microsoft .NET resources from O'Reilly

RESTful .NET

Jon Flanders

O'REILLY®

Beijing · Cambridge · Farnham · Köln · Sebastopol · Taipei · Tokyo

RESTful .NET
by Jon Flanders

Copyright © 2009 Jon Flanders. All rights reserved.
Printed in the United States of America.

Published by O'Reilly Media, Inc., 1005 Gravenstein Highway North, Sebastopol, CA 95472.

O'Reilly books may be purchased for educational, business, or sales promotional use. Online editions are also available for most titles (*http://safari.oreilly.com*). For more information, contact our corporate/institutional sales department: (800) 998-9938 or *corporate@oreilly.com*.

Editor: John Osborn	**Indexer:** Lucie Haskins
Production Editor: Sumita Mukherji	**Cover Designer:** Karen Montgomery
Copyeditors: Amy Thomson and Audrey Doyle	**Interior Designer:** David Futato
Proofreader: Emily Quill	**Illustrator:** Robert Romano

Printing History:

    November 2008:   First Edition.

ISBN: 978-0-596-51920-9

[M]   [5/10]

1273440445

Table of Contents

Foreword

I'm an RPC guy in my bones. I spent years of my life working with various remote procedure call technologies, so when SOAP came along, it seemed like the obvious next step on this path. To me, web services meant SOAP, period.

Then REST appeared.

When the RESTful approach first hit the scene, I wrote a short article describing it. At the end, I noted SOAP's broad support, then closed with this:

> Still, even though SOAP is already quite well established, the ideas embodied in REST are worth understanding. Web services are still new, and REST makes a remarkably interesting contribution to the technology.

For a SOAP guy in 2002, I thought I was being quite open-minded. The REST fans didn't see it this way. My inbox sizzled with mail telling me that I was stupid for not immediately seeing REST's innate superiority over the pure evil that was SOAP.

My response was to completely ignore REST for the next several years. I didn't write about it, I didn't speak about it, and I wouldn't even take questions on the topic during talks on web services. I was convinced that REST was the religion of a small band of fanatics, and rude ones at that. The common appellation for a REST fan—RESTafarian—seemed very appropriate to me, derived as it was from the name of an actual religion. These people were true believers, and I couldn't share their faith.

Yet REST was too cool to ignore forever. Once you get your mind around the approach (which doesn't take long—it's simple), REST's beauty is evident. More important, REST's utility is also evident. While SOAP and the WS-* protocols still have a significant role, REST is useful in many, many situations. To one degree or another, we're all RESTafarians now.

There's no better evidence of this than Microsoft's embrace of REST in Windows Communication Foundation (WCF). While it's wrong to view this as marking the end of SOAP, WCF's REST support is a big endorsement from what was once the strongest bunch of SOAP advocates. Developers now have a single foundation on which to build all kinds of web services.

But while REST is simple, WCF is not. To really understand and exploit this part of WCF requires a knowledgeable and experienced guide. I don't know anybody who's better suited to this role than Jon Flanders. Along with being one of the smartest people I know, and one of the most capable developers, Jon is first-rate at explaining complicated things.

Even to a long-time RPC guy like me, it's clear that RESTful services will be a big part of the future. This book is the best introduction I've seen to creating and using these services with WCF. If you're a WCF developer looking to enter the RESTful world, this book is for you.

—David Chappell
Chappell & Associates

Preface

I've been working with the Web throughout my entire software engineering career. I started out writing ASP pages and COM components. I then moved into the world of .NET with ASP.NET and ASMX web services.

In 2004, I got involved with BizTalk Server, which pushed me even more into the world of services and XML. I worked with Windows Communication Foundation (WCF) in its early beta stages, before its release in 2007. At that time, the Microsoft world of services was focused on service-oriented architecture (SOA), SOAP, and the WS-* specifications as the preferred methods for building services.

Had I been paying attention, I would have noticed that in 2000 a man named Roy Fielding had written a doctoral dissertation describing the architecture of the Web. By 2000, the Web had arguably become the world's biggest and most scalable distributed application platform. In his dissertation, Fielding examined this platform and distilled from it an architectural style based on the factors that led to its success. He named this architecture REST and suggested it as a way of building not only websites, but also web services.

REST is an architecture that uses the strengths of the Web to build services. It proposes a set of constraints that simplifies development and encourages more scalable designs.

Developers (the majority of whom were outside the Microsoft world) began to adopt this set of architectural constraints shortly after it was proposed (although, to be fair, there were a few inside the Microsoft camp who jumped on the REST technology). Many toolkits embraced REST as the major driver for building applications and services, especially Ruby on Rails, which soared in popularity.

Although WCF isn't tied to SOAP and WS-*, the majority of its programming model was initially geared toward building those kinds of services. The WCF channel model actually did have support for building services using REST, but the WCF programming model lacked explicit support for doing so.

In 2007, a Microsoft program manager named Steve Maine spearheaded an effort to build a REST programming model on top of the WCF infrastructure. This model was released with WCF 3.5 in early 2008.

It was around that time that I read *RESTful Web Services* by Leonard Richardson and Sam Ruby (O'Reilly). After reading and digesting that book, I finally, truly "got it." The "it" that I got wasn't about the technological details, since I understood that part pretty well even before reading the book. The "it" was why people are so enthusiastic about REST. These people are often referred to as RESTafarians, and I now consider myself one of them.

To me, a RESTafarian isn't someone who is religious and argumentative about REST on web forums and blogs (or someone who sends nasty emails to smart people like David Chappell). A RESTafarian is someone who really knows the REST architecture and knows when to apply it in building services. A RESTafarian is someone who understands that using REST's architectural constraints to build services provides a big advantage over RPC-type technology for a large number of systems.

I confess, I am indeed now a RESTafarian. I'll admit it openly and freely. I think using REST should be the first choice when building services, and that RPC should be chosen only if the system requires some particular feature exclusive to RPC technology (like SOAP and WS-*).

After coming to this conclusion, I knew I needed to write this book. I think that all developers deserve to have the tools they need to build highly scalable, loosely coupled services using REST techniques. Hopefully this book will help you learn the ways of REST and how to apply them when developing applications and services using .NET and WCF.

Who This Book Is For

This book is written for .NET developers who are familiar with WCF and REST and who want to learn about using the REST programming model in WCF 3.5.

This book does not teach the fundamentals of WCF. If you aren't familiar with WCF, I highly recommend you read *Learning WCF* by Michele Leroux Bustamante (O'Reilly). Also, while this book does provide some background on REST (in Chapter 1), the book does not focus on the basics of REST. For that, I recommend reading *RESTful Web Services*, followed by Roy Fielding's dissertation, available at *http://www.ics.uci.edu/ ~fielding/pubs/dissertation/top.htm*.

This book is intended to be a companion to both of the books listed above. The samples in this book are all in C#. All of the samples are available on this book's website at *http://www.rest-ful.net/book* in both C# and VB.NET.

How This Book Is Organized

The main chapters of this book are all about WCF 3.5, and the appendixes cover the new features of the WCF 3.5 SP1 upgrade.

Chapter 1, *REST Basics*

Chapter 1 is an introduction to the basic concepts of REST. Again, this book is not intended to be a "learn everything about REST" book. This chapter is a gentle introduction to the concepts of REST. From this chapter you should get the basic ideas of REST, including how resources are identified by unique URIs and how to interact with those resources using the uniform interface of HTTP.

Chapter 2, *WCF RESTful Programming Model*

This chapter introduces the WCF channel and programming models. The purpose of this chapter is to get you oriented in terms of how WCF processes messages and uses those messages to call methods on your services. This chapter should give you a good idea of the plumbing that was added in WCF 3.5 to support this new programming model. It introduces the bindings and hosting infrastructure for building RESTful services as well as the `UriTemplate` class, which is used to map resource URIs onto your methods.

Chapter 3, *Programming Read-Only Services*

`GET` is arguably the most important of the verbs in the HTTP uniform interface. For a high percentage of services, most or all of the functionality is to return read-only data. This chapter will introduce you to the `WebGetAttribute`, which is the mechanism for building resources that return read-only representations.

Chapter 4, *Programming Read/Write Services*

WCF supports the remainder of the uniform interface (`POST`, `PUT`, and `DELETE`) through the `WebInvokeAttribute`. Combined with the `UriTemplate` class, this attribute will enable you to build a complete RESTful service that supports the whole uniform interface.

Chapter 5, *Hosting WCF RESTful Services*

Although this book isn't about WCF in general, one of the key decisions any WCF developer will make is how and where to host services. The RESTful programming model influences that decision, since it is based on HTTP. This chapter will examine special considerations for hosting this type of endpoint.

Chapter 6, *Programming Feeds*

One of the most interesting and exciting features enabled by the RESTful programming model of WCF is the ability to work with feeds. Feeds today are not your father's feeds. Feeds have historically been used (if any technology less than 10 years old can have real history) for publishing web logs (blogs), small technical articles, and the like. Feeds have expanded to include news and other kinds of website data, and are now quickly moving into the Enterprise. Feed readers are built into every modern browser, so they can provide a powerful way to expose corporate data. In this chapter, I'll show you how to build and consume feeds using the WCF feed programming model.

Chapter 7, *Programming Ajax and Silverlight Clients*

Many people see RESTful services as being useful only for exposing data to Ajax-based applications such as mashups, but REST does have reach beyond this type of application. In this chapter, we'll examine WCF 3.5's ability to return data as XML- or JSON-encoded results, as well as the integration between WCF and ASP.NET Ajax.

Chapter 8, *Securing REST Endpoints*

Despite the fact that anti-REST forces often point to a lack of security as a drawback of REST, this is a false argument. RESTful services take advantage of the Web, and the Web has tried-and-true security features.

In this chapter, we'll examine the WCF settings for enabling security and for creating an endpoint that is highly secure.

Chapter 9, *Using Workflow to Deliver REST Services*

Another new piece of functionality in .NET 3.5 is the ability to use Windows Workflow Foundation (WF) workflows to implement and consume services. The RESTful programming model can be used on top of this facility.

This chapter focuses on both stateless and stateful workflow models for implementing RESTful services.

Chapter 10, *Consuming RESTful XML Services Using WCF*

WCF is used as much for building service clients as it is for building services themselves. The same is true of the RESTful programming model. In this chapter, we'll take a RESTful service, SQL Server Data Services (which is a cloud-based storage system), and decompose it into a WCF service contract that can invoke the service through the WCF programming model.

Chapter 11, *Working with HTTP*

Most RESTful implementations use HTTP as the application protocol. In this chapter, I'll talk about how to interact between the WCF programming model and the HTTP request and response messages. Also, we'll look at a couple of slightly more advanced HTTP features and how to use them with your RESTful services in WCF.

Appendix A, *WCF 3.5 SP1*

WCF 3.5 SP1 was released just as this book was being finalized. Appendix A discusses the SP1 improvements and contains a list of new features found in the upgrade, including the new `UriTemplate` syntax and the new support for AtomPub.

Appendix B, *ADO.NET Data Services*

.NET 3.5 SP1 includes ADO.NET Data Services (codename *Astoria*), which provides you with the ability to use a prebuilt WCF service contract to expose a data-backed object model through AtomPub. This appendix shows you how to use ADO.NET Data Services and discusses why you might choose to use it instead of writing your own custom RESTful service endpoints.

Appendix C, *ADO.NET Entity Framework Walkthrough*

ADO.NET Data Services will use any data-backed object model to expose an AtomPub service, but is optimized for use with the ADO.NET Entity Framework (EF). Although EF doesn't have anything to do with RESTful services, I have included this appendix to demonstrate how you can use EF to implement the types of services that are explained in Appendix B.

What You Need to Use This Book

To run the samples provided throughout this book, you need to have Visual Studio 2008 (any version) installed. If you want to work with the code in the appendixes, you will require .NET 3.5 SP1, Visual Studio 2008 SP1, and SQL Server Express or above.

Conventions Used in This Book

The following typographical conventions are used in this book:

Plain text
> Indicates menu titles, menu options, menu buttons, and keyboard accelerators (such as Alt and Ctrl).

Italic
> Indicates new terms, URLs, email addresses, filenames, file extensions, pathnames, directories, and Unix utilities.

`Constant width`
> Indicates commands, options, switches, variables, attributes, keys, functions, types, classes, namespaces, methods, modules, properties, parameters, values, objects, events, event handlers, XML tags, HTML tags, macros, the contents of files, or the output from commands.

`Constant width bold`
> Shows commands or other text that should be typed literally by the user.

`Constant width italic`
> Shows text that should be replaced with user-supplied values.

 This icon signifies a tip, suggestion, or general note.

 This icon indicates a warning or caution.

Using Code Examples

This book is here to help you get your job done. In general, you may use the code in this book in your programs and documentation. You do not need to contact us for permission unless you're reproducing a significant portion of the code. For example, writing a program that uses several chunks of code from this book does not require permission. Selling or distributing a CD-ROM of examples from O'Reilly books *does* require permission. Answering a question by citing this book and quoting example code does not require permission. Incorporating a significant amount of example code from this book into your product's documentation *does* require permission.

We appreciate, but do not require, attribution. An attribution usually includes the title, author, publisher, and ISBN. For example: "*RESTful .NET* by Jon Flanders. Copyright 2009 Jon Flanders, 978-0-596-51920-9."

If you feel your use of code examples falls outside fair use or the permission given above, feel free to contact us at *permissions@oreilly.com*.

How to Contact the Author

Feel free to look at this book's web page at *http://www.rest-ful.net/book*. You can also email me at *jon.flanders@gmail.com*.

Comments and Questions

Please address comments and questions concerning this book to the publisher:

> O'Reilly Media, Inc.
> 1005 Gravenstein Highway North
> Sebastopol, CA 95472
> 800-998-9938 (in the United States or Canada)
> 707-829-0515 (international or local)
> 707-829-0104 (fax)

We have a web page for this book, where we list errata, examples, and any additional information. You can access this page at:

> *http://www.oreilly.com/catalog/9780596519209*

To comment or ask technical questions about this book, send email to:

> *bookquestions@oreilly.com*

For more information about our books, conferences, Resource Centers, and the O'Reilly Network, see our website at:

> *http://www.oreilly.com*

Acknowledgments

There are a number of people I'd like to thank for helping to make this book possible.

I'd like to thank John Osborn, my editor at O'Reilly, for helping me to write this book and, of course, for putting up with the delays.

Thanks to David Chappell for writing an incredible Foreword. David is one of the smartest people I run into in my travels, and is also one of the nicest and most sincere. Thanks David.

I want to thank all of the technical reviewers: Aaron Lerch, Dare Obasanjo, Aaron Skonnard, Drew Miller, Matt Milner, Michele Bustamante, Julia Lerman, Dominick Baier, Sam Gentile, Dave Chappell, Brian Noyes, Steve Resnick, and Matthew Fowle. If you think part of the book is good, the reviewers deserve credit. If there is any part of the book that you don't like, the fault is exclusively my own.

I also want to thank some people at Microsoft: Steven Maine for pushing to get this programming model into WCF, and Don Box for being the person who helped to get my career started.

The people who deserve the most thanks are members of my family. I want to thank my wife Shannon Ahern for enabling me to do the things I love to do, through her love and support (and also for being an incredible technical editor—if there are any spelling or grammar mistakes in this book, they were introduced after her editing pass). I also need to thank our children: Christian, Raiden, Austin, Parker, and Catherine for putting up with long hours of writing, and having to quiet their normal level of enthusiasm to give me an environment in which to work.

CHAPTER 1

REST Basics

Representational State Transfer (REST) is an architectural style first laid out in the dissertation of a man named Roy Fielding at the University of California Irvine, just a few miles from Monterey Park, CA, where I live (not that it matters—it's just a fun fact for me).

REST is a set of constraints based on the architectural style of the World Wide Web. Writing this book in 2008, I don't need to go into much detail about the success of the Web; it is a ubiquitous system for hypermedia and applications built on hypermedia. In this chapter, we'll examine the basics of the REST architecture and its constraints, which are based on resource design and uniform interface interaction. This chapter is an introduction to the concepts of REST, and the remainder of the book will concentrate on applying those concepts to building RESTful services using Windows Communication Foundation (WCF).

Architecture of the World Wide Web

The success of the Web can be attributed in part to luck and timing, but some of the credit for its success can be attributed to its architecture. The architecture of the Web is based on a few fundamental principles that have taken it from its small beginnings to the large mass of information and functionality that exists today. These principles include:

- Addressable resources
- Standard resource formats
- A uniform interface for interacting with those resources
- Statelessness in the interaction between clients and services
- Hyperlinking to enable navigation between resources

Everything on the Web is addressable. Uniform Resource Identifiers (URIs) are used to define the locations of particular resources. Resources can be things like HTML documents, images, or other media types. Addressability is one of the important parts of the Web's success. How easy is it for us to find things on the Web based on partial knowledge of URIs? How many advertisements or commercials have a URI placed prominently for our consumption? The fact that you can take a URI from an advertisement, type it into a browser, and have the browser return the information you wanted is actually pretty amazing.

Part of the power of the Web stems from the fact that the resources on the Web are standard media types. This makes it possible for vendors to build new web browsers (a.k.a. *user agents*) without having to ask any particular company or authority for permission. It means that programs and users can access a web server's resources using any modern operating system and browser. There are certainly some real issues here in terms of the way different browsers interpret resources, but clearly those issues haven't done much to stop the ubiquity of the Web.

Based on HTTP (Hypertext Transfer Protocol), the uniform interface of the Web also plays into this openness and interoperability. HTTP is an open and well-known protocol that defines a standard way for user agents to interact with both resources and the servers that produce the resources. These interactions are based on the verbs (or methods) that accompany each HTTP request.

GET is probably the most commonly used and well-known verb, and its name is descriptive of its effect. A GET for a particular URI returns a copy of the resource that URI represents. One of the most important features of GET requests is that the result of a GET can be cached. Caching GET requests also contributes to the scalability of the Web. Another feature of GET requests is that they are considered safe, because according to the HTTP specification, GET should not cause any side effects—that is, GET should never cause a change to a resource. Certainly, a resource might change between two GET requests, but that should be an independent action on the part of the service.

 Some site maintainers fail on this part of the uniform interface and use GET requests from a user agent to change a resource. These are incorrect implementations, and those individuals should have their web programming licenses revoked.

POST, which indicates a request to create a new resource, is probably the next most commonly used verb, and there are a whole host of others that we will examine later in this chapter and throughout this book.

HTTP and the Web were designed to be *stateless*. A stateless service is one that can process an incoming request based solely on the request itself. The concept of per-client state on the server isn't part of the design of HTTP or the Web.

Session State

Vendors have attempted to implement state management techniques on top of the Web. In a typical scenario, a user's browser stores a small piece of data known as a *cookie*. The data contained in the cookie is presented to the server on each subsequent request. Using server-side session management techniques, information contained in the cookie or a unique URI can be mapped to a set of name-value pairs on the server and thus associated with a particular user agent.

If the cookie contains all of the required state information, its usage can be considered RESTful since the request itself still contains all the information the server requires to process it (it doesn't require an external store or server-side data structure).

Some implementations attempt to maintain stateful sessions for the scalability of an application. The architectural constraints of the Web are goals to strive for, and sometimes there are good reasons to use techniques that conflict with these constraints. Per-client sessions are useful because they greatly simplify the programming model for building websites or web services, but when you adopt them you are limiting your ability to scale your application.

If a request from a particular user agent contains all of the state necessary to retrieve (or create) a resource, that request can be handled by any server in a farm of servers, thus creating a scalable, robust environment.

Statelessness also improves visibility into web applications. If a request contains everything needed for the server to make a proper reply, the request also contains all the data needed to track and report on that request. There is no need to go to some data source with some key and try to recreate the data that was used as part of a request in order to determine what went right, or what went wrong (this wouldn't be ideal anyway, since that data may have changed in the meantime). Statelessness increases a web application's manageability because the entire state of each request is contained in the request itself.

Hyperlinking between resources is also an important part of the Web's success. The fact that one resource can link to another, enabling the user agent (often through its human driver, but sometimes not) to navigate between related resources, makes the Web interconnected in a very significant way.

The Web is the world's largest, most scalable, and most interoperable distributed application. The success of the Web and the scalability of its architecture have led many people to want to build applications or services on top of it.

SOAP

Many individuals and organizations have tried to build on the success and scalability of the Web by describing architectures and creating toolkits for building services. Services are endpoints that can be consumed programmatically rather than by a person sitting at a computer driving an application like a web browser. The two main approaches used in these attempts have been either the SOAP protocol or the architectural style of REST.

 While a chapter on the subtle differences between protocols such as REST and POX (Plain Old XML over HTTP) might make for an interesting read, this chapter is more specifically focused on the architectural differences between REST and its main competitor, SOAP.

SOAP, which at one point in its history stood for Simple Object Access Protocol (before its acronym status was revoked in the 1.2 version of its specification), is what many developers think of when they hear the term *web service*. SOAP was born out of a coordinated attempt by many large vendors to create a standard around a programmatic Web.

In many ways, SOAP doesn't follow the architecture of the Web at all. Although there are bindings for using SOAP over HTTP, many aspects of SOAP are at odds with the architecture of the Web.

Rather than focusing on URIs (which is the way of the Web), SOAP focuses on *actions*, which are essentially a thin veneer over a method call (although of course a SOAP client can't assume a one-to-one relation between an action and a method call). In this and many other ways, SOAP is an interoperable cross-platform remote procedure call (RPC) system. SOAP-based services almost always have only one URI and many different actions. In some ways, actions are like the HTTP uniform interface, except that every single SOAP service creates new actions; this is about as un-uniform and variable as you can get.

When used over HTTP, SOAP limits itself to one part of the Web's uniform interface: POST. This creates a limitation because results, even those that are read-only, can't be safely cached. In many SOAP services, most actions should really use GET as the verb because they simply return read-only data. Because SOAP doesn't use GET, SOAP results cannot be cached because the infrastructure of the Web only supports caching responses to GET requests. To be honest, you can't really call a SOAP-based service a *web* service since SOAP intentionally ignores much of the architecture of the Web. The term "SOAP service" is probably a more accurate description.

When confronted with the fact that SOAP doesn't follow the architecture of the Web, SOAP proponents will often point out that SOAP was designed to be used over many different protocols, not just HTTP. Because it is meant to be generic and used over many different protocols, SOAP can't take advantage of many of the Web's features since many of those features are particular to HTTP.

REST

REST is an architectural style for building services. This style is based on the architecture of the Web, a fact that creates a fairly sharp contrast between REST and SOAP. While SOAP goes out of its way to make itself protocol-independent, REST embraces the Web and HTTP. Although it's certainly possible to use some or all of the principles of REST over other protocols, many of its benefits are greatest when used over HTTP.

Another significant contrast is that SOAP isn't an architectural style at all. SOAP is a specification that sets out the technical details on how two endpoints can interact in terms of the message representation, and it doesn't offer any architectural guidance or constraints. In contrast, REST services are built to follow the specific constraints of the REST architectural style.

> Services that follow this style are known as *RESTful*. Note that these architectural constraints are more what you'd call "guidelines" than actual rules. Some services will use all of these constraints, and some will use only some of the constraints.
>
> In their book *RESTful Web Services* (O'Reilly), Leonard Richardson and Sam Ruby lay out something they call the Resource Oriented Architecture (ROA), which is a stricter set of rules for determining whether a service is really RESTful.

While SOAP services are based on a service-specific set of actions and a single URI, RESTful services model the interaction with user agents based on resources. Each resource is represented by a unique URI, and the user agent uses the uniform interface of HTTP to interact with a resource via that URI. Put another way, REST services are more concerned with nouns (e.g., resources) than verbs (e.g., HTTP methods or SOAP actions) since the design of a service is about the URIs rather than a custom interface.

Resources and URIs

The first thing to do when designing a RESTful service is to determine which resources you are going to expose. A *resource* is any information that you want to make available to others, such as:

- All the movies playing in or near your zip code
- The current price of a particular stock
- All the photos Jon took on June 1, 2008
- A list of all the products your company sells

As you can see, some resources are static, like pictures taken on a particular day in the past, and some resources are dynamic, like the movies playing in or near a particular zip code. Many resources are dynamic in nature, so having an addressable set of resources for your service doesn't mean that you know all the particular resource instances when you sit down to design your service. A resource is a conceptual mapping to a particular entity or entity set that you want your service to be able to work with.

When designing a RESTful service, you will identify the resources that your service will expose and use. Once you've identified the resources you'll map them to URIs.

URI design

One of the things I like most about RESTful services is the fact that all resources are uniquely identified by a URI. The capability to retrieve a resource via a unique address is one of the big reasons the Web has been so successful.

Additionally, the use of RESTful services builds on our existing experience in using the Web. Nothing is more satisfying than using a website that has nicely designed URIs (yes, websites can be as RESTful as web services can). The utility of well-designed URIs is fairly self-evident. You can appreciate this if, like me, you have "hacked" a URI on a website to find a particular resource, even if the page you started with had no hyperlink to that resource.

An excellent example of a website that employs this resource-URI association is Flickr (*http://www.flickr.com*). Flickr allows you to store, view, and share photos on the Web. Here are a few of the resources that Flickr exposes for me:

- All Jon's photos
- All Jon's photos from a particular date
- All Jon's photos in a named set
- All Jon's photos with a particular tag

Here are the corresponding URIs for those resources:

- *http://www.flickr.com/photos/jonflanders*
- *http://www.flickr.com/photos/jonflanders/archives/date-posted/2008/06/05/*
- *http://www.flickr.com/photos/jonflanders/sets/72157605450493091/*
- *http://www.flickr.com/photos/jonflanders/tags/rest/*

I think these are pretty good URIs (although I'd prefer it if I could put in the name of a set rather than using Flickr's identifier for a named set). This URI design allows me to find easily whichever resources (photos) I want to see. For example, if I wanted to see all of my photos taken on January 1, 2008, I would request the resource at *http://www.flickr.com/photos/jonflanders/archives/date-taken/2008/06/05/*.

I mention Flickr in a book ostensibly about services, even though Flickr is a website, to emphasize two points. First, good URI design is important, as it can greatly increase the usability of a website (and therefore a RESTful service as well). Second, our human experience in using the Web can help us in designing and using RESTful services, which is one of the points in my "Why REST matters to me" list.

 The ironic thing about Flickr's very RESTful URI design is that its programmatic API (which Flickr claims is based on REST) isn't very RESTful at all from a URI point of view.

Flickr uses a design that is often referred to as a REST-RPC hybrid because it uses GET even when it modifies a resource. Flickr doesn't rely on the uniform interface to define interactions with resources; it basically adds an action to the Query string of GET requests.

The idea behind REST is to design your URIs in a way that makes logical sense based on your resource set. The URIs should, if possible, make sense to any user looking at them. If they make sense to a user looking at the URIs, they will make sense to the program that consumes the URIs programmatically. When designing the associations between resources and URIs, it may be useful to map them as if you were designing a browsable website. Even if the URIs will never be entered into a browser, this type of mapping will be useful for the person or persons writing the code to consume your service. Human-readable URIs are not strictly required for a service to be considered RESTful; they are just generally helpful when testing and debugging.

Uniform Interface

In REST, resources are identified by a unique URI. This is one of the constraints of the REST architectural style. Another constraint limits how a user agent interacts with your resources. User agents only interact with resources using the prescribed HTTP verbs. The main verbs are what we call the uniform interface. The verb that is used in a request to a particular URI indicates to the service what the user agent would like to do. When using the REST architectural style we do not make up our own verbs, we use the verbs prescribed by the HTTP standard.

The four main verbs of the uniform interface are GET, POST, PUT, and DELETE. Recall that GET is the verb that tells the service that the user agent wishes to get a read-only representation of a resource. DELETE indicates that a client wishes to delete a resource. POST indicates the desire to create a new resource. PUT is typically used for modifying an existing resource. If, however, the user agent has the knowledge to specify the URI for the new resource, PUT is used for resource creation. See Figure 1-1.

What is the advantage of the uniform interface of REST over any other service creation architecture? Why is it a useful constraint?

One reason that the uniform interface is so useful is that it frees us from having to create a new interface every time a new service is created. Creating an interface for a service endpoint is the equivalent of creating a new API, and can be hard work. Even when the

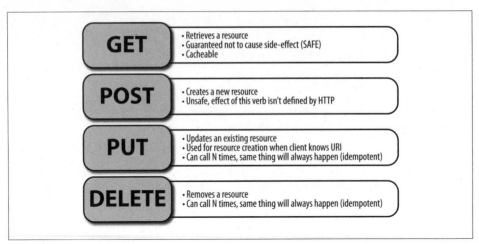

Figure 1-1. Uniform interface

API has limited scope, it can be hard work. Whole books and research papers are written on the correct approach to creating a reusable API. Doing it properly is not a trivial exercise.

On a related note, when consuming REST-based services, you don't have to learn a new API every time you want to use a new service. Instead, you have to determine the URIs and the format of the resources (more on this later in this chapter), as well as which parts of the uniform interface the URIs will allow you to use. In some ways, once you learn how to build and use one RESTful service, you've learned how to build and use them all.

Another benefit of the uniform interface is the comfort you can take from the fact that GET is always safe, and the knowledge that the rest of the uniform interface's verbs other than POST are idempotent.

 Idempotent means that the effect of doing something more than once will be the same as the effect of doing it only once.

You can call GET on a service or resource as many times as you want with no side effects. You can update a resource over and over with no ill effects. Deleting a resource that has already been deleted is a no-op. The only unsafe verb continues to be POST, and because the effect of POST is undefined by the HTTP specification, you'll need to decide when implementing a service what the exact effect of POST should be (see Chapter 4 for more information about writing read/write services with REST).

POST is unsafe because there aren't any rules about what will happen when you do a POST. The service can really do anything when a POST request comes in, and the resource could be radically changed.

As well as being safe, GET also allows caching (see Chapter 11 for more information about caching and its benefits). In order to scale, a service has to be able to cache, and SOAP services, no matter what you do with them, cannot be safely cached, even when the action is one that is essentially read-only. This is because SOAP always uses POST, which can't be cached at any level.

Another important point about the uniform interface is that not every single resource has to implement the entire uniform interface. In fact, in many cases the only part of the uniform interface you'll implement on a resource is GET. If a resource already exists, and will not be created, modified, or deleted by the user agent, the only job of the RESTful service will be to return that resource in response to a GET request.

Hopefully you're beginning to see the architectural constraints of REST to take shape. The constraints comprise a checklist for building a RESTful service. First, you decide what your resources are. Then you map those resources to URIs. For each of those URIs you determine which media type, or representation, you are going to accept and return.

Resource Representations

REST has no architectural constraints on physical representations of resources. This makes sense considering the varied needs of applications and users on the Web. A RESTful service's resource type is technically known as its *media type*. The media type is always returned in an HTTP response as one of the HTTP headers (Content-Type).

The media type for your resources is variable, but there are a few pretty popular and commonly used ones.

XML

XML is probably the most popular format for representation of resources. It's a well-known format, and there are libraries for processing XML on every mainstream platform. The formal media type for XML is application/xml (it used to be text/xml, but that media type has been deprecated).

When choosing XML as your data format, one of the things you'll decide is whether to use a custom XML schema or one of the XML formats that has been standardized across applications.

RSS/Atom

Feeds are a popular beast on the Web today; they are usually associated with what are called *feed readers*, and with a particular kind of web application known as a *web log* (or just blog for short). Blogs (and other types of data exposed as feeds) syndicate (broadcast) their data, and feed readers consume that syndicated data.

The two XML schemas that are used for feed syndication are Really Simple Syndication (RSS) and the Atom Syndication Format. Atom is the more recent standard and seems to be winning the hearts and minds of most developers and companies. It is accompanied by the Atom Publishing Protocol (commonly known as APP or AtomPub), which is more than just a format specification, but is an additional set of constraints built on top of REST architecture. AtomPub dictates the media types for a service, as well as the required uniform interface implementation for content publishing. AtomPub has grown to be used in many different applications besides classic content publishing like blogs.

See Chapter 6 for more information about feeds, and Chapter 11 for an example of the usage of Atom in a nonBlog blog scenario.

The media type for RSS is application/rss+xml. Atom's is application/atom+xml.

XHTML

Extensible Hypertext Markup Language (XHTML) is an HTML media type that is also valid XML. HTML is the media type (text/html) that has driven the human-readable Web for many years. HTML can be challenging to parse if you've ever tried it, since the rules about tags, closing tags, attributes, and so on are all very loose. XML, on the other hand, has a very strict set of format requirements. XHTML (application/xhtml +xml) is the merger of HTML and XML. It is primarily intended for display by a browser, but is easily parsed by an XML library. It is also fairly commonly used in programmatically accessible services. Some services are written to return XHTML to both browser and programmatic user agents.

JSON

JavaScript Object Notation (JSON) is a media type (application/json) that is a text-based resource format for representing programmatic data types. It's a very simple and basic network data representation for objects.

Although often associated with the JavaScript language, JSON is actually used as a media type in many different programming languages and environments.

One of JSON's selling points is its ease of use from JavaScript and Ajax-type browser-based applications. Another selling point is the size of the representation over the network. As a media type, XML tends to be much larger than the compact, terse format of JSON. Many services now return JSON exclusively, regardless of the media type requested by the user agent, even when the user agent isn't an AJAX application in the browser. Chapter 7 covers more about JSON as a media type.

Other media types

The four media types discussed in this section are not exhaustive. There are many other media types such as binary media types and images. When building a RESTful service, you have great latitude to choose your media type based on the particular application you are building. If you aren't sure about which media type to use, try viewing some *microformats* at *http://www.microformats.org/*. Microformats are standardized media types based on common usage and behaviors. The nice thing about choosing a microformat as your media type is that it will be more well known than an XML schema that you create on your own, since tools and libraries may already exist to aid you in working with those formats.

Implementing a Simple RESTful Service Example

To help you understand the concepts introduced in this chapter, let's walk through an example that employs the basic steps of designing a RESTful service. For this example, we will use an easy-to-understand domain: a membership system that stores information about its users.

Resources

This user system will expose the following set of resources:

- All users
- A particular user delineated by the user's unique identifier

This is a fairly simple set of resources, but it actually turns out that many real-life services include only a handful of resources. Of course, because a resource is a conceptual entity, there will likely be near infinite URIs based on those resources.

URIs and Uniform Interface

For our example service, I'm going to start with the relative segments of the URIs, and I'm going to use a simple template syntax (curly braces {}) to indicate parts of the URI that will be replaced by context-specific variables (such as user ID). Table 1-1 contains a listing of the different URIs and the parts of the uniform interface we will implement for each URI.

Table 1-1. User service example URIs

URI	Method	Description	Output	Input
/users/	GET	Returns a representation of all users in the system	users collection	n/a
/users	POST	Creates a new user in the system, expects a representation of the user in the HTTP body	user	user (without the user_id specified)
/users/{user_id}	GET	Returns the representation of a particular user, based on the user's identifier in the system	user	n/a
/users/{user_id}	PUT	Modifies a user resource	user	user
/users/{user_id}	DELETE	Deletes a user from the system	user	user

This service has a small surface area, but you can see that it implements all the parts of the uniform interface for the user resource.

PUT or POST for Creation?

Note that in our example, the URI for creating a user is different from the URI for getting a user. In this case, the URI for creating the user acts as a factory because it represents all users.

Whether you use the same or different URIs for creating and getting resources will depend partially on the design of your system. If our example service allowed the users of the service to specify the identifier for a new user, the URI for PUT and GET would be the same (*/user/{user_id}*). For resource creation the user agent would use PUT instead of POST because that is the expected RESTful semantic when the user knows the URI of the new resource.

In our example, we do not allow the user agent to determine the identifier for a user. Rather, we will create that identifier ourselves (perhaps it's an identity column in my database table that represents users) and return it as part of the response. For this reason, we will stick with POST for resource creation.

Representations

If we were working with a hierarchy or linked data for the users, XHTML would be a good choice for resource representation, since it would allow us to link to related data. However, our example domain will not contain these types of links, so we will use a simpler custom XML format.

Notice that I'm using the term *custom XML format* instead of *custom XML schema*. XML schemas are another media type altogether. They are XML documents that provide constraints on the format of other XML media type instances. XML schemas are very important in the SOAP world; you might say they are essential, but they are optional in a RESTful service. If you want to create XML schemas for your representations

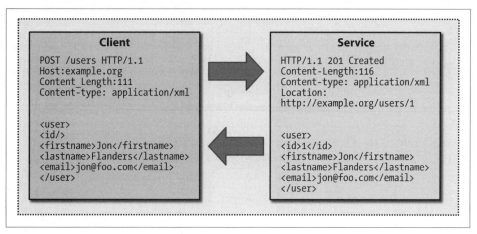

Figure 1-2. Using POST to create a resource

and provide them to your consuming user agents, that's fine. Nothing in the set of REST architectural constraints mandates it or forbids it.

Having metadata like XML schemas and Web Service Description Language (WSDL) is one of the features of SOAP services that people find very useful. The lack of such metadata in RESTful services is somewhat troubling to people who come from that world. In Chapter 9 we'll examine the options for building up the client's API for consuming a service that doesn't expose a schema.

Interaction

Now that we have the basis for our RESTful service example, let's examine the interaction that will occur between the user agent and the service.

If the service is deployed at the host example.com (*http://example.com*), the first interaction (assuming there are no users yet) will be a POST to the */users* URI to create a new user (see Figure 1-2).

The user agent will send an HTTP request using POST to the */users* URI, passing in the media type, as well as the resource it wishes to create as the HTTP request body. Assuming there are no error conditions, the service will return a 201 Created status code. It's convention for a service to return the newly created resource as the response to a POST. The service can also return a Location header, which specifies the URI of the new resource. A user agent can make a GET request to the */users* URI to get a list of all the resources available, which at this point will be one. This is shown in Figure 1-3.

Since we can GET all the users, we should also be able to GET a specific user. A GET request to the URI that represents user 1 will simply be a GET request to */users/1* (see Figure 1-4).

The last two parts of the uniform interface that this service implements are PUT and DELETE. Figure 1-5 shows a PUT request and Figure 1-6 shows DELETE.

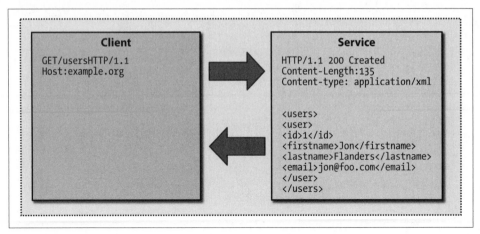

Figure 1-3. GET to /users

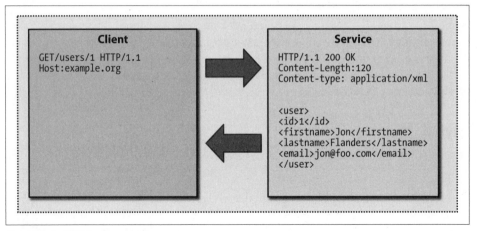

Figure 1-4. GET for a particular user

Wrap-Up

One of the things I really enjoy about REST as an architecture is the exercise I just went through. When designing a RESTful service, first determine the resources that the service will expose. Next, determine how you will map those resources to URIs, and decide which part of the uniform interface each URI should implement. Finally, choose the resource format.

This set of steps follows the architectural constraints of REST, and can help you determine what the service should look like (URIs) and how it should behave (the uniform interface). The verbs are preset, so you can concentrate solely on the nouns (resources), and you don't have to create a new API for every service. SOAP, on the other hand,

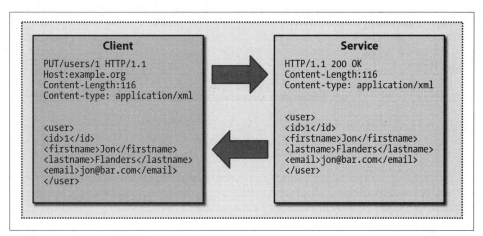

Figure 1-5. Changing a resource using PUT

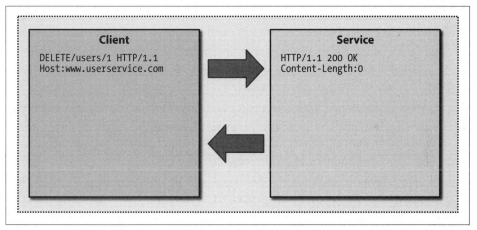

Figure 1-6. Removing a resource using DELETE

provides no real guidelines for what a service should look like or do. Each of the actions are created out of nothing with no real guidance for what they should be. REST builds on knowledge that you already have about URIs, and tells you exactly what each of those URIs can potentially do by restricting you to the uniform interface. This is one of the design constraints of REST, and, if I can interject a little personal opinion into this chapter, it's one that I enjoy.

Admittedly, there is still data variability in RESTful services, since REST does not impose constraints on resource media types. However, this lack of data constraints is outweighed by the great utility of the REST interface and addressing constraints.

Another benefit of using REST constraints is that it becomes easier to use with each service that you build. Once you learn REST, you can easily identify which parts of the architectural constraints are being used on a service, which makes it increasingly easy to determine which constraints you should use in the future.

Processes

One criticism some people have about REST is its lack of support for the concept of a *processing* endpoint that models a particular process. Services can sometimes expose functionality that either doesn't seem to fit well within the concept of a resource or doesn't seem to fit well within the semantics of the uniform interface. For example, consider a service that is designed to implement bank transfers from one account to another. Clearly, you can create each account as a separate resource and use the uniform interface to specify the operations that users can perform on each account. But what resource represents a transfer between two accounts?

This is really a matter of having the right point of view. If you view this type of operation as a function, it will not fall neatly into the REST model. You can, however, treat it as a temporary resource.

 In a typical distributed system, this type of operation would generally be wrapped in a transaction. Of course, REST doesn't use the concept of transactions, but you could also represent transactions as resources.

This idea doesn't resonate with some people, even when all the other parts of REST as an architecture do. This is a design decision you may encounter and be faced with. It also may be that you never will run into this kind of decision, or that you are completely happy with the idea of a transaction as a resource.

Some people look at this problem and decide to stick with SOAP services. Others look at it and decide simply to overload on POST. And others try to push REST and the concept of resources to their fullest, and will model everything as resources (even processes).

Summary

This chapter discussed the basics of creating RESTful services and using REST as an architecture. There are some core tenets of REST that you'll want to keep with you as you read through the book.

First, REST uses the same tenets for building services as the Web. Resources are named entities that we'd like to interact with. Resources are addressable using URIs. The interaction between our code and those URIs is done using the uniform interface. The constraints of the REST architectural style are simple, elegant, and easy to remember, and are the foundations with which arguably the world's largest, most scalable distributed application was built.

REST employs architectural constraints for building services, and you are free to use as many or as few of the constraints as you like (although, if you only use a few, you may have to argue with purists if you want to advertise your service as RESTful).

CHAPTER 2

WCF RESTful Programming Model

In Chapter 1, I introduced the concepts fundamental to using REST to build services. WCF in .NET 3.5 includes a sophisticated built-in mechanism that allows you, a .NET developer, to build RESTful services using the WCF programming model.

Isn't WCF All About SOAP?

You might be thinking, "Isn't WCF all about SOAP?" While you will probably find many people who think WCF is only used for building SOAP-based services (and many who think WCF is only for building RPC-styled SOAP-based services), it turns out that WCF is much broader than either of those communication styles. WCF is really a highly extensible framework with a common programming model and a totally pluggable communication infrastructure.

To illustrate the high-level extensibility of WCF, let's look at some technical details on particular pieces of WCF's plumbing. Although most of the time you won't be working at this low level, looking at this code will help your understanding of REST and WCF.

Channels and Dispatching

So what does WCF do, from a server-side perspective? The basic job of the WCF runtime is to listen for (or retrieve) messages from a network location, process those messages, and pass them to your code so that your code can implement the functionality of a service (Figure 2-1).

> WCF's client-side programming model is symmetrical to that on the server side, but the processing of messages is in the opposite direction. Chapter 10 discusses the WCF programming model from the client perspective.

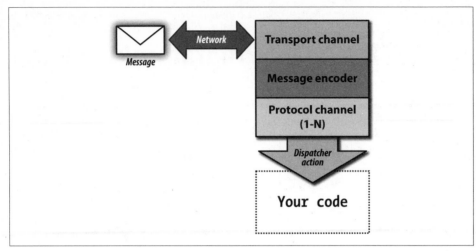

Figure 2-1. The WCF server-side stack

The transport channel

When you open a WCF server-side endpoint, WCF uses a *channel listener* to create a network listener called the *transport channel* to accept network traffic or use a network protocol to retrieve messages. When WCF is accepting messages (for example, when listening on a socket), it is acting as a *passive listener*. When WCF is looking for messages (for example, when using the MSMQ—Microsoft Message Queuing—protocol to connect to a named queue to retrieve messages), it is acting as an *active listener*. Regardless of listening style, the job of listening for messages is performed by what WCF refers to as a transport channel. Common transport channels include HTTP and MSMQ. In the case of the server side, the transport channel is created by a channel listener. The channel listener is a factory pattern object that is responsible for setting up the server-side listening infrastructure.

The message encoder

Next is the *message encoder*, which takes a network message and wraps it in an object that the rest of the WCF infrastructure can understand. This object is an instance of `System.ServiceModel.Channels.Message`. Although `Message` is modeled somewhat after a SOAP message pattern, with a header and a body, it isn't necessarily tied to the SOAP protocol.

The `Message` object can be used to deserialize a message into a .NET object or retrieve it as XML (even if the underlying message is not formatted as XML). One important property of `Message` is `Version`. When this property is set to `MessageVersion.None`, the object will ignore the `Headers` property (in fact, an exception is raised if the `Headers` property is used when `Version` is set to `MessageVersion.None`).

Another interesting property is `Properties`. This is a collection that can contain arbitrary objects, so it acts like a per-instance state bag. Interesting data can be placed into this collection, and other components up and down the stack can then communicate information indirectly through data on the message itself.

Protocol channels

Optional objects follow the message encoder. WCF refers to these objects as *channels*, and to disambiguate them from transport channels, they are called *protocol channels*. Protocol channels implement protocols that might be useful for a particular service, such as security or reliable-messaging protocols. These objects are optional, but in certain services may be helpful or even required to implement a particular style of architecture.

The dispatcher

The dispatching layer is responsible for invoking the proper methods on incoming message objects. First, the `IDispatchOperationSelector` object determines which method is appropriate. Next, a pluggable component implements `IDispatchMessageFormatter` to deserialize the `Message` object into the proper .NET type. Finally, the `IOperationInvoker` object actually invokes the service.

Together, the transport channel, message encoder, protocol channels, and dispatcher are called the *channel stack*. WCF uses *bindings* to create the stack. A binding is really a piece of configuration, although it can be represented in memory as an object or serialized into an application configuration file. Based on the configuration of your service, through both attributes and another type of configuration called a *behavior*, WCF constructs the dispatching layer.

The infrastructure that creates the channel stack is not reliant on any particular programming model or communication mechanism. In other words, WCF is a pluggable pipeline-like architecture for creating channels of communication.

Using this programming model, WCF supports a wide variety of communication mechanisms. Suppose, for example, that you want the implementation to listen for SOAP-formatted messages over HTTP at a particular URI and then route those messages based on the SOAP action header's name. To do this, you can use either the `WsHttpBinding` or `BasicHttpBinding` objects, which derive from the binding base class and provide SOAP-based communication over HTTP.

If you use the default dispatch layer configuration, the `IDispatchOperationSelector` looks at the incoming `Message` object for the SOAP action header and then uses .NET metadata to match the action header value to the name of a .NET method (this could be an exact match or could be customized using the `OperationContractAttribute`). The dispatch layer then uses this information to deserialize the message into the accepted .NET types, and the `IOperationInvoker` actually invokes the correct object.

The name of the default implementation is `OperationSelector`, which might indicate that there is only one, but this is actually just one potential implementation.

Although many of the WCF defaults in the dispatch layer lean toward a SOAP model, the channel stack has no real notion of anything "SOAP-y" in the least. It's only some of the WS-* protocols and WCF out-of-the-box (OOTB) bindings and objects that are aware of the SOAP protocol.

Given my assertion that WCF isn't tied to SOAP, what would it take to create a RESTful-based service using WCF? Not a whole lot, actually, since WCF has an HTTP listener (in the form of the HTTP transport channel), which isn't tied to POST (i.e., it can handle other HTTP verbs). It also has a message encoder that understands XML messages, even when those messages aren't based on SOAP. Putting both of those pieces together gives us the basic building blocks for doing RESTful services with WCF.

 You might be wondering about other incoming HTTP message body formats like form or JSON-encoded bodies—we'll deal with those in later chapters.

HTTP Programming with WCF 3.0

It turns out that the facility to use REST existed in WCF even before .NET 3.5. (For clarity, I'll refer to the version that shipped with .NET 3.0 as WCF 3.0, and the version that ships with .NET 3.5 as WCF 3.5.) WCF 3.0 actually has the infrastructure for doing RESTful-style programming, but it lacks any sort of standard RESTful programming model. Most of the remainder of this book will focus on the WCF programming model rather than on the communication infrastructure. In this section we'll spend some time on the communication layer to illustrate a few key points. First, WCF isn't tied to SOAP, even in WCF 3.0. Second, the communication infrastructure of WCF was written well enough to support different communication styles without modification in WCF 3.5. WCF 3.5 adds a programming model for REST that we could build without Microsoft's help if we were so inclined.

It is possible to use WCF 3.0 to put together an HTTP endpoint that doesn't use SOAP. To do this, we first require a binding to create the correct channel stack. However, WCF 3.0 doesn't include any OOTB bindings that fit the bill (they all default to using SOAP), so we will have to create a custom binding using a `CustomBinding` object and adding the correct `BindingElements`. These `BindingElements` will be used to build the channels in the channel stack.

 We could also build a class that derives from the binding base class, which would be the right thing to do if we were going to reuse this binding in more than one project.

For this binding we will need, at minimum, a message encoder and a transport channel. These two objects are the only required elements for a channel stack. For most RESTful services, that's all we'll ever need in the channel stack—there are very few situations in which we would want to use other protocol channels. The `BindingElements` have to be added to the binding in the reverse order that they will be used, so we add the `TextMessageEncodingBindingElement` first, followed by `HttpTransportBindingElement` (which specifies the use of the HTTP transport in the channel stack). Example 2-1 shows the code that creates the custom binding (as always, this could instead be part of a configuration file).

Example 2-1. Creating a custom binding

```
CustomBinding b = new CustomBinding();
TextMessageEncodingBindingElement msgEncoder;
msgEncoder = new TextMessageEncodingBindingElement();
msgEncoder.MessageVersion = MessageVersion.None;
b.Elements.Add(msgEncoder);
HttpTransportBindingElement http;
http = new HttpTransportBindingElement();
b.Elements.Add(http);
```

Note that this code changes the `MessageVersion` property to `MessageVersion.None`. This instructs the `TextMessageEncoder` not to look for anything "SOAP-y," although it still will only process incoming messages that are formatted as XML (since this is what the `TextMessageEncoder` is programmed to do).

Next, we must construct an endpoint. A WCF endpoint has three parts: an address, a binding, and a contract. The binding dictates the look of the channel stack and determines how the endpoint will communicate. The address is the URI at which the endpoint will listen, and the contract contains information about the type that WCF will use to route messages. In WCF, the contract will be a .NET type with the `ServiceContractAttribute`, and this type can be either an interface or a .NET class. In this case I am specifying a .NET class as the contract.

The next step is to host the endpoint so that WCF will create a channel listener to start the channel stack. In most cases, the class named `ServiceHost` will carry out this part (see Chapter 5 for more information about hosting WCF endpoints).

After creating the `ServiceHost` instance, add a `ServiceEndpoint` using the `CustomBinding`, an HTTP-based URI as the address, and a type named `SimpleHTTPService` as the contract. This code also uses `Console.ReadLine` as the mechanism to keep the process alive while requests are being processed. We can create a console application to host my WCF endpoint. Example 2-2 shows the `Main` method from my console application.

Example 2-2. SimpleHTTPService using WCF

```
static void Main(string[] args)
{
CustomBinding b = new CustomBinding();
TextMessageEncodingBindingElement msgEncoder;
msgEncoder = new TextMessageEncodingBindingElement();
msgEncoder.MessageVersion = MessageVersion.None;
b.Elements.Add(msgEncoder);
HttpTransportBindingElement http;
http = new HttpTransportBindingElement();
b.Elements.Add(http);
ServiceHost sh = new ServiceHost(typeof(SimpleHTTPService));
ServiceEndpoint se = null;
se = sh.AddServiceEndpoint(typeof(SimpleHTTPService),
    b,
    "http://localhost:8889/TestHttp");
sh.Open();
Console.WriteLine("Simple HTTP Service Listening");
Console.WriteLine("Press enter to stop service");
Console.ReadLine();
}
```

This code may lead you to wonder what `SimpleHTTPService` looks like. `SimpleHTTPService` is a class that includes one method (this is typically referred to in WCF terminology as a *universal operation*). Instead of having regular .NET types as input and output parameters to the method, we are using `System.ServiceModel.Channels.Message`.

Using `Message` means that the WCF dispatch layer doesn't have to deserialize the incoming message into specific .NET types. Adding the `OperationContractAttribute` and setting its `Action` property equal to * and the `ReplyAction` property equal to * indicates that all messages, regardless of action, will be routed to this method. Admittedly, having to use SOAP header information is kind of non-RESTful, since we are annotating the class with SOAP-based attributes, but the values of these properties actually short-circuit any SOAP-based routing. Example 2-3 shows the code for the `SimpleHTTPService`.

Example 2-3. SimpleHTTPService implementation

```
[ServiceContract]
public class SimpleHTTPService
{
[OperationContract(Action = "*", ReplyAction = "*")]
Message AllURIs(Message msg)
{
    HttpRequestMessageProperty httpProps;
    string propName;
    propName = HttpRequestMessageProperty.Name;
    httpProps = msg.Properties[propName] as HttpRequestMessageProperty;
    string uri;
    uri = msg.Headers.To.AbsolutePath;
    Console.WriteLine("Request to {0}", uri);
```

```
if (httpProps.Method != "GET")
{
    Console.WriteLine("Incoming Message {0} with method of {1}",
        msg.GetReaderAtBodyContents().ReadOuterXml(),
        httpProps.Method);
}
else
{
    Console.WriteLine("GET Request - no message Body");
}
//print the query string if any
if (httpProps.QueryString != null)
    Console.WriteLine("QueryString = {0}", httpProps.QueryString);
Message response = Message.CreateMessage(
    MessageVersion.None,
    "*",
    "Simple response string");
HttpResponseMessageProperty responseProp;
responseProp = new HttpResponseMessageProperty();
responseProp.Headers.Add("CustomHeader", "Value");
return response;
}
```

Figure 2-2 shows the results of testing the client (which is just a browser in this case) and the output from the service in the console application.

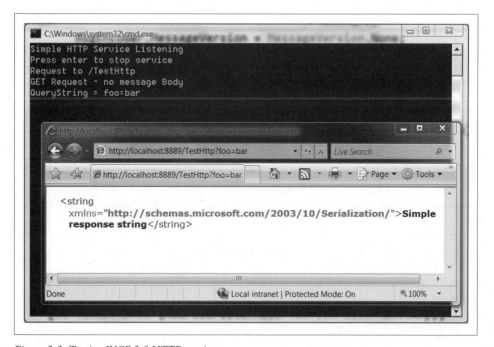

Figure 2-2. Testing WCF 3.0 HTTP service

Due to the structure of WCF 3.0, the endpoint created here will route all incoming network requests to the single method. While it would be possible to use .NET 3.0 to automatically dispatch different network messages to different methods without using SOAP (since the default dispatching is based on the concept of Action), it requires adding a fair amount of custom code into the WCF channel stack and dispatching layer. This is one of the things included in WCF 3.5, which we'll examine in a moment.

There is something else to note about the code in the body of the AllURIs method in the earlier code sample. Notice how I am asking the Message object for a property from its Properties collection. The property is an instance of the HttpRequestMessageProperty type, which is a property populated by the HTTP transport channel. As you can see from the code, this property has all the information about the current HTTP request, including the Method and the incoming HTTP headers. Message properties are indexed by name, so the static Name property of the HttpRequestMessageProperty is used to find the property inside of the Message (of course my code is assuming the binding being used has the HTTP transport channel in use and that the property will always be there). If I wasn't using Message as the parameter type I could access the property via the OperationContext.Current.IncomingMessage Properties collection. Example 2-4 is the full definition of the HttpRequestMessageProperty.

Example 2-4. HttpRequestMessageProperty definition

```
namespace System.ServiceModel.Channels
{
    public sealed class HttpRequestMessageProperty
    {

        public WebHeaderCollection Headers { get; }
        public string Method { get; set; }
        public static string Name { get; }
        public string QueryString { get; set; }
        public bool SuppressEntityBody { get; set; }
    }
}
```

The code at the end of the AllURIs method in Example 2-2 creates an HttpResponseMessageProperty object, which is the corollary object to the HttpRequestMessageProperty object. The HTTP transport channel will use this property to set parts of the HTTP response. The code creates and sets the value of a custom HTTP header. Example 2-5 includes the full definition of the HttpResponseMessageProperty.

Example 2-5. HttpResponseMessageProperty definition

```
namespace System.ServiceModel.Channels
{
    public sealed class HttpResponseMessageProperty
    {
        public static string Name { get; }
        public HttpStatusCode StatusCode { get; set; }
```

```
        public string StatusDescription { get; set; }
        public bool SuppressEntityBody { get; set; }
    }
}
```

`HttpWebRequestMessageProperty` and `HttpWebResponseMessageProperty` are important tools when using WCF for HTTP, and since RESTful services use HTTP, we'll find them helpful there as well. You'll see these properties being used throughout this book to enhance our RESTful services.

So, what insight into WCF does the code in Examples 2-1 and 2-2 provide? Mainly, that WCF is not just about SOAP, and that WCF has included most of the facilities to support RESTful services since the beginning. What was lacking in 3.0 was an explicit programming model for REST.

Web Programming in WCF 3.5

With the introduction of WCF 3.5, the WCF channel stack and dispatching layer look like the drawing in Figure 2-3.

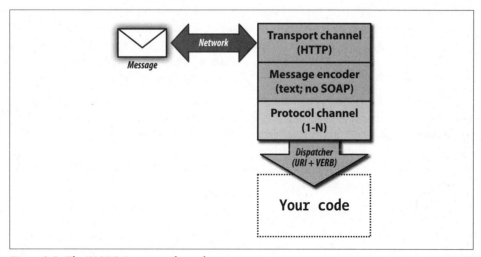

Figure 2-3. The WCF 3.5 server-side stack

The WCF 3.5 web programming model provides features that build on the 3.0 model to make RESTful programming possible with WCF without adding a significant amount of custom code. These are contained in the *System.ServiceModel.Web.dll* assembly, which is new for WCF 3.5. Here is a list of the features that make it easier to build RESTful services:

`WebHttpBinding`
    An OOTB binding that uses the HTTP transport and text message encoder (with its `MessageVersion` set to `None`). This is something that could be done in 3.0 with a

`CustomBinding`, as shown in the previous section. Having an OOTB binding is definitely a timesaver.

WebBehavior

This is an endpoint behavior that will modify the dispatch layer on all operations on a contract. The modifications cause messages to be dispatched to methods on your service based on URIs and HTTP verbs (rather than the default, which is to dispatch based on the SOAP action header).

WebServiceHost

This is a `ServiceHost`-derived class that simplifies the configuration of a web-based service. Also included is a `WebServiceHostFactory` for IIS/WAS hosting scenarios (hosting is discussed in more detail in Chapter 5).

WebOperationContext

This is a new context object, which contains the state of the incoming request and outgoing response, and simplifies coding against HTTP using WCF.

WebGetAttribute *and* WebInvokeAttribute

Two new operation behaviors that are applied as attributes on a `ServiceContract`'s methods that already are operations because they have the `OperationContractAttribute` applied. On each method, using these attributes declares which part of the uniform interface (`GET`, `POST`, `PUT`, and `DELETE`) the CLR method should implement. `WebGetAttribute` is for `GET` and `WebInvokeAttribute` is for all the other parts of the uniform interface. It also tells the dispatcher how to match the methods to URIs, and also how to parse the URI into method parameters.

You can see this set of objects applied in Figure 2-3. The code shown in my next example reimplements the WCF 3.0 HTTP-based service from Example 2-2 using WCF 3.5. Example 2-6 shows the `Main` method of the Console Application host, after adding a reference to *System.ServiceModel.Web.dll* and adding a `using` statement to the code file for `System.ServiceModel.Web`.

Example 2-6. WCF 3.5 version of Main

```
static void Main(string[] args)
{
    WebHttpBinding binding;
    binding = new WebHttpBinding();
    WebServiceHost sh;
    sh = new WebServiceHost(typeof(SimpleHTTPService));
    sh.AddServiceEndpoint(typeof(SimpleHTTPService),
        binding,
        "http://localhost:8889/TestHttp");
    sh.Open();
    Console.WriteLine("Simple HTTP Service Listening");
    Console.WriteLine("Press enter to stop service");
    Console.ReadLine();

}
```

This code contains considerably fewer lines than the WCF 3.0 version shown in Example 2-2. Instead of having to create a `CustomBinding`, this code uses the `WebHttpBinding`, which uses the HTTP transport, as well as a text encoder with its `MessageVersion` set to `MessageVersion.None`.

This code also uses the new `WebServiceHost` class. The `WebServiceHost` API is exactly the same as the standard `ServiceHost` class based on how you program against it, as it still requires `AddServiceEndpoint` (or the configuration file) for all the endpoints it will host. But when the code calls `WebServiceHost.Open`, some behind-the-scenes magic happens (well not really magic, but stuff happens automatically). `WebServiceHost` overrides the `ServiceHostBase.OnOpening` method, loops through all the endpoints, and adds a special new behavior to each endpoint. This behavior, named `WebHttpBehavior`, modifies the WCF dispatching layer to route messages to methods on your service based solely on the URI. It adds the `WebHttpBehavior` to all endpoints of the service, so use `WebServiceHost` only when hosting RESTful endpoints. If the service contains any non-RESTful endpoints, use `ServiceHost` and add the `WebHttpBehavior` manually to only the endpoints that require it.

Example 2-7 shows the WCF 3.5 version of my service.

Example 2-7. WCF 3.5 SimpleHTTPService implementation

```
[ServiceContract]
public class SimpleHTTPService
{

    [OperationContract()]
    [WebGet(UriTemplate="*")]
    Message AllURIs(Message msg)
    {
        WebOperationContext webCtx;
        webCtx = WebOperationContext.Current;
        IncomingWebRequestContext incomingCtx;
        incomingCtx = webCtx.IncomingRequest;
        string uri;
        uri = incomingCtx.UriTemplateMatch.RequestUri.ToString();
        Console.WriteLine("Request to {0}", uri);
        if (incomingCtx.Method != "GET")
        {
            Console.WriteLine("Incoming Message {0} with method of {1}",
                msg.GetReaderAtBodyContents().ReadOuterXml(),
                incomingCtx.Method);
        }
        else
        {
            Console.WriteLine("GET Request - no message Body");
        }
        NameValueCollection query;
        query = incomingCtx.UriTemplateMatch.QueryParameters;
        //print the query string if any
        string queryName;
        if (query.Count != 0)
```

```
{
    Console.WriteLine("QueryString:");
    var enumQ = query.GetEnumerator();
    while(enumQ.MoveNext())
    {
        queryName = enumQ.Current.ToString();
        Console.WriteLine("{0} = {1}", queryName, query[queryName]);
    }
}
Message response = Message.CreateMessage(
    MessageVersion.None,
    "*",
    "Simple response string");
OutgoingWebResponseContext outCtx;
outCtx = webCtx.OutgoingResponse;
outCtx.Headers.Add("CustomHeader", "Value");
return response;
    }
}
```

One big difference between the 3.0 and 3.5 versions of this code is that the `Operation
ContractAttribute` on the CLR method doesn't have to use * as the values for the
`Action` and `ReplyAction` properties, since the new dispatch layer doesn't `Action` for
routing at all. In the 3.5 version, the dispatching is based on the URIs and the HTTP
verbs rather than the SOAP action header value. WCF will ignore all of the SOAP-
specific properties when `WebHttpBinding` is used.

WebHttpBinding

The `WebHttpBinding` class is a new OOTB binding in WCF 3.5, designed to be the
binding for RESTful WCF endpoints.

The binding is pretty simple, and is very much like the `CustomBinding` used in my WCF
3.0 example earlier in the chapter (Example 2-1). `WebHttpBinding` contains a binding
element that creates the HTTP (or HTTPS) WCF transport channel to listen for or send
messages over HTTP(S). It also contains a message-encoder binding element that sets
the channel stack's encoder to `TextMessageEncoder`, with the `Version` set to
`MessageVersion.None` (no SOAP expected).

In some cases, you may still have to create a `CustomBinding`, but the `WebHttpBinding` type
will suffice the majority of the time.

WebHttpBehavior

`WebHttpBehavior` is one of the key pieces of the WCF 3.5 programming model. The job
of the `WebHttpBehavior` is to modify the WCF dispatching layer to use RESTful-based
context to route messages to the CLR methods of the service object, and to modify the
serialization layer to use the correct objects to deserialize requests and serialize
responses.

Although the `WebHttpBehavior` itself can't be customized, it is influenced by other settings, mostly the new attributes for `OperationContractAttribute` methods, which I'll discuss in a moment.

The code shown in Example 2-3 does not explicitly use the `WebHttpBehavior` type; rather, the `WebServiceHost` added it automatically.

WebServiceHost

`WebServiceHost` is a new class in WCF 3.5 that derives from the `ServiceHost` class. Recall that `ServiceHost` is the piece of the WCF infrastructure that starts channel listeners for each endpoint.

`WebServiceHost` is similar in functionality to `ServiceHost`, but it simplifies the configuration of its endpoints by assuming the `WebHttpBinding` and automatically applying the `WebHttpBehavior` to all the endpoints. `WebServiceHost` can also auto-configure endpoints in cases where the service type (the type that is passed to its constructor) only has one contract. Chapter 5 goes into much more detail on `WebServiceHost`.

WebOperationContext

In terms of programming against the HTTP API in WCF, the implementation of the `AllURIs` method remains fairly unchanged between the WCF 3.0 and WCF 3.5 versions. However, in WCF 3.5, you can use the `WebOperationContext` object inside the method body to interrogate the incoming request, instead of having to rely on information from both `OperationContext` and the HTTP message properties (`HttpRequestMessageProperty` and `HttpResponseMessageProperty`). `WebOperationContext` attaches itself to the `OperationContext` using `IExtension<OperationContext>`. IExtension of *t* is used to attach one object to another as an extension.

As an extension of `OperationContext`, `WebOperationContext` wraps the `HttpRequestMessageProperty` and `HttpResponseMessageProperty` with other, more explicitly typed properties that simplify programming against commonly used HTTP constructs. Chapter 11 includes more information about programming against these constructs.

`WebOperationContext` has four properties, each of which represents a different part of an HTTP request/response message exchange sequence. Example 2-8 is the full definition of `WebOperationContext`.

Example 2-8. WebOperationContext definition

```
namespace System.ServiceModel.Web
{
    public class WebOperationContext : IExtension<OperationContext>
    {
        public static WebOperationContext Current { get; }
        public IncomingWebRequestContext IncomingRequest { get; }
```

```
        public IncomingWebResponseContext IncomingResponse { get; }
        public OutgoingWebRequestContext OutgoingRequest { get; }
        public OutgoingWebResponseContext OutgoingResponse { get; }

    }
}
```

The static `Current` property will retrieve the correct `WebOperationContext` instance for the currently executing request. The remaining properties represent the four potential call points in an incoming or outgoing HTTP request. `IncomingRequest` and `Outgoing` `Response` are server-side properties for introspecting and modifying HTTP properties. `OutgoingRequest` or `IncomingResponse` are responsible for setting the properties on the HTTP request or looking at the HTTP response on the client side. See Chapter 11 for more information about these important context objects.

Another simplification provided by WCF 3.5 is that `WebOperationContext` parses the `QueryString`. While you can view this data in WCF 3.0 using the `OperationContext`, you must write the code to parse those parameters. In WCF 3.5, you can use the `QueryParameters` collection on the `IncomingRequest` property to view the data in a more easily readable format. Additionally, you can use the `OutgoingResponse` property to set a custom HTTP header on the response, instead of having to create and set the `HttpResponseMessageProperty`.

WebGetAttribute

Also note that I added a new attribute to the method on the service in Example 2-7: `WebGetAttribute`. The new dispatch layer will use this attribute to determine which method to call for a particular incoming request.

If you don't customize `WebGetAttribute`, the URI of the service (since there is only one method at this point) will be *http://localhost:8889/TestHttp/AllURIs*. By default, WCF 3.5 uses the CLR method name as part of the URI. This is true for both `WebGetAttribute` and `WebInvokeAttribute`.

If you want the resource URI model of your RESTful service to follow the constraints and guidelines of REST, you should customize the URI. If you use the default URIs, you can end up with two URIs for a single resource if you want to use more than one verb from the uniform interface. Having two URIs for a single resource would violate one of the most important constraints of REST. Also, if you stick with the default URI the CLR method names in the URIs become more like custom verbs again, instead of the noun-based approach we want to use with REST.

WCF 3.5 allows you to customize the URI for each CLR method. You can do this by customizing the `UriTemplate` property, which is a property on both `WebGetAttribute` and `WebInvokeAttribute`.

WebGetAttribute and WebInvokeAttribute annotate service operations (methods that include the OperationContractAttribute). These attributes form the base of the new dispatching model built into 3.5.

WebInvokeAttribute includes all of the same properties that WebGetAttribute has, but it also includes a Method property. WebGetAttribute is pretty obviously about which part of the uniform interface it implements: GET. The Method property indicates which verb (other than GET of course) the associated method will implement from the uniform interface. If the Method property isn't set, the default is POST. Table 2-1 shows the properties of both WebGetAttribute and WebInvokeAttribute.

Table 2-1. WebGetAttribute and WebInvokeAttribute properties

Property name	Type	Default value	Description
BodyStyle	WebMessage BodyStyle	Bare	Specifies whether the request and the response data should be wrapped in an element with the same name as the CLR method name. Bare is typically used with RESTful services.
ResponseFormat	WebMessage Format	Xml	Specifies the format for serializing the response.
RequestFormat	WebMessage Format	Xml	Specifies the format for deserializing the request.
UriTemplate	string	null (assumed to be the name of the CLR method)	The definition of the URI the CLR method should respond to.
Method	string	null (assumed to be POST if null)	The HTTP verb the method should respond to (again this property is not on WebGetAttribute).

The UriTemplate property on WebGetAttribute is a simple string, but is arguably the most important property in the whole WCF web programming model. The string is going to be parsed into a type (also named UriTemplate) during the creation of the endpoint. This type is used at runtime to route messages to methods based on matching the template to the requested URI.

UriTemplate

It makes sense to take a moment to look at the UriTemplate class in detail. It is important to get a good idea of its mechanics and how you can use it to your advantage when designing your services.

Note that UriTemplate is in the System namespace even though the class is contained in the *System.ServiceModel.Web.dll* assembly.

`UriTemplate` enables you to make a template out of part of a URI by declaring a pattern-matching syntax. When passed a URI, the `UriTemplate` class parses the URI and determines if its pattern matches the URI. If the pattern matches, `UriTemplate` parses the matched parts into a data structure, indexed by order and possibly indexed by name (depending on the type of template used). This is a little bit like regular expression matching of a string, and although it's not quite as powerful as regular expressions, it doesn't really have to be. Let's start out with a URI example.

Imagine we had a web service that served up data about the biological taxonomy (e.g., Domain, Kingdom, Phylum, etc.). The URIs of this service should be:

> *http://example.org/Domain/Kingdom/Phylum/Class/Order/Family/Genus/Species*

Users could specify any level of this hierarchy and get the data appropriate for that level. Some valid URIs would be:

- *http://example.org/*
- *http://example.org/Eukaryote/Animalia*
- *http://example.org/Eukaryote/Animalia/Chordata*
- *http://example.org/Eukaryote/Animalia/Chordata/Mammalia/Carnivora/Canidae/
  Canis/C.%20lupus*
- *http://example.org/Eukaryote/Animalis/Chordata/Felidae/Felis/F%20silvestris*

The idea is to have each of these URIs return the appropriate data when an HTTP `GET` request is made to my service (we'll discuss the data format later in the chapter; for now we'll focus on the URIs). The service should return data that is appropriate for the specified hierarchy level. So, for example, if a user makes a request for the root, the service will return data about all the Domains (Archaea, Eubacteria, and Eukaryota), and if a user requests *http://example.org/Eukaryote*, the service will return data only about the organisms in the Eukaryote domain.

I'm going to use the following template string to make this URI scheme work with `UriTemplate`:

```
"/{Domain}/{Kingdom}/{Phylum}/{Class}/{Order}/{Family}/
{Genus}/{Species}"
```

Notice that the whole URI is not included in the template—only the path after the scheme, host, and port portion of the URI. The `UriTemplate` infrastructure assumes that part of your complete URI can and will probably change (as it would typically when you moved from dev to test to production as each environment would have a different host name). The curly braces between each level of hierarchy of the URI are the `UriTemplate` syntax. This syntax enables the `UriTemplate` to parse a particular URI for a match and, if a match is found, to bind the parts of the URI into a collection of variables.

UriTemplate also includes wildcard capabilities. UriTemplate="*" (used in Example 2-7) will route all URIs to one method. The wildcard character can also be used at the end of a URI to allow a catch-all method for an unknown number of URI path segments (e.g., UriTemplate="/{Domain}/*"). The wildcard (*) must be either the only string or the last string in the UriTemplate—additional path segments aren't allowed after a wildcard.

Example 2-9 shows some of the code from a console application that attempts to match URIs based on UriTemplate.

Example 2-9. Exercising UriTemplate

```
Uri baseUri = new Uri("http://example.org");
UriTemplate template = new UriTemplate("/{Domain}/{Kingdom}/
{Phylum}/{Class}/{Order}/{Family}/{Genus}/{Species}");
Console.WriteLine("URI path segments are:");
foreach (var pathSeg in template.PathSegmentVariableNames)
{
    Console.WriteLine(pathSeg);
}
Console.WriteLine("type in a URI to test");
string uri = Console.ReadLine();
Uri testUri = new Uri(uri);
UriTemplateMatch match = template.Match(baseUri, testUri);
if (match != null)
{
    var bound = match.BoundVariables;
    string keyValue;

    foreach (var key in bound.Keys)
    {
        keyValue = key.ToString();
        Console.WriteLine("{0} = {1}", keyValue, bound[keyValue]);
    }
}
else
    Console.WriteLine("URI not a match");
```

The output of running this application is shown in Figure 2-4.

The code in Example 2-9 is pretty simple. It creates a UriTemplate instance, then prints all the path segments to the console. UriTemplate uses **path segment** internally for each part of the URI that is denoted by the curly braces ({}). The program will then receive input from the console and turn that input into a URI. Finally, the code will attempt to match the URI against the UriTemplate that was set with the hierarchy we are trying to parse.

Figure 2-5 shows the results of passing in the URI *http://example.org/Eukaryote/Animalia/Chordata/Actinopterygii/Siluriformes/Malapteruridae/Malapterurus/minjiriya.*

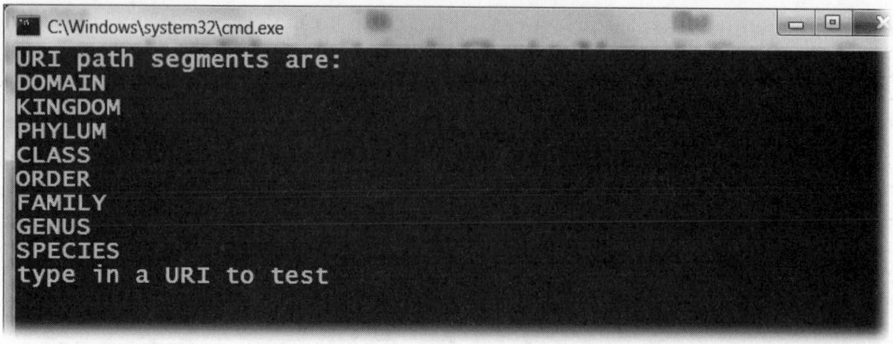

Figure 2-4. *UriTemplate testing output based on Example 2-9*

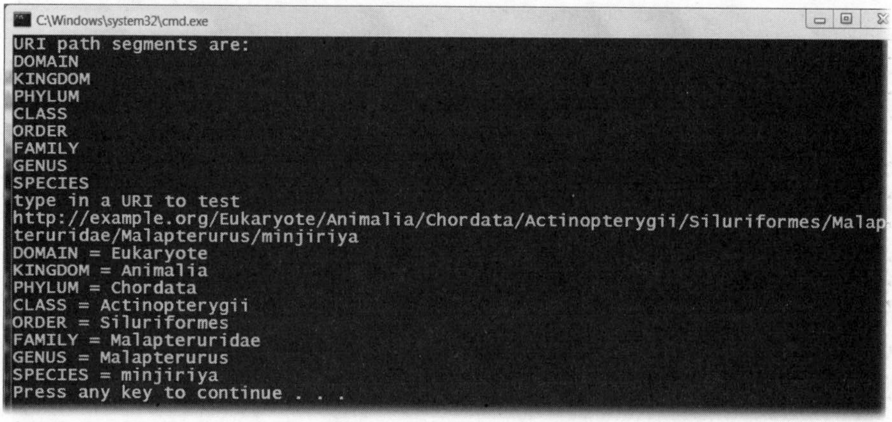

Figure 2-5. *UriTemplate testing full URI*

When I type a string into a console and press Enter, the code takes the string and turns it into an URI. It then uses `UriTemplate.Match` to determine whether the URI matches the template definition. If there is a match, the returned `UriTemplateMatch` object can be used to inspect the results of the match, which would allow the code to use the matched path segment values. This program loops through the `UriTemplateMatch.Bound Variables` collection, which contains all the data that has been bound to each path segment. Table 2-2 shows the complete list of `UriTemplateMatch` properties.

> In Chapter 10, when we talk about using WCF to invoke RESTful services, I'll show you how to turn `UriTemplate` around the other way—to get a full URI from a template by passing in the bound variables.

Table 2-2. UriTemplateMatch properties

Property	Type	Description
BaseUri	Uri	Contains the base URI passed to UriTemplate.Match
BoundVariables	NameValueCollection	A collection of name/value pairs, where the names are the path segments from the UriTemplate and the values are the parsed data
Data	Object	Arbitrary application-specific data that can be associated with a UriTemplate
QueryParameters	NameValueCollection	A name/value collection of items from the query string of the parsed URI
RelativePathSegments	Collection<string>	A union of the results of template matching and wildcard matching
RequestUri	Uri	The request URI passed to Match
UriTemplate	UriTemplate	A reference to the UriTemplate instance on which Match was called
WildCardPathSegments	Collection<string>	All the data that matched against the wildcard part of the UriTemplate (if any)

Compound Path Segments

Some RESTful services employ a URI feature known as *compound path template syntax*, which is useful when the URI resource you are modeling has more than one piece of data at a single level, or when you'd like to template the final URI extension. If, for example, you were working with the latitude and longitude of geographical locations, you might include the following in the UriTemplate:

    "/{lat}/{long}"

However, it doesn't make much sense to have a URI formatted this way because longitude isn't part of a hierarchy under latitude. The general rule of thumb with URIs is that if there are multiple same-level pieces of data for a particular resource, and order matters, use a semicolon to separate them. If order doesn't matter, use a comma.

Unfortunately, WCF does not inherently support this type of functionality. If it did, the UriTemplate might look like the following for latitude and longitude:

    "/{lat};{long}"

Another common practice is to expose different resource formats using the file extension:

    "/map.json"
    "/map.xml"

It would be nice to template these URIs like this:

    "/map.{format}"

Chapter 7 discusses why this syntax might not be the optimal solution when using WCF when returning different media types (like JSON and XML) from the same method.

Because `UriTemplate` doesn't support either of these `UriTemplate` values in .NET 3.5, you can use the following workaround:

```
"/{latlong}"
```

You can then parse the data from the combined latitude/longitude string into its component parts by using `String.Split` or other string parsing mechanism. This is not an optimal solution, but at least WCF will not reject a particular path segment's data if it contains a comma or semicolon. I should also note here that WCF 3.5 SP1 adds additional support for compound path segments (see Appendix A).

If you pass an incomplete URI (a URI that doesn't contain all of the predefined levels) to the testing program, things don't go so well. Figures 2-6 and 2-7 show the results of passing *http://example.org/* and *http://example.org/Eukaryote*, respectively.

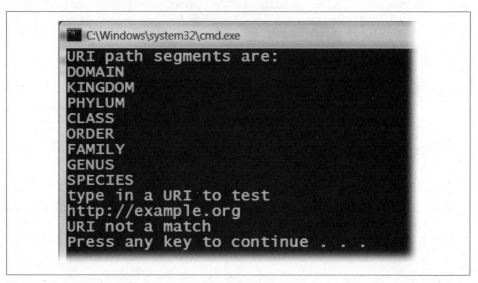

Figure 2-6. Result of passing the root URI to UriTemplate

From Figures 2-6 and 2-7, you can see that in order to consider a URI a match, `UriTemplate` requires a match on all of the path segments (assuming there is no wildcard in the template). So how do we deal with the problem of producing a URI that matches only the specified levels? This is precisely the function of the `UriTemplateTable` class.

`UriTemplateTable` is, as its name suggests, a table or collection of related `UriTemplate` objects. `UriTemplateTable` allows you to build up a collection of `UriTemplate` instances, and then run a match against the whole table. When you build up this table of

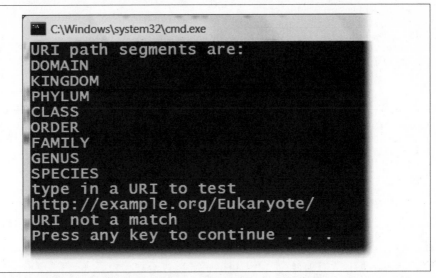

Figure 2-7. *Result of passing the first-level URI to UriTemplate*

UriTemplate instances, you associate each UriTemplate with an arbitrary (but hopefully useful) object. This object is then used to set the UriTemplateMatch.Data property if there is a match for a particular UriTemplate. The WCF infrastructure uses UriTemplateTable to store all the UriTemplate definitions for ServiceContract, and uses matches to route requests to methods based on a template match (as well as an HTTP verb match).

Right now, I am just going to use UriTemplateTable to illustrate how this works.

Example 2-10 represents version 2 of my code from Example 2-6. It creates an array of strings and a UriTemplate instance for each string. It then adds all the UriTemplate instances (and each UriTemplate's associated object) to a UriTemplateTable instance using its KeyValuePairs property. The code then includes a simple loop logic that waits for a URI and, when entered, tries to match that URI against the UriTemplateTable using UriTemplateTable.MatchSingle.

> UriTemplateTable also has a Match method that can return a collection of UriTemplateMatch instances if more than one UriTemplate matches. Using MatchSingle will cause the service to throw an exception if more than one UriTemplate matches, so if you plan to use MatchSingle, you should use UriTemplateTable to ensure only one UriTemplate will match.

Example 2-10. *Using UriTemplateTable*

```
string[] stemplates = new string[]{
"/",
"/{Domain}",
"/{Domain}/{Kingdom}",
```

```
  "/{Domain}/{Kingdom}/{Phylum}",
  "/{Domain}/{Kingdom}/{Phylum}/{Class}",
  "/{Domain}/{Kingdom}/{Phylum}/{Class}/{Order}",
  "/{Domain}/{Kingdom}/{Phylum}/{Class}/{Order}/{Family}",
  "/{Domain}/{Kingdom}/{Phylum}/{Class}/{Order}/{Family}/{Genus}",
  "/{Domain}/{Kingdom}/{Phylum}/{Class}/{Order}/{Family}/{Genus}/{Species}"
};
Dictionary<UriTemplate, object> templates =
  MakeTemplates(stemplates);
Uri baseUri = new Uri("http://example.org");
//create the UriTemplateTable
UriTemplateTable tt = new UriTemplateTable(baseUri);
//add all the UriTemplate/Value pairs to it
foreach (var kvp in templates)
{
    tt.KeyValuePairs.Add(kvp);
}
bool done = false;
while (!done)
{
    Console.WriteLine("type in a URI to test ('Q' to exit)");
    string uri = Console.ReadLine();
    if (uri == "Q")
    {
        done = true;
    }
    else
    {
        Uri testUri = new Uri(uri);
        UriTemplateMatch match = tt.MatchSingle(testUri);
        if (match != null)
        {
            Console.WriteLine(match.Data);
        }
        else
        {
            Console.WriteLine("No match found!");
        }
    }
}
```

Before discussing the execution of the program shown in Example 2-10, let's look at Example 2-11, which is the method (called MakeTemplates) that I used to create the UriTemplate instances.

Example 2-11. The MakeTemplates method

```
static Dictionary<UriTemplate, object> MakeTemplates(string[] templateStrings)
{
    Dictionary<UriTemplate, object> templates =
      new Dictionary<UriTemplate, object>();
    UriTemplate uriTemplate = null;
    string msg = null;
    int lastPathSegment = 0;
    string segment = "ROOT";
```

```
    foreach (string template in templateStrings)
    {
        uriTemplate = new UriTemplate(template);
        if (uriTemplate.PathSegmentVariableNames.Count > 0)
        {
            lastPathSegment = uriTemplate.PathSegmentVariableNames.Count - 1;
            segment = uriTemplate.PathSegmentVariableNames[lastPathSegment];
        }
        msg = segment + " MATCH!";
        templates.Add(uriTemplate, msg);
    }
    return templates;
}
```

There isn't anything special about the `MakeTemplates` method in Example 2-11, but it shows the logic I am using in my code to associate an object with each `UriTemplate` instance. Basically, the code creates a string that is logically associated with each URI you want to match. You can now use this new code to match against all the different URIs that are part of the logical URI scheme.

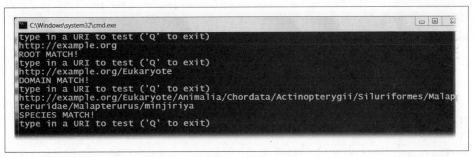

Figure 2-8. Using UriTemplateTable to match multiple URIs

`UriTemplateTable` allows you to match multiple URIs at multiple levels in the same program. The output of Example 2-10 is shown in Figure 2-8.

Now, what if the string associated with each `UriTemplate` was the name of a method instead of just a string with no particular meaning? When a match is found, the code could dynamically invoke the associated method on a particular object. This is pretty much the way in which WCF 3.5 URI dispatching works. In WCF 3.5, `WebHttpBehavior` adds the object to the WCF server-side dispatching layer. `WebHttpDispatchOperationSelector` returns the name of the method selected (based on the `UriTemplateMatch`), and the `IOperationInvoker` invokes the method on the service instance object.

This implementation is inside the `WebHttpDispatchOperationSelector` type. It is the part of the WCF dispatching layer that determines which method is to be called on a service instance based on the `UriTemplate` match and the HTTP verb of the incoming request. The dispatcher keeps a special class (`WCFLookupResult`) that keeps track of which method is associated with a particular template and also which HTTP verb. I can't use

WCFLookupResult because it is a private class (it's actually a nested class inside WebHttpDispatchOperationSelector), but I like knowing about it since it helps me to understand how the 3.5 dispatching model works. Here is the full definition of WCFLookupResult:

```
private class WCFLookupResult
{

    public WCFLookupResult(string method, string operationName);

    // Properties
    public string Method { get; }
    public string OperationName { get; }
}
```

As the WCF channel stack is opening, the WebHttpDispatchOperationSelector uses reflection on all the service methods on the contract associated with the current endpoint, and uses that information to construct the UriTemplateTable. It then adds a KeyValuePair instance for each method creating an UriTemplate and a WCFLookupResult. The UriTemplate comes from the UriTemplate property in either WebGetAttribute or WebInvokeAttribute. If WebGetAttribute is used, the WCFLookupResult.Method will be GET; otherwise, it's the value of WebInvokeAttribute.Method. The WCFLookup.OperationName is the name of the function on the service contract. This is how the WebHttpDispatchOperationSelector is able to implement its functionality.

UriTemplate Literal Values

Another UriTemplate feature that is worth mentioning is the capability to mix literal values with variable (path segment) values. In all of the preceding examples in this chapter, the UriTemplate has either been a wildcard value or a template in which all segments are variable values.

Building on the biological taxonomy example, imagine that instead of having all Domain requests routed to the same method, we want each discrete Domain value routed to its own method. Here's an example of using UriTemplate to mix literal and variable values to enable this type of dispatching:

```
UriTemplate levelOne = new UriTemplate("/Animalia");
UriTemplate levelTwo = new UriTemplate("/Animalia/{Kingdom}");
```

In this example, only those URIs containing the literal value Animalia as the first path segment after the base URI will be routed to the ProcessAnimalia method. URIs with the literal value Animalia will match on the first UriTemplate. URIs with the literal value Animalia followed by another path segment will be routed to the match on the levelTwo UriTemplate. In this way, you can combine literal values with variable path segments as dictated by your URI scheme.

Another thing you can do is use a string literal at a particular path level on one method when another method uses a variable path segment at that same level. For example, to expose a special resource under the /Animalia resource, change the code to:

```
UriTemplate levelOne = new UriTemplate("/Animalia");
UriTemplate levelTwo = new UriTemplate("/Animalia/{Kingdom}");
UriTemplate specialLevel = new UriTemplate("/Animalia/special");
```

There is now a third UriTemplate, which extends the top-level template, but it has a literal path segment instead of a variable path segment. According to the rules of Uri TemplateTable matching, any URI with Animalia and another path segment that isn't the literal value special will continue to match on the UriTemplate with the variable name of levelTwo that has the variable path segment. If the literal value special is the value of the path segment in a URI after the segment with the literal value Animalia, the UriTemplate named specialLevel (the third one in this list) will be a match. This rule comes in handy when special-casing a particular path segment literal value. You could just use a variable path segment and check the value of the variable path segment in the levelTwo template match for the literal value special, but since WCF can handle that for you, you can partition your code into two methods and instead of having to write the conditional code yourself, WCF will conditionally route the request automatically.

UriTemplate Special Values

Two special characters for UriTemplate are what I call the *root template* and the *wildcard template*.

The first UriTemplate in the UriTemplateTable in Example 2-10 uses the root template, which is simply the forward-slash character:

```
UriTemplate root = new UriTemplate("/");
```

This template is used quite often in a RESTful service to represent the root resource of a particular hierarchy, or the factory URI for creating new resources.

The other special template, the wildcard template, uses the wildcard character (*), either alone or in conjunction with literal and variable path segments. When the wildcard character is used alone, UriTemplate will match every URI:

```
UriTemplate matchAll = new UriTemplate("*");
```

UriTemplate QueryString

Yet another UriTemplate feature is the capability to parse the path portions of the URI along with the QueryString. Conventional wisdom is that the QueryString should be reserved for indicating to the client that the data being passed includes algorithm variables rather than resource hierarchy variables.

To illustrate this capability, imagine a RESTful endpoint with search capabilities. Which URI makes more sense, a or b?

a) *http://example.org/search/Don%20Box*
b) *http://example.org/search?q=Don%20Box*

Sometimes URI design is based on aesthetics, and in this case, I prefer option b. Also, option b follows the convention of having resources that perform algorithms take parameters as query parameters.

The URIs in both options could be parsed successfully with `UriTemplate`, but I prefer the syntax to support option b):

```
UriTemplate search = new UriTemplate("/search={y}");
```

Contrast this to the syntax to support option a:

```
UriTemplate search = new UriTemplate("/search/{q}");
```

Again, both options will accomplish the same thing (that is, route the request to the `Add` method and pass both `x` and `y` to the method), but the `QueryString` version just feels better because `x` and `y` aren't part of the resource, they are just values being passed to a resource.

Summary

In this chapter you learned about the basic functionality of the new WCF 3.5 programming model, and how that model builds on the extensibility of the basic WCF channel stack. WCF 3.5 includes several features that enable you to build RESTful services, including `WebHttpBinding`, which creates a channel stack that will support HTTP programming with variable URIs (and without any hint of SOAP).

- `WebServiceHost` provides an easy hosting environment for RESTful services, and adds the `WebHttpBinding` and `WebHttpBehavior` to service endpoints automatically.

- `WebHttpBehavior` replaces the default dispatching infrastructure of WCF, which is based on routing messages to CLR methods based on the SOAP action header. Instead, `WebHttpBehavior` allows routing of messages to CLR methods based on the URI and the HTTP verb.

- `WebGetAttribute` and `WebInvokeAttribute` operation behaviors are the pieces of the infrastructure that enable annotating CLR methods on the service contract type with the information used by the new dispatching layer. This allows incoming network requests to be routed to the correct method on your service instance. The `WebGetAttribute` indicates the CLR method will response to HTTP `GET` requests. When a method has the `WebInvokeAttribute` associated, the `WebInvokeAttribute.Method` property indicates which part of the uniform interface that method will respond to. The `UriTemplate` facility adds to this functionality by also allowing customization of the URI for each service method, with the variable path segments and query string capabilities to customize the URIs for RESTful services.

Now that I've shown you the basics of the REST architectural constraints, and the basics of how WCF provides a programming model for those constraints, I can start to show you how to build services using both.

CHAPTER 3

Programming Read-Only Services

Many RESTful services are designed only to return read-only data and implement `GET` from the uniform interface for all or a majority of their resources. `GET` is by far the most commonly used verb in the uniform interface.

In this chapter, we'll look at how to create this type of service using the constraints of REST using WCF as the implementation. By using the `WebGetAttribute` and the URI customization of `UriTemplate`, we will build up a simple but fairly deep set of resources. We will also examine serialization options in WCF and how they relate to RESTful services. We will continue to use the biological taxonomy example from Chapter 2, since it has a rich hierarchy that shows off the power of the `UriTemplate` system. Chapter 4 will focus on read/write services.

Using WebGetAttribute and UriTemplate

The process of building resources that expose themselves through HTTP `GET` using WCF is fairly straightforward. You build up a service contract definition using the normal WCF constructs of `ServiceContractAttribute` and `OperationContextAttribute`. If you are used to building SOAP-based services with WCF you might be used to customizing these attributes by changing their properties. Although you can do this when building a RESTful service using WCF, doing so won't help you when using REST.

In addition to these existing attributes, WCF 3.5 adds the `WebGetAttribute` for building read-only RESTful endpoints. This attribute is added to each CLR method on a `ServiceContract` definition that already has the `OperationContextAttribute`. The `WebGetAttribute` has the `UriTemplate` property, which allows you to modify the URI that the method will respond to. WCF uses this attribute to enable a method on your service type to become part of a RESTful endpoint. You can use the `WebGetAttribute` on the methods you want to expose via an HTTP `GET` request. The `WebGetAttribute.UriTemplate` property allows you to specify the exact URI to represent the resource. This combination allows you to be exact about which resource (or resources) the method will return a representation of.

Going back to the biological taxonomy system example from Chapter 2, imagine that we want a unique method on the service to handle each level of the resource hierarchy. To do this, we need to build up the service contract and add one CLR method for each resource. Next, we add the `OperationContractAttribute` to each method, along with the `WebGetAttribute`. Finally, we customize the `UriTemplate` property to provide the correct number of variable path segments for each resource. The service contract might look like the code shown in Example 3-1.

Example 3-1. IBioTaxService definition

```
[ServiceContract]
public interface IBioTaxService
{
    [OperationContract]
    [WebGet(UriTemplate = "/")]
    Message GetRoot();
    [OperationContract]
    [WebGet(UriTemplate = "/search?q={query}")]
    Message Search(string query);
    [OperationContract]
    [WebGet(UriTemplate = "/{Domain}")]
    Message GetDomain(string domain);
    [OperationContract]
    [WebGet(UriTemplate = "/{Domain}/{Kingdom}")]
    Message GetKingdom(string Domain,string Kingdom);
    [OperationContract]
    [WebGet(UriTemplate = "/{Domain}/{Kingdom}/{Phylum}")]
    Message GetPhylum(string Domain, string Kingdom,string Phylum);
    [OperationContract]
    [WebGet(UriTemplate = "/{Domain}/{Kingdom}/{Phylum}/{Class}")]
    Message GetClass(string Domain, string Kingdom, string Phylum,string Class);
    [OperationContract]
    [WebGet(UriTemplate = "/{Domain}/{Kingdom}/{Phylum}/{Class}/{Order}")]
    Message GetOrder(string Domain, string Kingdom, string Phylum,
 string Class,string Order);
    [OperationContract]
    [WebGet(UriTemplate = "/{Domain}/{Kingdom}/{Phylum}/{Class}/{Order}/{Family}")]
    Message GetFamily(string Domain, string Kingdom, string Phylum,
 string Class, string Order, string Family);
    [OperationContract]
    [WebGet(UriTemplate = "/{Domain}/{Kingdom}/{Phylum}/
{Class}/{Order}/{Family}/{Genus}")]
    Message GetGenus(string Domain, string Kingdom, string Phylum,
 string Class, string Order, string Family,string Genus);
    [OperationContract]
    [WebGet(UriTemplate = "/{Domain}/{Kingdom}/{Phylum}/{Class}
/{Order}/{Family}/{Genus}/{Species}")]
    Message GetSpecies(string Domain, string Kingdom, string Phylum,
 string Class, string Order, string Family, string Genus,string Species);
}
```

Note that the names of the methods are totally unrelated to the dispatching method. The contract definition uses a custom method-naming convention (**Get*XXX***, where ***XXX*** is the name of the resource) for readability only—it provides no benefit to either WCF or the service clients because the URI that each method will respond to is customized using the `UriTemplate` property.

Because the templates for each method have replaceable path segments, the parameters on each method must have the same name as the name of each path segment, and must be in the same order that the replaceable `UriTemplate` path segments are in. When WCF makes the `UriTemplate` match for a particular request, it uses the names and variables of the `UriTemplateMatch.BoundVariables` collection to invoke the matched method. All the method parameters that relate to replaceable path segments had to be string only. In Chapter 4, we'll examine how complex types from the HTTP request body are deserialized and passed to CLR methods as arguments. Since we are only concerned with `GET` right now, there won't be any request bodies.

Notice that in the Example 3-1 code the second method on the contract is `Search`. The `UriTemplate` property on the `Search` method's `WebGetAttribute` is using two interesting features of the `UriTemplate` system. First, it is using a `string` literal, which overrides the variable path segment used by the third method (`GetDomain` with a `UriTemplate` of `"/{Domain}"`). Since there is no biological domain named "search" it is safe to use a `UriTemplate` value of `"/search"` as a literal path segment. The special feature is that any request with a URI of `"/search"` will be dispatched to the `Search` method, and any other URI with just one path segment will be routed to `GetDomain`. It also uses the query string feature of `UriTemplate` by adding the string `"?q={query}"` to the end of its template definition. The feature allows replaceable query string parameters to be used as well as replaceable path segments. Like variable path segments, variable query string templates must have names that match the variable names of the CLR method parameters exactly.

Another interesting thing to note about Example 3-1 is that we are using the `System.ServiceModel.Channels.Message` type as the return value for all the methods. This type is not used as commonly as other WCF facilities for serialization because, although `Message` is very powerful, it also requires a fair amount of heavy lifting. However, this type is very useful when you want fine-grained control over the serialization of a resource. However, this is only one of the ways to define the serialization of return values. Let's look at some WCF serialization options and how they interact in a RESTful environment.

Data Formats

Inputs come into methods that use the `WebGetAttribute` when WCF takes the `UriTemplateMatch.BoundVariables` collection after the URI has been matched against a `UriTemplate` and passes them into your method as strings, based on either the URI path segments or query string parameters. As we saw in Example 3-1, these parameters must always be simple strings.

You could also use `string` for the return type from your methods, as WCF does support returning scalar types like `string` and `int` from RESTful service methods. However, it is more likely that you will want to use more complex return types from a RESTful service than just a scalar type.

The default behavior in WCF 3.5 is exactly the same as in WCF 3.0 in terms of returning complex types from the CLR methods on a service contract. WCF receives the object passed as the return value from the CLR method and attempts to serialize it into an XML instance using one of a few well-known and documented approaches.

WCF uses either the `DataContractSerializer` or the `XmlSerializer` when serializing and deserializing input and output parameters, depending on how we define the service contract. Another approach that is somewhat more advanced is to use the WCF `Message` type `System.ServiceModel.Channels.Message`, which leaves the message processing in our hands instead of WCF's. Let's take each of these approaches in turn, starting with the most complex: `Message`.

 This chapter only deals with the format of the response messages. In Chapter 4, we will examine the ways in which WCF can deserialize incoming HTTP message bodies into .NET types.

WCF 3.5 does add some additional functionality in the area of serialization. In addition to XML, it adds support for an additional serialization format: JavaScript Object Notation (JSON). Chapter 7 will discuss JSON in more detail.

Message

In Chapter 2, I introduced the `Message` type as the underlying representation of a network message to the WCF channel stack, and demonstrated the creation of a `Message` object as the return value of an HTTP `GET` request.

It is relatively rare to find `Message` as a parameter type or return type in most WCF services because, in general, most WCF-built services use strongly typed .NET types for their input and output parameters. This is mostly because the generated metadata, the Web Services Description Language (WSDL), can be used by clients to autogenerate client code to simplify the client development experience, and because the service developer's programming experience is also simplified by only having to deal with .NET types and not the underlying message types.

In the RESTful world, there is no WSDL, so using strongly typed contracts doesn't have the same benefits as it does when using SOAP, since the client will not be able to generate a proxy using WSDL for metadata.

Some RESTful services are starting to support something called *WADL*. WADL stands for Web Application Description Language, and is used to generate clients automatically. WCF doesn't currently have any support for WADL. Chapter 10 will discuss options for building clients using WCF.

Another reason that `Message` isn't used very often in WCF service implementations is that `Message` requires a fair amount of heavy lifting in terms of using XML APIs to create the message (although there is a hybrid approach that allows you to combine the definition of `Message` as the return value from your methods with strongly typed serialization, and newer APIs like LINQ to XML that further simplify the XML heavy lifting).

LINQ to XML (or XLINQ) stands for Language Integrated Query for XML, which is part of the overall LINQ subsystem added to .NET 3.5.

The flip side to this extra complexity is that `Message` gives you total control over the XML returned to the client from your operations. `DataContractSerializer` is somewhat limited in this area because it doesn't allow the full range of XML constructs—for example, it doesn't allow you to use XML attributes. `XmlSerializer` provides more flexibility in terms of the XML format, but it requires extensive attributing to your .NET data types. Another drawback of the `XmlSerializer` is dealing with the generation of the special assembly that it uses to do its work, either by letting it dynamically generate the assembly at runtime or by using the *sgen.exe* tool to pregenerate it. These limitations also apply when using WCF with SOAP, but the advantage of using strongly typed WSDL generally overrides them. Since there is no WSDL in the RESTful case, `Message` becomes a more attractive construct.

`Message` also has the advantage of giving you much more control over versioning resource representations. Many developers build REST clients in other languages and runtimes using constructs like `Message` or raw XML APIs, because these create a much more loosely coupled service and client. And even if a client does use an object serialization construct, the service can still use `Message` because the service then has the option to return new data to new clients and continue to use the old data format for old clients.

Example 3-2 shows what it might look like if we used `Message` in the biological taxonomy service.

Example 3-2. Using Message as the return type

```
public Message GetRoot()
{
    MemoryStream ms = new MemoryStream();
    XmlDictionaryWriter xw = XmlDictionaryWriter.CreateTextWriter(ms);
    xw.WriteStartDocument();
```

```
    xw.WriteStartElement("Domains");
    string[] domains = new string[] { "Archaea", "Eubacteria", "Eukaryota" };
    foreach (string domain in domains)
    {
        xw.WriteStartElement("Domain");
        xw.WriteAttributeString("name", domain);
        xw.WriteAttributeString("uri", domain);
        xw.WriteEndElement();
    }
    xw.WriteEndElement();
    xw.WriteEndDocument();
    xw.Flush();
    ms.Position = 0;
    XmlDictionaryReader xdr = XmlDictionaryReader.CreateTextReader
      (ms, XmlDictionaryReaderQuotas.Max);
    Message ret = Message.CreateMessage(MessageVersion.None, "*", xdr);
    return ret;
}
```

Example 3-2 isn't the only way to write code that uses `Message`. You could, for example, use LINQ to XML. Whatever the XML technology used, the basic operations will be the same: create or retrieve the XML as a stream, create an `XmlDictionaryReader`, and then call the `Message.CreateMessage` factory method. Note that in the Example 3-2 code the `MessageVersion` is set to `MessageVersion.None`. This allows `MessageVersion` to function properly with the `TextEncoder` in this non-SOAP scenario. Also, `Action` is set to "*" because the action header is irrelevant to the WCF components when using REST.

Figure 3-1 shows the results of running the Example 3-2 code.

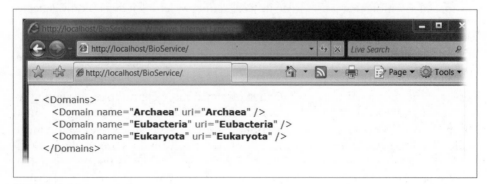

Figure 3-1. Message result

DataContract

The `DataContract` serialization system was built specifically for WCF 3.0 (and continues without any visible changes in WCF 3.5). The idea behind this system was to create a fast and simple serialization layer that could turn .NET objects into XML and XML into .NET objects. It is pretty heavily constrained in terms of support for XML schema features.

The biggest restriction of `DataContract` serialization is that `DataContract` only supports elements, so you can't use XML attributes. This means that you can't recreate the same XML format as you can when you use `Message`. Is this necessarily bad? It depends on your point of view, but I'd rather have the option to use attributes when it makes sense. Also, I often prefer XHTML for read-only services, especially since browsers can read it and XHTML can't be generated using the `DataContractSerializer`.

Another limitation of `DataContract` (although not one that matters much in the REST world) is that all of the elements must be schema-qualified. This means that you must set `elementFormDefault="qualified"` at the global schema level or on each element. However, this limitation doesn't matter much when programming RESTful services because, in general, XSD is not always used to represent the format of XML-based resources. There are other restrictions when using `DataContract`, most of which deal with parts of the XSD specification that, although useful, tend to reduce interoperability with other SOAP toolkits.

> The `DataContractSerializer` will also serialize types that are marked with the `Serializable` attribute (in addition to the `DataContract` attribute). This is useful for scenarios where you are using existing types. The downside of relying on `Serializable` is that you don't have any control over issues like namespaces or the order of items in the resulting XML.
>
> `DataContractSerializer` will also use `IXmlSerializable` or `ISerializable` if implemented on a type.
>
> Another feature added to .NET 3.5 SP1 that complicates this discussion somewhat is that `DataContractSerializer` can be used to serializer Plain Old CLR Objects (POCOs). See Appendix A.

To use `DataContract` you must use a type that has the `DataContract` attribute, and you must attach the `DataMember` attribute to all of the fields or properties that you want to include in the serialization. A Domain type definition with these attributes would look like this:

```
[DataContract()]
public class Domain
{
    [DataMember]
    public string Name;
    [DataMember]
    public string Uri;
}
```

One nice feature of WCF is the capability to return generic collection types from methods and have the `DataContract` serialization layer deal with them directly. This means that you can change the `GetRoot` method to this:

```
[OperationContract]
[WebGet(UriTemplate = "/")]
List<Domain> GetRoot();
```

And you can change the implementation to this:

```
public List<Domain> GetRoot()
{
    List<Domain> ret = new List<Domain>();
    string[] domains = new string[] { "Archaea", "Eubacteria", "Eukaryota" };
    foreach (string domain in domains)
    {
        ret.Add(new Domain { Name = domain, Uri = domain });

    }
    return ret;
}
```

Figure 3-2 shows the resulting XML.

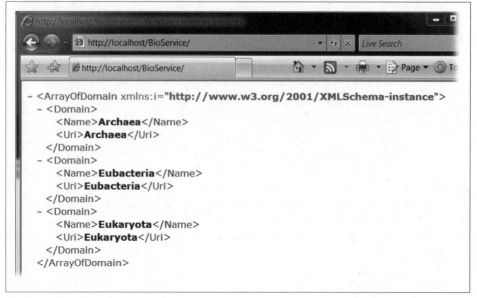

Figure 3-2. DataContract serialization result

There are two things I don't like about the XML format displayed in Figure 3-2. First, I don't really want an XML namespace for the XML, and if I did, I certainly wouldn't want it to be the default that the DataContract serialization layer puts in. The namespace can be changed by modifying the DataContract attribute on the Domain type:

```
[DataContract(Namespace="")]
public class Domain
{
    [DataMember]
    public string Name;
```

```
        [DataMember]
        public string Uri;
    }
```

The other thing I don't really like is that the root element is **"ArrayOfDomain"**. I'd much rather see `Domains` as the root element name. To change the root element name, create a new type that derives from `List<Domain>` and use the `CollectionDataContract` attribute to dictate the name used for serialization:

```
    [CollectionDataContract(Name = "Domains", Namespace = "")]
    public class DomainList : List<Domain>
    {
    }
```

Set the `Namespace` property on this attribute to an empty string and change the contract and service to use this new type:

```
    public DomainList GetRoot()
    {
        DomainList ret = new DomainList();
        string[] domains = new string[] { "Archaea", "Eubacteria", "Eukaryota" };
        foreach (string domain in domains)
        {
            ret.Add(new Domain { Name = domain, Uri = domain });

        }
        return ret;
    }
```

Figure 3-3 shows the result of the changes to the XML format. Unfortunately, there is no way to get rid of the `xmlns` attribute for the XSD instance schema, although that shouldn't really hurt anything.

When building RESTful services, using `Message` is often a better option than using `DataContract`. If you want to use .NET types to represent your data and have more control over the XML format, `XmlSerializer` is the recommended approach.

XmlSerializer

`System.Xml.Serialization.XmlSerializer` has been in the .NET Framework since .NET 1.0. It's a reliable and tried-and-true way to serialize .NET instances into XML and vice versa.

WCF supports the `XmlSerializer` system in order to support existing .NET types that already have associated `XmlSerializer` attributes, for example, in services that port web services written using .NET's ASMX web service infrastructure to WCF. `XmlSerializer` also supports parts of the XSD specification that `DataContract` doesn't support. When using SOAP and consuming WSDL from web services that were written in other toolkits, you will often have to deal with XML schemas that use those parts of the XSD specification. This can also be the case when you want to expose or consume RESTful resources that are XML and use those XSD constructs.

Figure 3-3. Improved DataContract result

XmlSerializer is one of my favorite tools for carrying out RESTful serialization because it provides more control over how objects are serialized into XML than DataContract.

Here are the Domain and DomainList types rewritten using the XmlSerializer attributes:

```
[XmlRoot(Namespace="",ElementName="Domain")]
public class Domain
{
    [XmlAttribute(AttributeName="name")]
     public string Name;
    [XmlAttribute(AttributeName = "uri")]
     public string Uri;
}
[XmlRoot(Namespace = "", ElementName = "Domains")]
public class DomainList : List<Domain>
{
}
```

This is a pretty simple matter of using the XmlSerializer attributes instead of the DataContract attributes. Instead of being limited to attributes, by using the XmlAttribute we can make the XmlSerializer turn those fields into XML attributes instead of elements.

Next, we change the service contract definition. WCF's default serialization method is to use the DataContractSerializer. If you want WCF to use the XmlSerializer, we need to annotate the method or the whole service contract with the XmlSerializerFormat attribute:

```
[OperationContract]
[WebGet(UriTemplate = "/")]
```

```
[XmlSerializerFormat()]
DomainList GetRoot();
```

`XmlSerializerFormat` instructs the serialization infrastructure to use an `XmlSerializer` instance to carry out the serialization of objects to XML. Figure 3-4 shows the results of requesting the root resource when the `XmlSerializer` is used to serialize the return value.

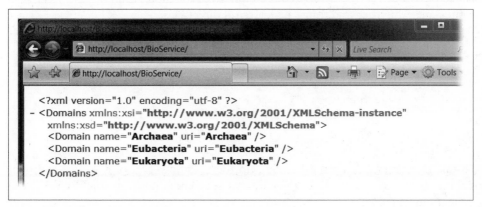

Figure 3-4. XmlSerializer usage

As with the `DataContract` XML, the `XmlSerializer` XML contains extra `xmlns` attributes. These are nuisances I'd rather not see, but they shouldn't affect any toolkits' XML processing since they are perfectly legal and correct.

Hybrid Approach

You can also use a hybrid approach, where you use `Message` for the return type and `DataContract` for serialization. This works because the `Message.CreateMessage` static factory method will use whatever serialization is appropriate, based on the data type that is passed in. Note that `DataContract` also supports types that are marked with a `Serializable` attribute like `System.String`.

The hybrid approach combines the flexibility of `Message` with the simpler programming model of using serialization. Example 3-3 shows the `GetRoot` method again, this time rewritten to use the `DataContract` types, but with `Message` as the return value.

Example 3-3. Serialization/Message hybrid

```
//hybrid version
public Message GetRoot()
{
    DomainList ret = new DomainList();
    string[] domains = new string[] { "Archaea", "Eubacteria", "Eukaryota" };
    foreach (string domain in domains)
    {
        ret.Add(new Domain { Name = domain, Uri = domain });
```

```
    }
    Message realRet = Message.CreateMessage(MessageVersion.None, "*", ret);
    return realRet;
}
```

The result will be exactly the same as in the `DataContract` return value approach shown in Example 3-2. This hybrid approach simply gives you more flexibility and is easier to write (since you can avoid using the XML API directly).

 There are two other special return types for WCF service methods: `Stream` and `byte[]`. These allow you to send back arbitrary binary and text data. See Chapter 7 on JSON for more information about using those return types.

Summary

In this chapter, we discussed building up the read-only part of a service endpoint (which, in some cases, might be the only part of an endpoint) using the WCF 3.5 web programming model.

The first step is to determine which resources will be returned by the service, and then model those resources with unique URIs. Next, create the WCF service contract and add the `WebGetAttribute` to the CLR methods. Then modify the `UriTemplate` property with the appropriate template value so that each CLR method can be called in response to the correct URIs for each resource.

Next, decide on the resource representation. The format of the representation will dictate which WCF serialization systems you can use. The `DataContractSerializer` is the newest and probably fastest serialization method, but it is somewhat limited in terms of the XML it can output. `XmlSerializer` is more flexible in terms of XML output, but it is slightly more complex than using the `DataContractSerializer`. Use the `Message` type if you want complete control over the serialization of the message.

In Chapter 4, we'll examine the steps for creating read/write resources. The process is very similar to the process outlined here for creating read-only resources: determine the resources, model them using URIs, determine the representation, and decide on which parts of the uniform interface to implement.

CHAPTER 4

Programming Read/Write Services

In the previous chapter, you were introduced to the WCF 3.5 web programming model and the major pieces of its infrastructure. You used the programming model to write a read-only RESTful service, and used the infrastructure to deploy and expose it.

While it could be that some of the services you build will be read-only, it is more likely that your services will include other parts of the uniform interface in addition to GET. In this chapter, I'll show you how to put the WCF 3.5 web programming model to work in building a read/write service that allows user agents to create, modify, and delete resources.

POST, PUT, and DELETE

Chapter 1 discussed REST and the architectural constraints of the uniform interface. See Figure 4-1 to refresh your memory about the uniform interface and how it should work.

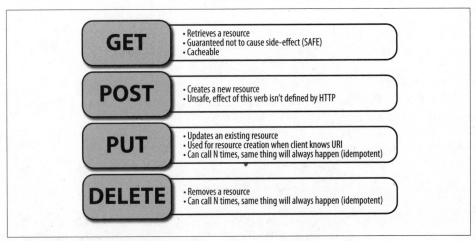

Figure 4-1. REST uniform interface

Recall from Chapter 3 that WCF enables a RESTful programming model by allowing annotation on methods via attributes. These attributes specify which method should be invoked for each URI, and which part of the uniform interface each method implements. For example, `WebGetAttribute` will implement `GET`, and its `UriTemplate` property value specifies the URI to which the method will respond.

All other verbs in the uniform interface (`POST`, `PUT`, and `DELETE`) are implemented using the `WebInvokeAttribute`. `WebInvokeAttribute` also allows you to customize the URI that the method will respond to through its own `UriTemplate` property. It also allows you to set the HTTP verb so that you can not only implement the remainder of the uniform interface, but you can implement HTTP verbs that are not part of the uniform interface. Because we already examined `GET` and `WebGetAttribute` at length in Chapter 3, this chapter will focus on `WebInvokeAttribute`.

Using WebInvokeAttribute

For this discussion, we will revisit the user/membership system example from Chapter 1 by creating the code to implement that service using WCF, instead of just discussing it in the abstract. The service from the last chapter is really a read-only service for the most part (although not being overly familiar with the biological taxonomy system perhaps there are more changes than I am aware of), so I think this example is better for a read/write service. To refresh your memory, the sample service is a membership system that stores information about users. First, let's walk through the RESTful design steps for this service in a slightly abbreviated fashion.

Resources

Our example service will expose the following resources:

- All users
- A particular user delineated by the user's unique identifier

URIs and Uniform Interface

Table 4-1 shows the URIs and the parts of the uniform interface that we will implement for each URI in our example.

Table 4-1. User service URIs

URI	Method	Description	Output	Input
/users	GET	Returns a representation of all users in the system	users collection	n/a
/users	POST	Creates a new user in the system, expects a representation of the user in the HTTP body	user	user (without the user_id specified)

URI	Method	Description	Output	Input
/users/ {user_id}	GET	Returns the representation of a particular user, based on the user's identifier in the system	user	n/a
/users/ {user_id}	PUT	Modifies a user resource	user	user
/users/ {user_id}	DELETE	Deletes a user from the system	n/a	n/a

It is important to reiterate here that you don't have to implement the entire uniform interface for all resources; the same service may expose read-only resources alongside read/write resources. For example, the /users resource is read-only and does not implement the DELETE method, because even if there aren't any users, we still want that resource to be there.

Representations

For this particular application, let's use a custom XML format. The following code defines two .NET classes you'll use to represent the data: User represents each user, and Users represents the collection of users.

```
[CollectionDataContract(Name = "users", Namespace = "")]
public class Users : List<User>
{
}
[DataContract(Name = "user", Namespace = "")]
public class User
{
    [DataMember(Name="id",Order=1)]
    public string UserId;
    [DataMember(Name = "firstname", Order = 2)]
    public string FirstName;
    [DataMember(Name = "lastname", Order = 3)]
    public string LastName;
    [DataMember(Name = "email", Order = 4)]
    public string Email;
}
```

Implementation

Next, we need a class annotated with the ServiceContractAttribute that has the ability to keep track of users. For this example we'll use a static data member with the list of users:

```
[ServiceContract]
public class UserService
{
    static Users _users = new Users();
    //rest of the implementation to follow
}
```

Yes, this implementation flies in the face of the concept of statelessness in REST because the service holds onto state (the list of users). Right now, however, we need to focus on the semantics of writing the service infrastructure pieces of code with WCF. Instead of this stateful implementation, imagine instead that we are storing the list of users in a backend database and that the service implementation is totally stateless.

POST

POST is the part of the uniform interface that is typically used to create a new resource. To implement POST as part of our RESTful WCF service, we annotate the CLR method with the WebInvokeAttribute. We set the WebInvokeAttribute.Method property to the string "POST" (although POST is the default, being explicit is usually a better policy) and then we set the UriTemplate property to the template we want this method to respond to. This will cause WCF to call the method on our service instance when a request comes to the endpoint with a URI that matches the template when the HTTP verb used in the request is POST.

The UriTemplate follows the same rules on the WebInvokeAttribute as it does on WebGetAttribute. In fact, all of the UriTemplate definitions from all methods are parsed and added to the endpoint's UriTemplateTable in exactly the same way. When matching against the UriTemplateTable, not only does the WCF web-dispatching infrastructure look at the URI, it also looks at the HTTP verb from the request. This is why the UriTemplate value can be the same for multiple service methods, as long as each accepted HTTP verb is different. Example 4-1 shows the first part of the UserService definition, which relates to the top-level URI ("/users").

Example 4-1. Top-level URI implementation

```
[WebGet(UriTemplate = "/users")]
[OperationContract]
public Users GetAllUsers()
{
    return _users;
}
[WebInvoke(UriTemplate = "/users", Method = "POST")]
[OperationContract]
public User AddNewUser(User u)
{
    u.UserId = Guid.NewGuid().ToString();
    _users.Add(u);
    return u;
}
[WebGet(UriTemplate = "/users/{user_id}")]
[OperationContract]
public User GetUser(string user_id)
{
    User u = FindUser(user_id);
    return u;
}
```

Note that `UriTemplate` value is the same for both `GetAllUsers` and `AddNewUser`, but one uses the `WebGetAttribute` and one uses `WebInvokeAttribute`. The `Method` property of `WebInvokeAttribute` on `AddNewUser` is `POST`, which is the method we're most interested in at the moment. The WCF web-dispatching infrastructure will use the HTTP verb to differentiate requests to this URI and will route them to the appropriate method.

 The code in Example 4-1 sets `WebInvokeAttribute.Method` to `POST`, even though `POST` is the default. Explicitly defining default values (which would be used even if you left them out) makes it easier to scan a contract for the uniform interface.

Another interesting thing about this design is that it does not allow the service client to set the resource identifier (in this case `User.UserId`). This is why the URI for both getting all users and creating a new user is the same. In this case, the `"/users"` resource acts like a factory when `POST` is used, and even if the `UserId` property is set, it will be overwritten.

Your own design might end up being different in this regard. If you decide to allow users to select the identifier for the resource, the URI for creating the new resource will include the identifier and will thus be different from the collection URI. If the design used here followed that pattern, the `UriTemplate` for the `AddNewUser` method would be `"/users/{user_id}"`. It would also be expected that the HTTP verb would be `PUT` instead of `POST` to create the user resource. In most cases, it is difficult to design a service that allows clients to decide on the identifiers because each identifier must be unique.

Because of this choice, the `AddNewUser` method in Example 4-1 doesn't have a `UriTemplate`-based parameter for *user_id*, but it does have a parameter: the complex `User` type, which we defined earlier. It's expected that when you implement `POST` and `PUT` from the uniform interface you will accept a request body as part of the incoming HTTP request message (`DELETE` on the other hand isn't expected to have a request body). When you use the `WebInvokeAttribute` on a method, the first parameter(s) of the method are expected to be the template matches from the `UriTemplate` definition if there are any. The last parameter is expected to be deserialized from the incoming HTTP message body.

In Chapter 1, we looked at hypothetical images of what the requests and responses to this service would look like. Let's now look at images of actual interactions between a user agent and the service, using a special user agent called *Fiddler*.

Fiddler is an incredibly useful tool for carrying out complex interactions between websites and web services. Not only can it spy on requests going from a user agent to a server, it can also allow you to build arbitrary HTTP requests using its Request Builder functionality. See *http://www.fiddlertool.com/* for more information about this useful tool.

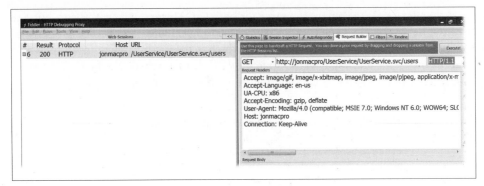

Figure 4-2. Using Fiddler to GET to root URI

Figure 4-3. Fiddler Session Inspector view of GET request

The Fiddler Request Builder tab allows you to create arbitrary HTTP requests using different HTTP verbs and different representations as the request body. It also allows you to see the response that the service returned from those requests. This is an invaluable tool when building services of any kind, but with RESTful services it can become the first path testing client.

In Chapter 10, I'll show you how to implement clients using WCF. For now, we will concentrate on the service syntax and programming model using the Fiddler tool.

The first thing we will do is view the current collection of users by passing a GET request to the root URI. Figure 4-2 shows the Request Builder HTTP GET request, and Figure 4-3 shows the Session Inspector tab view for the same request.

Figure 4-4. Creating a new user resource with HTTP POST to the root URI

Figure 4-5. POST request and result in Fiddler Session Inspector

 In this case we are hosting the WCF RESTful service inside of IIS, using the *.svc* file capabilities instead of self-hosting, primarily for ease of deployment and because using Fiddler is slightly easier when using port 80 for HTTP requests. See Chapter 5 for more details about hosting options.

In Figure 4-3, you can see that the response to the HTTP GET request is an empty collection. Our next step, then, is to add a user to the collection using a POST request to the same URI, including an entity body of the right media type. Figure 4-4 shows this request, and Figure 4-5 shows the response.

One important thing to note in Figure 4-4 is the Content-Type header. The Content-Type header is essential when using RESTful services in general, but is especially

Figure 4-6. Fiddler Session Inspector view of a GET request showing a newly added user resource

important when making requests to RESTful services. If you don't have a Content-Type header in your HTTP request to a WCF service, you'll always get a "415 Missing Content Type" status code. You don't need the Content-Type header when making a GET request, since there isn't any entity body when making a GET request.

---

201 status code

I said in Chapter 1 that a call to POST should return a "201 Created" status code. This is a pretty typical convention for RESTful services. In general, it is a good idea to take advantage of the range of available HTTP status codes and be very explicit.

Unfortunately, WCF always returns either a "200 OK" HTTP status code (if a method completes with no exceptions, regardless of the part of the uniform interface being invoked) or a "400 Bad Request" code (if an exception is thrown).

You may want to be more expressive with the code you return to your clients. I'll show you how to customize status codes in Chapter 11.

In Figure 4-5 you can see the Fiddler Session Inspector tab. The raw option is selected, and the service responded with a user resource (as shown by the new unique value in the id element).

If we make another GET request to the root URI, we will see the newly added member. Notice that in Figure 4-6 in the response content body that the id element now has a value, and the unique identifier that is now part of the newly created user resource.

We can now use this identifier as part of a GET request for that particular resource (Figure 4-7).

PUT

At this point, the service has one user resource, created via a POST request. Let's now turn our attention to using PUT.

Figure 4-7. Single resource GET request

Example 4-2 shows the service method that implements `PUT` and modifies a specific user resource.

Example 4-2. Service method that implements PUT

```
[WebInvoke(UriTemplate = "/users/{user_id}", Method = "PUT")]
[OperationContract]
public User UpdateUser(string user_id,User update)
{
    User u = FindUser(user_id);
    UpdateUserInternal(u, update);
    return u;
}
```

The details of the `UpdateUserInternal` aren't very important as it's just a simple copy of fields from the new user resource into the old, except for the `UserId` field. The more interesting bit of code from Example 4-2 is that the `UriTemplate` value of this `WebInvokeAttribute` is the same as the `UriTemplate` value on the single user resource `GET` method (the `GetUser` method from Example 4-1). Remember, you can have multiple methods with the same `UriTemplate` value, as long as the HTTP verb is different. The `GetUser` method uses the `WebGetAttribute`; its method will inherently implement `GET`, so requests to a particular user's URI will be routed to the `GetUser` method when the HTTP verb in the request is `GET`. The `UpdateUser` method will be called when a request arrives for a specific user's URI when the HTTP verb is `PUT` because the `WebInvokeAttribute.Method` on the `UpdateUser` method is set to `PUT`.

To modify a resource, we can make a `PUT` request to the user's URI, passing the correct user resource representation (which in this case is XML). On success, the service returns the same resource as the body of its response. You can see the request in Figure 4-8 and the response in Figure 4-9.

Figure 4-8. Using a PUT request to modify a user resource

Figure 4-9. PUT request and response in the Fiddler Session Inspector view

You can see in Figure 4-8 that we changed the resource by modifying the email address. The service returns a "200 OK" response code and returns the newly modified resource as the response body.

DELETE

At this point, you probably have a pretty good idea of how the implementation of DELETE is going to progress. Example 4-3 shows the code used to implement DELETE.

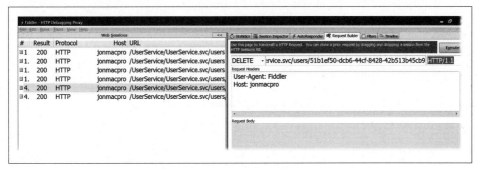

Figure 4-10. Using DELETE in Fiddler

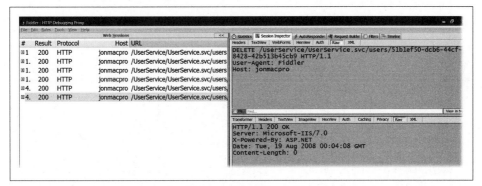

Figure 4-11. DELETE request and response in the Fiddler Session Inspector view

Example 4-3. Implementing DELETE

```
[WebInvoke(UriTemplate = "/users/{user_id}", Method = "DELETE")]
[OperationContract]
public void DeleteUser(string user_id)
{
    User u = FindUser(user_id);
    _users.Remove(u);
}
```

You can see the interaction between the client and the service using DELETE in Figures 4-10 and 4-11.

RESTful convention dictates that DELETE will not accept or return a representation. There really isn't anything else special about implementing DELETE, other than making sure to set the WebInvokeAttribute.Method property appropriately.

Full service implementation

Example 4-4 shows the entire service implementation from top to bottom.

Example 4-4. Full read/write service implementation

```
[ServiceContract]
public class UserService
{
    static Users _users = new Users();

    [WebGet(UriTemplate = "/users")]
    [OperationContract]
    public Users GetAllUsers()
    {
        return _users;
    }
    [WebInvoke(UriTemplate = "/users", Method = "POST")]
    [OperationContract]
    public User AddNewUser(User u)
    {
        u.UserId = Guid.NewGuid().ToString();
        _users.Add(u);
        return u;
    }
    [WebGet(UriTemplate = "/users/{user_id}")]
    [OperationContract]
    public User GetUser(string user_id)
    {
        User u = FindUser(user_id);
        return u;
    }
    User FindUser(string user_id)
    {
        User ret = null;
        var result = (from u in _users
                        where u.UserId == user_id
                        select u).Single();
        if (result != null)
            ret = result;
        else
            ret = new User();
        return ret;


    }
    [WebInvoke(UriTemplate = "/users/{user_id}", Method = "PUT")]
    [OperationContract]
    public User UpdateUser(string user_id, User update)
    {
        User u = FindUser(user_id);
        UpdateUserInternal(u, update);
        return u;
    }

    private void UpdateUserInternal(User u, User update)
    {
        u.Email = update.Email;
        u.FirstName = update.FirstName;
        u.LastName = update.LastName;
```

```
    }
    [WebInvoke(UriTemplate = "/users/{user_id}", Method = "DELETE")]
    [OperationContract]
    public void DeleteUser(string user_id)
    {
        User u = FindUser(user_id);
        _users.Remove(u);

    }
}
```

Summary

In this chapter, you learned how to finish implementing the uniform interface using WCF. Use `WebInvokeAttribute` to implement any HTTP method other than `GET`, and use the `WebInvokeAttribute.Method` property to specify which HTTP method the CLR method should respond to. You can customize the URI using the `WebInvokeAttribute.UriTemplate` property. WCF routes messages to the methods on instances of your service type by looking for a match based on the URI and the HTTP verb.

There is still more that you can do to make your services compliant with the constraints of REST. Chapter 11 has more information about extending beyond the basic infrastructure of the WCF web-programming model and using the full breadth of HTTP in your service.

CHAPTER 5

Hosting WCF RESTful Services

Once you're ready to deploy your RESTful service using WCF, you'll need to make a decision faced by every WCF service developer: where to host your service. The decision-making process should revolve around the capabilities that different hosting options can provide your endpoint. Those capabilities include process lifetime, process token, and security management, as well as general process management capabilities. In this chapter, we'll examine the issues around hosting WCF services in your own process, which is known as self-hosting. We'll also look at *managed hosting*, the name used to describe hosting WCF services inside of Internet Information Server (IIS).

WCF REST Hosting Isn't a Special Case

Hosting a WCF service involves loading and running endpoints inside of an executable process. Because WCF is a CLR-based technology, you can host your endpoint inside of any executable process that can load the CLR. The main options are Windows Services, Windowed applications (like Windows Forms or Windows Presentation Foundation), or IIS.

WCF processes messages through a construct known as an endpoint. To start a WCF endpoint in a particular process, you must create a channel listener. Although there are a few ways to do this, by far the most common is to rely on the `ServiceHost` class to provide the infrastructure for loading up and starting channel listeners for endpoints configured on the `ServiceHost` instance.

An important thing to keep in mind when thinking about hosting your WCF REST endpoint is that it is simply a WCF endpoint. By this I mean that an endpoint using the `WebHttpBinding` is just like any other WCF binding. From a technical aspect, hosting a `WebHttpBinding` endpoint is exactly the same as hosting any other WCF endpoint.

`ServiceHost`, or its web counterpart `WebServiceHost`, is the mechanism for getting your service up and running. You can load `ServiceHost`/`WebServiceHost` into any process that has loaded the CLR. You can load `ServiceHost`/`WebServiceHost` into any CLR `AppDomain`, and there is no limit to the number of `ServiceHost` instances you can have in a particular `AppDomain`; you can have as many as necessary based on your configuration needs. Even though `WebServiceHost` is specialized for use with RESTful endpoints, it isn't any different from the general WCF `ServiceHost` case from this point of view.

On the other hand, there are some special considerations you need to keep in mind when planning to host a `WebHttpBinding` that aren't pertinent when thinking about hosting other WCF bindings. Most of these considerations, in my opinion at least, end up pointing toward hosting your endpoints inside of IIS. First we'll discuss the responsibilities you'll have as a developer during self-hosting, and then we'll wrap up with the capabilities you get when you host in IIS.

Self-Hosting

Self-hosting is when you write the code that creates at least one instance of `ServiceHost` and calls `ServiceHost.Open` on that instance. The process that contains this code can be any kind of process that can load the CLR. The options are a Console Application, a Windows Form, Windows Presentation Foundation (WPF) application, or a Windows Service. Of course, your application might create and manage more than one `ServiceHost` instance, which is perfectly legal.

The flexibility of using different processes for your `ServiceHost` is one of the reasons to adopt self-hosting instead of managed hosting. The main responsibilities you will have when self-hosting are creating, configuring, and opening your instances of `ServiceHost`.

Because you will be writing all the code, you will also have to manage the process lifetime, including making sure the `ServiceHost` closes appropriately when the process shuts down. Another issue you'll have to deal with is process identity: Who does the process run as? It's pretty common for your service to access secure resources (e.g., files, databases) and depending on how your code is written, the user your process is running as may become the user that is accessing the secure resources.

Configuring, Opening, and Closing a ServiceHost

In earlier chapters, you learned the basics of hosting `WebHttpBinding` endpoints, and if you've worked with WCF before reading this book, you're probably already familiar with the `ServiceHost` class. The `ServiceHost` class is used for hosting WCF channel listeners, which listen for messages over a particular address and protocol. `ServiceHost` is used explicitly in the self-hosting case and implicitly in the managed hosting case. We'll get to the implicit usage later in this chapter.

To configure a `ServiceHost` instance, you call `ServiceHost.AddServiceEndpoint` once for each endpoint you want to expose from that service. You can configure endpoints using code, a configuration file, or both. You may also want to configure other parts of `ServiceHost`, such as service or endpoint behaviors, before you call `ServiceHost.Open`.

It is important to remember that the configuration of the `ServiceHost` is based on the type passed to the `ServiceHost`'s constructor, generally known as the service type. The fully qualified type name of the service type must match the name attribute on the service element in the configuration file to make the configuration happen. It is also important to note that it happens during the execution of the constructor of the `ServiceHost`. This means anything you do with code will overwrite whatever is in the configuration file.

When configuring each `ServiceHost` endpoint you must specify the binding. Recall that the binding indicates how the WCF hosting infrastructure should build the channel stack.

When hosting RESTful services you must also use `WebHttpBehavior` on each endpoint so that the WCF dispatching layer will appropriately route HTTP messages to the methods on your service instance. If you don't configure this behavior on each endpoint, the `WebGetAttribute`/`WebInvokeAttribute` routing declarations won't work.

Example 5-1 shows a simple example of hosting a `WebHttpBinding` endpoint inside of a Console Application using `ServiceHost`, rather than `WebServiceHost`.

Example 5-1. Simple use of ServiceHost

```
ServiceHost sh =
    new ServiceHost(typeof(HostingExample));
ServiceEndpoint se = sh.AddServiceEndpoint(typeof(HostingExample),
                    new WebHttpBinding(),
                    "http://localhost:8080/Hosting");
se.Behaviors.Add(new WebHttpBehavior());
sh.Open();
Console.WriteLine("Service is running...");
Console.ReadLine();
sh.Close();
```

The code in Example 5-1 is pretty straightforward and simple. First, you create the `ServiceHost` passing in the service type to the constructor (in this case the type is named `HostingExample`). Next you call `AddServiceEndpoint`, specifying the contract (which is the same as the service type in this case), binding (`WebHttpBinding`), and address (which needs to use HTTP).

Next, get the `ServiceEndpoint` object back from the call to `AddServiceEndpoint`. You need this object reference so you can add the `WebHttpBehavior` to the `ServiceEndpoint.Behaviors` collection.

Finally, a call to `ServiceHost.Open` is necessary to get the communication up and running. In this case we also need a way to keep the process alive while we want to process messages. A simple way to do this when using a Console Application is to call `Console.ReadLine`. When the service stops (after pressing Enter on the console in this particular case), we call `ServiceHost.Close` to clean up any remaining resources.

This code isn't very robust, because when it calls `ServiceHost.Open` or `ServiceHost.Close` all sorts of bad things could happen. What if the binding isn't compatible with a particular contract? What if the URI is already being listened on? The typical response to this problem would be to put the call to `ServiceHost.Open` in a `try` block and just call `ServiceHost.Close` inside of the `finally` block. That would be the correct way to write this code except for the fact that `ServiceHost.Close` is only to be used when gracefully shutting down a service (i.e., it will block and wait for currently executing requests to finish before shutting down). Calling `ServiceHost.Close` when something has gone wrong will actually cause another exception to be thrown, so we can't use a typical `try/catch/finally` block to deal with `ServiceHost` lifetime.

The way to deal with this problem is to write code that takes the various states of `ServiceHost` into account. The `ServiceHost.State` property will show you the current state of your `ServiceHost` instance. In fact, this property is part of an interface named `ICommunicationObject`. Each WCF communication class (each class that uses some sort of communication stack) implements this interface, including of course `ServiceHost` (inherited from the `ServiceHostBase` base class). Each `ICommunicationObject` implementation acts like a state-machine, and you can always check a communication object's state by using the `State` property. Table 5-1 shows the values for `Communication State`, which is the type of `ICommunicationObject.State` property. Note that `Service Host` also fires an event for all of its states except `Created`, so you can subscribe to those events on your `ServiceHost` instance if you are interested.

Table 5-1. CommunicationState values

Value	Description	Event
Created	The object has been created, but is not yet being used for communication	n/a
Opening	The object has started, but has not completed the process of opening	Opening
Opened	The object is open and ready for communication	Opened
Closing	The object has started, but has not completed the process of closing	Closing
Closed	The object is closed	Closed
Faulted	The object has faulted	Faulted

This can help us with the robustness issue because `ICommunicationObject` implementations allow some state transitions and disallow others. For example, you can't move from `Faulted` to `Open` because once an `ICommunicationObject` is in the `Faulted` state, it can't perform any communication. This rule also applies to the `ServiceHost.Close` method, since it initiates an ordered shutdown of a `ServiceHost`. The `ServiceHost` instance tries to perform communication cleanup when `ServiceHost.Close` is called, and if the `ServiceHost` is in the `Faulted` state, `ServiceHost.Close` will throw an exception (although it will move the state to `Closed` in the process).

But even if a `ServiceHost` instance is in the `Faulted` state, you can call `ServiceHost.Abort`, which is kind of like pulling the power cord on your computer (where calling Close is like shutting down your computer normally). You should only resort to ServiceHost.Abort when calling ServiceHost.Close would throw an exception, which is when the ServiceHost instance is in the Faulted state.

A more appropriate way to write the code to open a ServiceHost is shown in Example 5-2.

Example 5-2. More robust use of ServiceHost

```
ServiceHost sh =
  new ServiceHost(typeof(HostingExample));
//flag to check if call to Open succeeded
bool openSucceeded = false;
try
{
    ServiceEndpoint se = sh.AddServiceEndpoint(typeof(HostingExample),
            new WebHttpBinding(),
            "http://localhost:8080/Hosting");
    se.Behaviors.Add(new WebHttpBehavior());
    sh.Open();
    openSucceeded = true;
}
catch (Exception ex)
{
    Console.WriteLine("ServiceHost failed to open {0}",ex.ToString());
}
finally
{   //call Abort since the object will be in the Faulted state
    if (!openSucceeded)
        sh.Abort();
}
if (openSucceeded)
{
    Console.WriteLine("Service is running...");
    Console.ReadLine();
}
else
    Console.WriteLine("Service failed to open");
```

 I used a Boolean value in this code to check for success rather than checking the state of the object because when working with ICommunicationObject implementations (not ServiceHost, however), there can sometimes be failures without the object changing states. Although this isn't the case here, I have used the typical and well-documented pattern for consistency with other samples you might see.

The code in Example 5-2 calls ServiceHost.Open inside of a try block. Inside of the finally block we call ServiceHost.Abort if the call to ServiceHost.Open failed (indicated in this case by a local Boolean variable).

Another thing you can do to make this code more robust is to put in an automatic retry code that will attempt to open the ServiceHost if it fails initially (or a specified number of times). Whether you want to do this or simply log the failure for human intervention is up to you.

The call to ServiceHost.Close should be put inside of similarly robust code, as shown in Example 5-3.

Example 5-3. Robust ServiceHost.Close

```
bool closeSucceeded = false;
try
{//try to close
    sh.Close();
    closeSucceeded = true;
}
catch (Exception ex)
{
    Console.WriteLine("ServiceHost failed to close {0}",ex.ToString());
}
finally
{//abort if the call to close failed because we'll be in the Faulted state
    if (!closeSucceeded)
        sh.Abort();
}
```

The code in Example 5-3 follows the same pattern as the code we used to call ServiceHost.Open. This code places the call to ServiceHost.Close inside a try block and, if successful, will check the finally block to see if the call to ServiceHost.Close succeeded or not (again based on a local Boolean value set to true only if the call to ServiceHost.Close succeeds). If the ServiceHost is in the Faulted state, the code appropriately calls ServiceHost.Abort.

This pattern illustrates why you shouldn't put ServiceHost inside of a using block, even though your .NET development habits tell you to do this. ServiceHost implements IDisposable, and if we follow good .NET habits, this means we should always put objects that implement IDisposable in a using block like the one shown in Example 5-4.

Example 5-4. Incorrect management of ServiceHost lifetime

```
static void DontDoThis()
{
    try
    {
        //DON'T DO THIS - THIS IS AN EXAMPLE OF BAD CODE!!!!!
        using (ServiceHost sh =
            new ServiceHost(typeof(HostingExample)))
        {

            ServiceEndpoint se = sh.AddServiceEndpoint(typeof(HostingExample),
                                    new WebHttpBinding(),
```

```
                            "http://localhost:8080/Hosting");
            se.Behaviors.Add(new WebHttpBehavior());
            //what if call to Open fails?  We move to Faulted
            sh.Open();
            //This code never executes
            Console.WriteLine("Service is running...");
            Console.ReadLine();
            sh.Close();
            //when the using block exits,
            //IDisposable.Dispose will be called
            //ServiceHostBase.Dispose calls Close
            //Calling Close on a Faulted object causes
            //an exception to be thrown
        }
    }
    catch (Exception ex)
    {
        //this will be the wrong exception - the one that caused
        //ServiceHost.Open will be lost
        Console.WriteLine("Service host didn't open {0}", ex.Message);
    }
}
```

The comments in Example 5-4 lay out what is wrong with the code, but the basic problem is that if `ServiceHost.Open` or `ServiceHost.Close` fails, that exception will be lost, and the same exception (the one about not being able to use a communication object when it is in the faulted state) will always be available outside of the `using` block.

> The communication object, `System.ServiceModel.ServiceHost`, cannot be used for communication because it is in the `Faulted` state.

Seeing this generic exception instead of the real exception will lead to confusion since it is difficult to debug the real source of the problem, so the rule is, *never put* `Service Host` *in a using block*.

Base Addresses

When you are self-hosting, you can set up *base addresses*. Base addresses are just URIs, but rather than being the full URI that your service will be listening on, they are what their name implies: addresses that are used as the base path for a URI that will have additional relative path segments added after the base path. When you configure base addresses on your `ServiceHost` instance, you can specify relative URIs for your endpoints instead of fully qualified URIs. The WCF hosting infrastructure will then add the relative URIs to the base URIs, and the new full URIs will be used as the address for the endpoint. You can configure base addresses in the code or in the configuration file. In code, they are passed to the constructor of `ServiceHost`, as you can see in Example 5-5.

Example 5-5. Adding base addresses using code

```
//pass in a base address
ServiceHost sh =
    new ServiceHost(typeof(HostingExample),
        new Uri("http://localhost:8080/"));
ServiceEndpoint se = sh.AddServiceEndpoint(typeof(HostingExample),
                        new WebHttpBinding(),
                        "Hosting");
//"Hosting"will be added to base address to form the full URI
```

If you are using the configuration file to add base addresses, place them under the `host/ baseAddresses` element under each service element, as shown in Example 5-6.

Example 5-6. Configuring base addresses in the configuration file

```
<?xml version="1.0" encoding="utf-8" ?>
<configuration>
  <system.serviceModel>
    <services>
      <service name="SimpleWebHosting.HostingExample">
        <host>
          <baseAddresses>
            <add baseAddress="http://localhost:8080"/>
          </baseAddresses>
        </host>
      </service>
    </services>
  </system.serviceModel>
</configuration>
```

`ServiceHost` will look at the scheme of each endpoint's binding and attempt to match a relative address from an endpoint to a base address based on the scheme the binding exposes (each binding object has a `Binding.Scheme` property). Since we are using `WebHttpBinding`, its scheme is used, which is HTTP.

There are some rules to follow when using base addresses. First, you can have only one base address per scheme, which means when using `WebHttpBinding` you can have only one base address that uses HTTP. The result is that when building RESTful services, you can have only one base address, unless you are hosting endpoints that use other bindings on the `ServiceHost` instance you are using to host `WebHttpBinding` endpoints.

The second rule is that, if you use a relative address when configuring an endpoint, there must be a scheme match in the base addresses, otherwise the call to `ServiceHost.Open` will fail.

ServiceHost Versus WebServiceHost

So far in this chapter, we have discussed the `ServiceHost` type. .NET 3.5 includes a new `WebServiceHost` type that derives from `ServiceHost`. You will almost always use `WebServiceHost` as the `ServiceHost` type when hosting RESTful endpoints.

`WebServiceHost` has some extra functionality, but everything I've told you so far about `ServiceHost` (like how to properly call `Open/Close/Abort`) also applies when using `WebServiceHost`.

`WebServiceHost` does the following:

- Disables metadata (e.g., WSDL and mex) to make sure the metadata URIs won't interfere with your `UriTemplate` definitions. This only happens if code or configuration mistakenly tried to enable metadata publishing.

- Automatically creates endpoints for all your contract types using the `WebHttpBinding` so you don't have to call `AddServiceEndpoint` or add configuration to the configuration file.

- Adds the `WebHttpBehavior` to all endpoints so the URI+Verb routing of messages to service instance methods will work.

When choosing between using `ServiceHost` or `WebServiceHost`, the determining factor will typically be whether or not you have non-`WebHttpBinding` endpoints exposed via your service. If you do, use `ServiceHost`. See Figure 5-1.

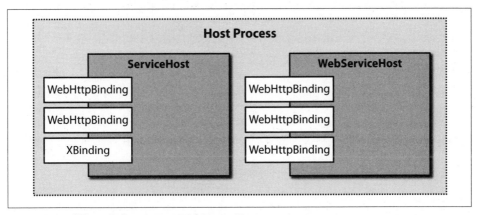

Figure 5-1. Self-hosting ServiceHost/WebServiceHost

 You should only use `ServiceHost` if you are hosting RESTful and non-RESTful endpoints from the same service (a practice that you might want to avoid in the first place, due to its complex nature).

If you are hosting `WebHttpBinding` endpoints only, `WebServiceHost` is the way to go. Example 5-7 shows the earlier "robust" open and close cases from Examples 5-4 and 5-5 with `WebServiceHost`. This allows us to remove the call to `AddServiceEndpoint` and `ServiceEndpoint.Behaviors.Add`.

Example 5-7. Using WebServiceHost

```
ServiceHost sh =
  new WebServiceHost(typeof(HostingExample),
      new Uri("http://localhost:8080/Hosting"));
bool openSucceeded = false;
try
{
    sh.Open();
    openSucceeded = true;
}
catch (Exception ex)
{
    Console.WriteLine("ServiceHost failed to open {0}", ex.ToString());
}
finally
{
    if (!openSucceeded)
        sh.Abort();
}
if (sh.State == CommunicationState.Opened)
{
    Console.WriteLine("Service is running...");
    Console.ReadLine();
}
else
    Console.WriteLine("Service failed to open");
bool closeSucceeded = false;
try
{
    sh.Close();
    closeSucceeded = true;
}
catch (Exception ex)
{
    Console.WriteLine("ServiceHost failed to close {0}", ex.ToString());
}
finally
{
    if (!closeSucceeded)
        sh.Abort();
}
```

If you are hosting multiple contracts (e.g., if your service type implements more than one contract interface type), the WebServiceHost auto-configuration of the service type will fail. When you are implementing multiple contracts on a service type and using WebServiceHost, you must use either AddServiceEndpoint or the configuration file explicitly for all your endpoints. An exception will be thrown on the call to WebService Host.Open in Example 5-8. Note that this sample doesn't use correct robust hosting code.

Example 5-8. Multiple contracts with WebServiceHost

```
class Program
{
    static void Main(string[] args)
    {
        WebServiceHost sh =
            new WebServiceHost(typeof(ServiceType),
                                new Uri("http://localhost:8080/Hosting"));
        sh.Open();
        Console.WriteLine("Service is running");
        Console.ReadLine();
    }
}

public class ServiceType : IWebOne, IWebTwo
{
    string IWebOne.One()
    {
        return "One";
    }
    string IWebTwo.Two()
    {
        return "Two";
    }
}
[ServiceContract]
public interface IWebOne
{
    [OperationContract]
    [WebGet(UriTemplate = "/conflict")]
    string One();
}
[ServiceContract]
public interface IWebTwo
{
    [OperationContract]
    [WebGet(UriTemplate="/conflict")]
    string Two();
}
```

Example 5-8 illustrates why `WebServiceHost` can't auto-configure both endpoints using the base address. There isn't anything in a RESTful service contract that would allow both sets of URIs to exist at the same base URI.

The specific exception thrown is:

> Service *ServiceType* implements multiple `ServiceContract` types and no endpoints are defined in the configuration file. `WebServiceHost` can set up default endpoints, but only if the service implements only a single `ServiceContract`. Either change the service to only implement a single `ServiceContract`, or else define endpoints for the service explicitly in the configuration file.

To resolve this issue, you must either use the configuration file or use `AddServiceEndpoint` explicitly from the code.

The only way to avoid this problem altogether is to be specific on each endpoint and create two unique URIs so that there won't be a URI conflict. When using WebService Host, I have to be explicit about using AddServiceEndpoint or the endpoint configuration element when my service type implements multiple service contracts.

Unfortunately, WebServiceHost has an implementation detail relating to this problem, which I consider to be a bug. When working with multiple contracts, you can't use a base address at all. Even if the relative addresses of the endpoints would create unique URIs for each endpoint, using a base address will result in the above-mentioned exception. This occurs whether you use code or configuration to create the endpoints. You can use the code in Example 5-9 to work around the bug.

Example 5-9. Using explicit addresses with multiple contracts

```
WebServiceHost sh =
    new WebServiceHost(typeof(ServiceType));
//Can't use base addresses if more than one contract
//new Uri("http://localhost:8080/Hosting"));
sh.AddServiceEndpoint(typeof(IWebOne),
                      new WebHttpBinding(),
                      "http://localhost:8080/Hosting/webone");
sh.AddServiceEndpoint(typeof(IWebTwo),
                      new WebHttpBinding(),
                      "http://localhost:8080/Hosting/webtwo");
sh.Open();
Console.WriteLine("Service is running");
Console.ReadLine();
```

Notice that in Example 5-9 the URIs for each contract actually use the same base address, so the endpoint addresses are exactly the same as if you were allowed to use a base address. This bug is annoying, but it isn't a show-stopping problem because there is a work-around, and since having multiple contracts shouldn't come up very often.

You might think that WebServiceHost loses some of its shininess if you have to use AddServiceEndpoint explicitly. Although that's probably true, it still performs two other main tasks: removing metadata URIs (if necessary) and adding the WebHttpBehavior to all the endpoints. The adding of the WebHttpBehavior automatically is the functionality I find most useful, since it's pretty easy to call AddServiceEndpoint or use the configuration file and forget to add the WebHttpBehavior.

Custom ServiceHost

Another technique you might use when self-hosting is to simplify the configuration of your ServiceHost even further by creating a class that derives from ServiceHost or WebServiceHost. You can then use that class instead of ServiceHost/WebServiceHost. This is advantageous when you find some repeatable pattern of configuration or usage that you can codify into a ServiceHost subclass, which will make your hosting code more compact and less error-prone.

Examples of things you might do with a custom `ServiceHost`/`WebServiceHost` type:

- Always add a particular behavior to the `ServiceHost` or to individual endpoints
- Validate configuration
- Override `Dispose` (you can modify `Dispose` to have correct behavior when your `ServiceHost` is created inside of a `using` block)
- Handle events in a consistent way

This is not an exhaustive list of things you can control in your hosting environment when you create a custom `ServiceHost`, merely a few examples. If you are building multiple services, or using multiple `ServiceHost` instances inside of a particular host process, you might find a custom `ServiceHost` very useful.

For example, suppose you were using `WebServiceHost` for its ease of configuration. Instead of having developers on the team write all the "safe" opening and closing code (which also means that code will have to be reviewed for those issues as well), you can simply build a "safe" `WebServiceHost`. See Example 5-10.

Example 5-10. "Safe" WebServiceHost-derived class

```
public class SafeCloseWebServiceHost : WebServiceHost
{
    public SafeCloseWebServiceHost(Type t, params Uri[] baseAddys)
        : base(t, baseAddys)
    {

    }
    public bool SafeOpen()
    {
        bool openSucceeded = false;
        try
        {
            this.Open();
            openSucceeded = true;
        }
        catch (Exception ex)
        {
            Console.WriteLine("ServiceHost failed to open {0}", ex.ToString());
        }
        finally
        {
            if (!openSucceeded)
                this.Abort();
        }
        if (this.State == CommunicationState.Opened)
        {
            Console.WriteLine("Service is running...");
            Console.ReadLine();
        }
        else
            Console.WriteLine("Service failed to open");
        return openSucceeded;
```

```
    }
    public bool SafeClose()
    {
        bool closeSucceeded = false;
        try
        {
            this.Close();
            closeSucceeded = true;
        }
        catch (Exception ex)
        {
            Console.WriteLine("ServiceHost failed to close nicely {0}",
                                                    ex.ToString());
        }
        finally
        {
            if (!closeSucceeded)
                this.Abort();
        }
        return closeSucceeded;
    }
}
```

If I built and mandated the use of `SafeCloseWebServiceHost` from Example 5-10 in my project instead of the `WebServiceHost` class, all the code that opens and closes `Service Host` instances would be greatly simplified.

Building a custom `ServiceHost` is probably overkill for a small project, but for a larger project (or several small projects), it can certainly be worthwhile to have your desired usage of `ServiceHost` codified into a custom `ServiceHost` class.

Hosting in IIS

The other way to host your WCF services is to configure them to run inside of IIS. This is referred to as *managed hosting*, since IIS is managing all of the following:

- Process startup and shutdown
- Process pooling and recycling
- `AppDomain` restart when code or configuration is changed
- Security identity

There are two additional significant advantages to hosting in IIS (there could be more, but I'm fixated on these two). One is that IIS has management capabilities already built in, both in terms of a management UI (the IIS Manager tool) and in terms of API (accessible from WMI and .NET code).

When discussing WCF in general, it's common to refer to managed hosting as *hosting in IIS/WAS*. WAS is the acronym for Windows Process Activation Services (I guess the acronym is really WPAS, but most people still refer to it by its early name, Windows Activation Services or WAS).

WAS is connected to IIS in that it uses the same process model (*w3wp.exe*) and the same administration tool. You can use WAS without having IIS installed. WAS allows you to use HTTP-type activation semantics for protocols other than HTTP (TCP and MSMQ, for example). Since in this book we are only concerned with HTTP, I'm not discussing WAS, but I wanted to address it briefly to be thorough.

The other advantage is the ease with which you can configure caching behavior for REST endpoints using IIS (for a more detailed discussion of caching see Chapter 11).

When hosting your services inside of IIS, you remove some of the responsibilities you have when self-hosting. The IIS infrastructure handles the creation, configuring, opening, and closing of the `ServiceHost` type.

WCF integrates with IIS using the same method ASP.NET uses to integrate with IIS. Although ASP.NET integrates into IIS differently depending on the version (ASP.NET and IIS are much more tightly integrated in IIS7 than in IIS6), conceptually IIS routes HTTP requests to ASP.NET based on the URI of the request being made. ASP.NET registers itself to handle particular URIs. If the URI being requested is registered as one that ASP.NET will handle, IIS transfers the request to ASP.NET.

In IIS, URIs are typically configured to be routed to ASP.NET based only on the file extension part of the URI (although it is possible to do wildcard and literal path mappings as well). Once ASP.NET receives a request, it uses a list of registered managed handlers to choose the .NET type to create to process the incoming request.

To host WCF inside of IIS, it must be registered to handle requests for particular URIs in both the IIS and ASP.NET configuration. This happens automatically when you install .NET 3.5, but WCF also comes with a command-line tool (`ServiceModelReg.exe`) that can be used to control and modify the WCF configuration with IIS/ASP.NET.

ASP.NET is an extensible framework for handling HTTP requests and routing them to instances of .NET types. A type handles requests inside of ASP.NET by registering itself as a handler for particular URIs. Handlers inside of ASP.NET are also generally based on the file extension of a particular URI. All handlers in ASP.NET implement the same interface, `IHttpHandler`. To get integrated with ASP.NET, WCF has registered the *.svc* file extension to be handled by its `IHttpHandler` implementation (`System.ServiceModel.Activation.HttpHandler` if you are interested). The *.svc* file mapping is also done in the IIS configuration to map requests to *.svc* files to be processed by ASP.NET, and then ASP.NET hands the request off to WCF's handler.

An *.svc* file is just a text file that is placed inside of an IIS virtual directory. In addition to its handler, WCF also installs an `IHttpModule` implementation. `IHttpModule` is a higher-level construct in ASP.NET than a handler, and is generally there to perform functions such as authentication and caching, as a module can handle more than just one type of request and generally doesn't actually process the request or generate a response. Modules register themselves to be called for various ASP.NET events before and after a handler does the actual processing of each request.

In the case of WCF, its `System.ServiceModel.Activation.HttpModule` registers itself to be notified of ASP.NET's `PostAuthenticateRequest` event.

 Authentication isn't done by the module, but actually takes place at the IIS/ASP.NET level (see Chapter 8 for more information about security).

In its event handler, the WCF module determines if the request is for an *.svc* file. If it is, the module that causes the request is passed to the WCF Channel Stack. The main purpose of the handler is to ensure that requests ending in *.svc* are actually sent to IIS/ASP.NET. When ASP.NET compatibility mode is enabled the handler actually executes the request (this is discussed in more detail later in this chapter). This configuration of objects (where the module actually processes the request) isn't typical when using ASP.NET and that is why we are discussing it here.

When ASP.NET receives an HTTP request for the *.svc* file extension, the WCF infrastructure that is loaded into ASP.NET will create, configure, and open a `ServiceHost` instance. The configuration of the `ServiceHost` is implicitly handled by the WCF configuration infrastructure when the `ServiceHost` instance is constructed.

The *.svc* file follows the ASP.NET convention of having a directive in the first line. In the case of the *.svc* file, this is the `ServiceHost` directive. The only required attribute on the directive line is `Service`, which has to point to a valid .NET type to implement one or more `ServiceContracts`. Here is a sample *.svc* file:

```
<%@ ServiceHost Service="SimpleWebHosting.HostingExample, SimpleWebHosting" %>
```

When a request is made to this URI, WCF creates a `ServiceHost` based on the type specified in the service attribute. This, of course, implies that this type can be loaded, so the assembly that contains the type must either be in the *bin* directory or the GAC (if it is fully qualified).

To make this service work an entry must be put into the *web.config* configuration file, as shown in Example 5-11.

Example 5-11. Web.config entries for svc file

```
<system.serviceModel>
  <behaviors>
    <endpointBehaviors>
```

```
      <behavior name="web">
        <webHttp/>
      </behavior>
    </endpointBehaviors>
  </behaviors>
  <services>
    <service name="SimpleWebHosting.HostingExample ">
      <endpoint address="" binding="webHttpBinding"
                contract="SimpleWebHosting.HostingExample "
                behaviorConfiguration="web"/>
    </service>
  </services>
</system.serviceModel>
```

Because ServiceHost is created automatically based on the *.svc*, we can only configure the endpoints using the *web.config* configuration file. The WCF infrastructure looks for a match between the Service attribute in the *.svc* file and the name attribute of a service element in the configuration file. If a service element match is found, an endpoint is configured according to the service/endpoint element (there can be multiple endpoint elements under a single service element).

 The Service attribute in the *.svc* file must have a more fully qualified name than the entries in the configuration file. WCF requires the assembly name as part of the service attribute in order to load the type into memory. Once it loads the type, WCF looks for the type name (without the assembly name) in the configuration file for both the name and contract attributes.

The configuration in Example 5-11 causes the endpoint to be configured using WebHttpBinding as the binding. The behaviorConfiguration attribute points to a behavior element by name (under the endpointBehaviors element). The behaviors found in that named behavior element will be added to the ServiceEndpoint.Behaviors collection. The WebHttpBehavior is then added to this endpoint based on this configuration. This is the exact configuration we need to build a RESTful endpoint (the WebHttpBinding and the WebHttpBehavior).

In this example, the service type is compiled into an assembly added to the bin directory of the ASP.NET virtual directory. If we were using a "web project," where ASP.NET dynamically compiles the code the first time the site is hit, the service type could be inside of a code file in the special *App_Code* directory. In this case, you can actually put the service type definition inline inside of the *.svc* file itself. In that case (shown in Example 5-12), WCF compiles the type on demand the first time the *.svc* file is requested (to do this, WCF has also registered a build provider with ASP.NET, which is how it can get involved in the compilation step).

Example 5-12. Inline service type definition

```
<%@ ServiceHost Service="InlineService" Language="C#" %>
using System;
using System.ServiceModel;
using System.ServiceModel.Web;

[ServiceContract]
public class InlineService{

[OperationContract]
[WebGet(UriTemplate="*")]
public string InlineServiceMethod()
{
    return "I got compiled by WCF into " + this.GetType().AssemblyQualifiedName;
}
}
```

When we access this endpoint, we get the following result. This result will be slightly different every time the page is recompiled based on **AppDomain** or a process restart.

```
<string xmlns="http://schemas.microsoft.com/2003/10/
Serialization/">I got compiled by WCF into InlineService, App_Web_ihhkOqkc,
    Version=0.0.0.0, Culture=neutral, PublicKeyToken=null</string>
```

This is a pretty interesting piece of functionality, but as is the case with the precompiled service type in Example 5-11, we still need to add the appropriate entry into the *web.config* file to make the code work as shown in Example 5-13.

Example 5-13. Inline service configuration

```
<system.serviceModel>
<behaviors>
    <endpointBehaviors>
        <behavior name="web">
            <webHttp/>
        </behavior>
    </endpointBehaviors>
</behaviors>
<services>
    <service name="SimpleWebHosting.HostingExample">
        <endpoint address=""
            binding="webHttpBinding"
            contract="SimpleWebHosting.HostingExample"
            behaviorConfiguration="web"/>
    </service>
<!--this is for the service that is inside of the .svc file -->
  <service name="InlineService">
    <endpoint address=""
            binding="webHttpBinding"
            contract="InlineService"
            behaviorConfiguration="web"/>
  </service>
</services>
</system.serviceModel>
```

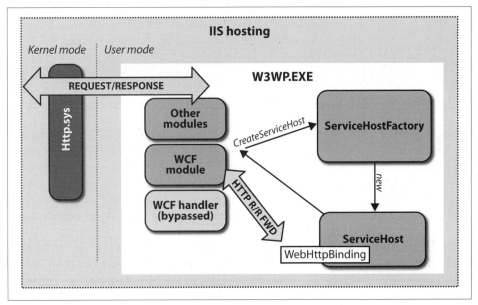

Figure 5-2. IIS WCF hosting architecture

Having to add configuration into the *web.config* file for each service becomes a little tedious. It would be nice to not have to put the entries into the *web.config* file. We already discussed how to use `WebServiceHost` to do this in the case of self-hosting. If we could use `WebServiceHost` in the managed hosting case it could help simplify the configuration of RESTful endpoints.

Earlier in this section, I described how the WCF infrastructure creates a `ServiceHost` instance and calls `ServiceHost.Open` on that instance based on the first incoming HTTP request. Neither the module nor the handler creates the `ServiceHost` directly; instead, they go through a well-known layer of indirection. That layer of indirection is a classic factory pattern that is implemented by a type named `ServiceHostFactory`.

WCF calls `ServiceHostFactory.CreateServiceHost` to access the `ServiceHost` instance. It then calls `ServiceHost.Open` on that instance. This interaction is shown in Figure 5-2, along with a general view of the interaction between the *http.sys* kernel mode HTTP listener built into Windows and how those requests are forwarded to the appropriate *W3WP.exe* process.

Notice that in both of the .*svc* files, we only specified the service attribute (although for the inline compiled example, Example 5-12, we also specified the language); nowhere did we specify a `ServiceHostFactory`, which means we get the default `ServiceHostFactory` type.

There is also a `ServiceHostFactoryBase` that you can use to customize the `ServiceHost` creation experience even more. Use this when you don't have a .NET type that implements your service. For example, the Workflow Services infrastructure in .NET 3.5 (see Chapter 8) has a `WebServiceHostFactory` named `WorkflowServiceHostFactory` that derives from `ServiceHostFactoryBase`.

We can specify a different `ServiceHostFactory` type by adding the `Factory` attribute to the `ServiceHost` directive (note that in Visual Studio 2008 without SP1, the `Factory` attribute is rejected by IntelliSense). You could create your own type that derives from `ServiceHostFactory` and use it to create `WebServiceHost` instead of a "regular" `ServiceHost` instance. It turns out you don't need to do that, though, because .NET 3.5 already includes one that does exactly what we want: `System.ServiceModel.Activation.WebServiceHostFactory`. Using `System.ServiceModel.Activation.WebServiceHostFactory` as the value of the `Factory` attribute, we can remove the `web.config` entries for the two services. Everything will be the same, but the configuration is much simpler, since we don't require any entries in the *web.config* file.

Example 5-14 shows the inline compiled *.svc* file (just the `ServiceHost` directive, since the rest of the file is exactly the same) using `System.ServiceModel.Activa tion.WebServiceHostFactory`.

Example 5-14. Using WebServiceHostFactory

```
<%@ ServiceHost Service="InlineService"
 Language="C#"
Factory="System.ServiceModel.Activation.WebServiceHostFactory" %>
```

For creating WCF service endpoints that return JSON-formatted messages instead of XML messages, you can use `WebScriptServiceHostFactory` (see Chapter 7 for more information about JSON, AJAX, and WCF).

This covers the basics of managed hosting. Let's see how these basics can apply to IIS-specific hosting issues that you might run into.

ASP.NET Compatibility

The ASP.NET context isn't available in the normal IIS WCF hosting mode. In fact, the WCF `HttpModule` explicitly nulls out `HttpContext.Current`, which is where you'd generally find the `HttpContext` for the currently executing request. This means that you don't have to enter code that is specific to a particular hosting environment in your services. Of course, WCF includes per-request context that you can use in a host-agnostic way. In the RESTful case, we have both the standard WCF `Operation Context` (available via `OperationContext.Current`) and the `WebOperationContext` (available via `WebOperationContext.Current`), with its various flavors of context based on the execution context. `WebOperationContext.IncomingRequestContext` and `WebOperationContext.OutgoingResponseContext` are available in the case of the execution of a service request (see Chapter 2 for a more detailed discussion of `WebOperation Context`).

In some cases, you might only be hosting inside of IIS and have a need for functionality that is available only on the `HttpContext`. This is probably more likely in the RESTful service case than in other WCF scenarios because of the very nature of `WebHttpBinding`, and friends might push you toward IIS hosting.

In the WCF context, the authentication information (see Chapter 8 for more information about authentication) and the entire HTTP programming model are exposed (see Chapter 11 for more information about interacting with HTTP), but the ASP.NET processing pipeline is not. See Chapter 11 for an example of using ASP.NET's pipeline instead of the `WebOperationContext`. If you want to use the functionality of ASP.NET's `HttpContext`, turn on `AspNetCompatibilityMode`. This is a global switch per *web.config*, which means that when you turn it on, it is turned on for all *.svc* files in that virtual directory. This is shown in Example 5-15.

Example 5-15. AspNetCompatibilityMode enabled

```
<system.serviceModel>
  <serviceHostingEnvironment aspNetCompatibilityEnabled="true"/>
</system.serviceModel>
```

Once you enable `AspNetCompatibilityMode`, the WCF `HttpHandler` becomes the request processor, rather than the `HttpModule`, and the `HttpContext.Current` becomes available (see Figure 5-3).

Unfortunately, after adding this configuration, you will get an exception if you try to use any of the services in the Virtual Directory:

> The service cannot be activated because it does not support ASP.NET compatibility. ASP.NET compatibility is enabled for this application. Turn off ASP.NET compatibility mode in the web.config or add the `AspNetCompatibilityRequirements` attribute to the service type with `RequirementsMode` setting as `'Allowed'` or `'Required'`.

Like many configuration settings in WCF, not only do we have to make the configuration changes, the contract definition must be changed to be consistent with those settings. In this case, the exception is pretty clear: you must add the `AspNetCompatibilityRequirementsAttribute` to the service type, as shown in Example 5-16. In a real deployment, you will have to add this attribute to each service in the Virtual Directory.

Example 5-16. Adding AspNetCompatibilityRequirementsAttribute

```
[ServiceContract()]
[AspNetCompatibilityRequirements(RequirementsMode=
AspNetCompatibilityRequirementsMode.Allowed)]
public class HostingExample
```

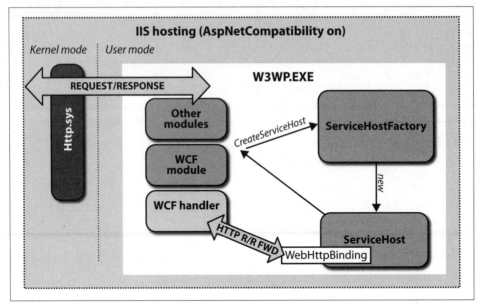

Figure 5-3. IIS hosting using handler

```
{
    [OperationContract]
    [WebGet(UriTemplate = "*")]
    public string TheMethod()
    {
        string ret = "Just testing service hosting ";
        if (HttpContext.Current != null)
            ret += " and HttpContext.Current isn't null!!!";
        return ret;
    }
}
```

Notice that Example 5-16 also includes code that will indicate whether or not the HttpContext is available. You can see the result of hitting this resource in Figure 5-4.

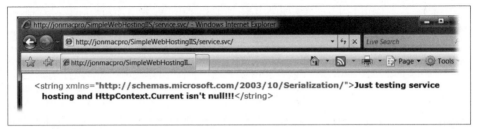

Figure 5-4. HttpContext enabled

Once you enable ASP.NET compatibility in both in the configuration file and the service type, you will have full access to ASP.NET's HttpContext.Current and all the

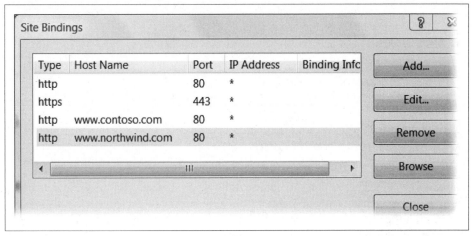

Type	Host Name	Port	IP Address	Binding Infc
http		80	*	
https		443	*	
http	www.contoso.com	80	*	
http	www.northwind.com	80	*	

Add...

Edit...

Remove

Browse

Close

Site Bindings

Figure 5-5. Multiple hostnames mapped to one site

functionality that is associated with that API. Using `HttpContext` means that you are tied to being hosted inside of ASP.NET, but you can still write code to execute different code paths depending on the availability of `HttpContext`. You can also check the `ServiceHostingEnvironment.AspNetCompatibilityEnabled` property if you want to see if `AspNetCompatibilityEnabled` has been turned on.

If your service is running in ASP.NET and you want to use some other feature of the ASP.NET pipeline, but still have the ability to actually host outside of ASP.NET, you can easily write the code to be conditional depending on whether the ASP.NET context is there (one way is to see if `HttpContext.Current` is null before using it, as we did in Example 5-16).

Multiple Hostnames

When building websites inside of IIS, it's pretty common to have multiple hostnames. When an HTTP client sends a request, it sends a host header value, which is set to the domain name of the requested URI (HTTP 1.0 clients don't send this value, so if you are supporting older clients this technique won't work). Most modern web servers (including IIS) allow you to configure one server to route requests to different websites based on the host header value. Figure 5-5 shows this configuration on an IIS 7.0 website (IIS versions 5 and 6 also support this feature).

Unfortunately, this will not work with WCF services. `ServiceHostFactory` and `Service Host` (and their derived versions) use the hostname for creating the HTTP listening endpoint when hosted in IIS, and an exception is thrown when there are multiple hostnames. This is because multiple URIs will be passed into the call to `ServiceHost Factory.CreateServiceHost`. Example 5-17 shows the exception details.

Example 5-17. System.ArgumentException thrown when multiple hostnames exist

```
"This collection already contains an address with scheme http.
 There can be at most one address per scheme in this collection.
Parameter name: item

Description: An unhandled exception occurred during the execution
 of the current web request. Please review the stack trace for more information
 about the error and where it originated in the code.
Exception Details: System.ArgumentException: This collection
 already contains an address with scheme http. There can be
 at most one address per scheme in this collection.
Parameter name: item"
```

The way around this problem is to not use multiple hostnames on one website. Instead, create multiple websites that all point to the same physical directory on the file system. Perhaps not the most elegant solution, but it doesn't really require any additional work than the multiple host headers on one site, just a different configuration.

Removing the .svc File Extension

The architectural style of REST centers on URIs; some people view URIs as the *key piece* of RESTful design. The REST architecture style is of course based on resources that are addressable using unique URIs, and how to interact with them through the uniform interface. URIs are a very important part of this style.

When creating RESTful services, it is important to design URIs very carefully. A lot of the work your clients do revolves around working with URIs. Additionally, having nice URIs is considered important in most REST circles.

This is why many people who use WCF inside of IIS find the *.svc* extension so abhorrent. Using *.svc* generally just makes the URIs inelegant, and inelegant URIs are just not cool (although technically speaking there isn't anything necessarily unRESTful about inelegant URIs). One problem with using the *.svc* file is that a URI in REST is supposed to represent the unique name of a resource. The *.svc* file extension does not look like part of the name of a resource; it just looks like the leaking of a particular implementation detail.

To avoid the issues that come with using *.svc* files, we can build a module for IIS/ASP.NET that rewrites URIs so that requests will come without the *.svc* file. Example 5-18 shows one potential implementation for such a module.

Example 5-18. IHttpModule to remove the .svc extension

```
using System.Web;

public class RestModule : IHttpModule
{

    public void Dispose()
```

```
    { }

    public void Init(HttpApplication app)
    {
        app.BeginRequest += delegate
        {
            HttpContext ctx = HttpContext.Current;
            string path = ctx.Request.AppRelativeCurrentExecutionFilePath;

            int i = path.IndexOf('/', 2);
            if (i > 0)
            {
                string svc = path.Substring(0, i) + ".svc";
                string rest = path.Substring(i, path.Length - i);
                string qs = ctx.Request.QueryString.ToString();
                ctx.RewritePath(svc, rest,qs,false);
            }
        };
    }
}
```

After making the type available to an ASP.NET application (by compiling it and putting it into the `bin` directory or using the `App_Code` functionality), you need to modify `web.config` to use this module:

```
<httpModules>
  <add name="NoMoreSVC" type="RestModule, SimpleWebHostingIIS"/>
</httpModules>
```

> Note that if you are using IIS 5 or 6 (XP or Windows Server 2003), you'll have to map a wildcard handler for *aspnet_isapi.dll* to make this module work.

This module removes the *.svc* extension from the URI that the clients use. For example, the URI *http://host/album.svc/instance/* will be changed to *http://host/album/instance/* after adding this module.

> In a book like this, I generally avoid including my own custom infra-structure code, because I think it takes away from learning about the underlying technology. However, I'm making an exception here be-cause you're likely to need this functionality once you adopt REST using WCF. I hope you find it useful. Don't feel obligated to use it; if you are happy with the *.svc* being part of your URIs, don't bother.

Custom ServiceHostFactory

Earlier in this chapter, we discussed building a custom ServiceHost in a self-hosting scenario. There are compelling reasons to use a custom ServiceHost type when using managed hosting as well.

Recall that there is no way to instruct the WCF hosting infrastructure in IIS to use a custom ServiceHost type (there is no ServiceHost type attribute in the .*svc* file). Fortunately, we can work around this issue using the Factory attribute.

Like ServiceHost, ServiceHostFactory is an open extensibility point. If you want WCF to use a custom ServiceHost, you can create a custom ServiceHostFactory. If you are only using managed hosting, you can often get the effect of a custom ServiceHost by building a custom ServiceHostFactory, since the factory contains the code that will build and configure a ServiceHost before it is opened by the WCF hosting infrastructure.

The applications of a custom ServiceHostFactory are as expansive as the applications of a custom ServiceHost. For example, suppose that your managed hosting environment doesn't include a method for specifying when a ServiceHost has been opened or closed. By implementing a custom ServiceHostFactory, you can hook up event handlers to the events of the ServiceHost being created, and your service will be notified when those lifetime events occur. See Example 5-19.

Example 5-19. Custom ServiceHostFactory

```
namespace SimpleWebHostingIIS
{
    public class EventHandlingServiceHostFactory : WebServiceHostFactory
    {
        public override ServiceHostBase CreateServiceHost(string constructorString,
            Uri[] baseAddresses)
        {
            //note that the base class returns ServiceHostBase, but its actually
            //WebServiceHost in this case
            ServiceHostBase sh =
                base.CreateServiceHost(constructorString, baseAddresses);
            //we can cast to WebServiceHost if we want
            WebServiceHost wsh = sh as WebServiceHost;
            //subscribe to events
            wsh.Opened += new EventHandler(wsh_Opened);
            wsh.Closed += new EventHandler(wsh_Closed);
            //I could subscribe to more events if needed
            return sh;
        }

        void wsh_Closed(object sender, EventArgs e)
        {
            Debug.WriteLine("WebServiceHost closed!");
        }

        void wsh_Opened(object sender, EventArgs e)
```

```
        {
            Debug.WriteLine("WebServiceHost opened!");
        }
    }
}
```

To use this `ServiceHostFactory`, you need only to change the value of the `Factory` attribute in the *.svc* file like this:

```
<%@ ServiceHost Service="SimpleWebHosting.HostingExample,
  SimpleWebHosting" Factory="SimpleWebHostingIIS.EventHandlingServiceHostFactory" %>
```

There are a large number of WCF and WCF RESTful extensibility scenarios that can be solved very simply by creating a custom `ServiceHost` and/or `ServiceHostFactory`.

Hosting Wrap-Up

In this chapter, I've laid out the issues you'll face when using self- or managed hosting. So which choice is the best? Obviously, there isn't always one right answer, but there are a couple of common pathways to the right choice.

One issue many developers run into is the lack of support some IT departments have for IIS (to be honest, there are some shops that stay away from IIS like the plague). If this is the case for you, self-hosting is obviously the only choice. Building a custom Windows service is generally the way to deploy your services, because you get support from the OS for startup, shutdown, management, and security identity. That's one pretty easy path.

What if your IT department does support IIS? What is the choice then? In general, I'd stick with IIS. IIS has a better management and deployment story than a custom Windows service would have. Another benefit of IIS is that it supports easy configuration for kernel and user mode caching (see Chapter 11).

If given the choice, I'd side with IIS for hosting unless there is a compelling reason to go with self-hosting.

Summary

In this chapter, we discussed the basics of hosting a WCF RESTful service. The two choices are self-hosting and managed hosting.

With self-hosting, you get a fair amount of control over the hosting process, which centers on the `ServiceHost` (or `WebServiceHost`) type for creating channel listeners with WCF. In many ways, hosting WCF web endpoints is no different than hosting any WCF endpoint from a self-hosting point of view. In both cases, you will be responsible for creating, configuring, opening, and closing the `ServiceHost` inside of the process. `WebServiceHost` is helpful in the RESTful case because its auto-configuration features can greatly simplify your hosting code and infrastructure. Using a custom

ServiceHost type can help encapsulate much of this infrastructure code into a nice, easy-to-use type.

The other option is to use managed hosting, in which the WCF infrastructure that is integrated into IIS/ASP.NET will manage interactions with the ServiceHost. The *.svc* file tells WCF which service to host, and the configuration file tells WCF how to host it. In the RESTful case, the WebServiceHostFactory helps to simplify managed configuration. For further customization in the managed hosting case, you can use a custom ServiceHostFactory type to interject your code into the hosting infrastructure, enabling you to customize the managed hosting experience when your scenario calls for deviation from the norm.

CHAPTER 6

Programming Feeds

Exposing data through a "feed" on the Web isn't a new idea. A machine-readable format that can push or pull data to or from a client application so that users can receive updated information about their favorite websites has been around for many years. In fact, over the past few years, this capability has solidified into something so ubiquitous that not only do bloggers and news sites expose feeds of their data, but many websites do as well (even my airline has a feed I can subscribe to for news and fare information).

In this chapter, we'll cover how you can use WCF 3.5 to build feeds. You may not be building the next great blogging engine, but feeds are so mainstream today that enterprises are now adopting them to expose internal data that you might not think of as classic feed data. Now that every browser has a feed reader, feeds can be an important tool in your toolbox for building your systems, even if you aren't building commercial websites or blog engines.

 If you haven't had a lot of exposure to feeds, I highly recommend opening your favorite browser and search engine and searching on "web feeds" or "RSS and Atom," which will likely turn up some pretty lively sources of information regarding the history and current use of feeds. Use your browser or download a feed reader (just search for "feed reader" to find one), and try it out before reading the rest of this chapter.

Building a Feed with WCF

Let's dive right into how to use the Web Programming Model in WCF 3.5 to build a feed. Two important pieces of the WCF infrastructure make it possible and easy-to-build feeds: the `WebGetAttribute` and a set of .NET types in the `System.ServiceModel.Syndication` namespace that represent the structure of a feed in memory and that WCF 3.5 can serialize into the correct XML formats for feed readers to understand.

We covered the `WebGetAttribute` in Chapter 2. Since you retrieve feeds via HTTP `GET` requests, the ability to build a service method that can return results based on such requests is key to building a feed. The `UriTemplate` mechanism will also come in handy if and when you want to do more than just expose a basic feed at a particular URI.

The second piece of the WCF 3.5 infrastructure you'll use is a set of .NET types in the `System.ServiceModel.Syndication` namespace that represents the structure of a feed in memory, and more importantly, that the WCF serialization infrastructure can serialize into the correct XML formats for feed readers to understand—namely, RSS 2.0 and Atom 1.0. These types—the most important of which is `SyndicationFeed`—are also extensible, which means that if new feed standards become available, or if you just want to use the standard formats in a repeatable way, you can derive from the appropriate class and plug it into this WCF system. You also can use these classes to consume feeds, which we'll cover in Appendix A.

The object model implemented by `SyndicationFeed` and the other types in the `System.ServiceModel.Syndication` namespace allows you take the data you want exposed as part of your feed and push it into the WCF feed object model. The object model will then take care of serializing those objects into the appropriate XML for your feed. This frees you from having to do any of the heavy lifting in terms of generating the appropriate XML for either feed format (or for other feed formats that might be created in the future).

The top level of this feed object model is the `SyndicationFeed` class. `SyndicationFeed` is modeled after the Atom 1.0 specification rather than RSS. Atom's format is more complex than the RSS specification, so the API is geared toward Atom so that it can represent the richness of Atom. The infrastructure will happily serialize either format, although when it serializes to RSS, the non-RSS data is serialized into the Atom 1.0 element names (with an `xmlns` attribute added to reference the Atom namespace URI). To be honest, the industry appears to be moving toward Atom and away from RSS, as every major feed reader now supports Atom, and the Atom Publishing Protocol (discussed in Appendix A) is beginning to take hold as the RESTful protocol on top of feeds for updates. Therefore, although we will spend some time talking about RSS, most of this chapter will focus on Atom.

`SyndicationFeed` has a number of properties, each of which is a collection of another type from the `System.ServiceModel.Syndication` namespace that represents a different part of a feed, as depicted in Figure 6-1.

`SyndicationFeed.Items` is perhaps the most important of these properties, and it contains the meat of the feed: the feed items. `SyndicationFeed.Authors` contains a list of `SyndicationPerson` objects, which represent the author(s) of this feed. You can categorize feeds and feed items for easy consumption (you may subscribe to a feed that exposes different feeds for some or all of the categories used in entries), so `SyndicationFeed.Categories` holds on to `SyndicationCategory` objects that represent those categories. Also, `SyndicationFeed` includes a `Links` collection, which comprises `SyndicationLink` objects that represent links to or from the feed. Table 6-1 lists the rest of the `SyndicationFeed` properties.

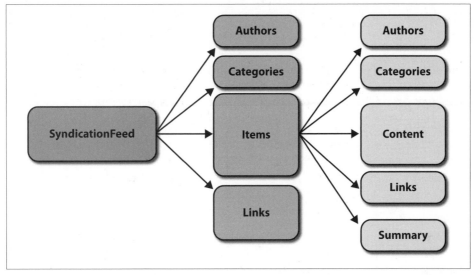

Figure 6-1. SyndicationFeed object model

All of these objects implement the `IExtensibleSyndicationObject` interface. This interface defines two read-only properties: `AttributeExtensions` and `ElementExtensions`. These two properties are like wildcards and support serializing objects into the feed XML attributes or elements that aren't "strongly typed" (i.e., known elements or attributes of either RSS or Atom).

Another type that is fairly important in this system is `SyndicationContent` and its derived classes. For each content-related item in a feed, the object model uses this class or one of its derived classes to represent the data in the feed. This data could be text, XML data, or a URI. Hence, the derived classes are `TextSyndicationContent`, `XmlSyndicationContent`, and `UriSyndicationContent`. These types are then serialized to the correct kind of element in the feed. Every other feed type uses these types appropriately for each piece of data to be serialized into the feed (we'll discuss this in more detail in a moment, when we look at the XML output from serialization).

Table 6-1 shows how all of the properties of `SyndicationFeed` are serialized into Atom or RSS feeds. The "atom" namespace prefix refers back to the Atom namespace URI (namely, *http://www.w3.org/2005/Atom*) inside an RSS document.

Table 6-1. How SyndicationFeed serializes/deserializes into RSS and Atom

Object/property	Atom	RSS
SyndicationFeed	`<feed/>`	`<rss/>`
AttributeExtensions	Attribute on `<feed/>`; one per object in the collection	Attribute on `<channel/>`; one per object in the collection
Authors	`<author/>`; one per object in the collection	`<managingEditor/>` if one element, or `atom:author` if multiple elements

Object/property	Atom	RSS
Categories	`<category/>`; one per object in the collection	`<category/>`; one per object in the collection
Contributors	`<contributor/>`; one per object in the collection	`<atom:contributor/>`; one per object in the collection
Copyright	`<rights/>`	`<copyright/>`
Description	`<subtitle/>`	`<description/>`
ElementExtensions	Element written as a child of `<feed/>`; one per object in the collection	Element written as a child of `<channel/>`; one per object in the collection
Generator	`<generator/>`	`<atom:generator/>`
Id	`<id/>`	`<atom:id/>`
ImageUri	`<logo/>`	`<image/>`
Items	`<entry/>`; one per object in the collection	`<item/>`; one per object in the collection
Language	Not serialized	`<language/>`
LastUpdatedDate	`<updated/>`	`<lastBuildDate/>`
Links	`<link/>`; one per object in the collection	`<link/>` element; if the link is an "alternate" link it uses `<atom:link/>`
Title	`<title/>`	`<title/>`

You can use the `SyndicationFeed` class to build up your feed without having to decide which feed format to use. For the example in this chapter, you'll build a feed on top of the Windows Event Log.

 The Event Log provides information regarding what is happening on a particular machine, so it seems useful to have a feed of that information, especially if we can subscribe to feeds from multiple machines.

Example 6-1 shows code for creating a top-level `SyndicationFeed` object from the `EventLog` data.

Example 6-1. Creating an EventLog feed

```
EventLog el = new EventLog(logName);
SyndicationFeed feed = new SyndicationFeed();
feed.Title =
    new TextSyndicationContent(String.Format("{0} {1} EventLog Feed",
        Environment.MachineName,
        el.Log));
feed.Description = new TextSyndicationContent("A feed of data from the EventLog");
feed.Authors.Add(new SyndicationPerson{Name=Environment.MachineName});
feed.Id = "urn:uuid:" + Environment.MachineName + el.Log;
```

The code in Example 6-1 uses `System.Diagnostic.EventLog` to open a particular log by name, and then sets the `Title` and `Description` properties and adds an author (i.e., the machine where the data is coming from). Next is the `Id` property, which is a string that will turn into the `<id/>` element inside an Atom feed. The Atom specification dictates that the `<id/>` element must be a unique, permanent URI (well, really it states that it must be an *Internationalized Resource Identifier*, or IRI, but we don't need to go into that much technical detail on the spec; suffice it to say that you can turn an IRI into a URI). We used the machine name and log name to create a recreatable, retrievable identifier.

Now that we've created the basic feed "envelope," let's move on to the data inside the feed.

SyndicationItem

Since feeds are all about serving up data, the most used property of `SyndicationFeed` is `Items`, which is a collection of `SyndicationItem`.

`SyndicationItem` is where most of the work with feeds is done, since each instance represents an item in the feed (`<entry/>` in the case of Atom or `<item/>` in the case of RSS). Table 6-2 shows the mapping between the properties of the `SyndicationItem` object model and the Atom and RSS XML formats.

Table 6-2. How SyndicationItem serializes/deserializes into RSS and Atom

Object/property	Atom	RSS
SyndicationItem	`<entry/>`	`<item/>`
AttributeExtensions	Attribute on `<entry/>`; one per object in the collection	Attribute on `<item/>`; one per object in the collection
Authors	`<author/>`; one per object in the collection	`<managingEditor/>` if one element, or atom:author if multiple elements
Categories	`<category/>`; one per object in the collection	`<category/>`; one per object in the collection
Content	`<content/>`	If text and Summary are null, `<description/>`; otherwise, `<atom:content/>`
Contributors	`<contributor/>`; one per object in the collection	`<atom:contributor/>`; one per object in the collection
Copyright	`<rights/>`	`<copyright/>`
ElementExtensions	Element written as a child of `<entry/>`; one per object in the collection	Element written as a child of `<item/>`; one per object in the collection
Id	`<id/>`	`<atom:id/>`
LastUpdatedDate	`<updated/>`	`<atom:updated/>`

Object/property	Atom	RSS
Links	`<link/>`; one per object in the collection	`<link/>`; if the link is an "alternate" link, it uses `<atom:link/>`
PublishDate	`<published/>`	`<pubDate/>`
SourceFeed	`<source/>`	`<source/>`
Summary	`<summary/>`	`<description/>` if not null
Title	`<title/>`	`<title/>`

The most used property of `SyndicationItem` is `Content`. `Content` is a `SyndicationContent` type, meaning that the `Content` of an item can be text, XML, or a URI, depending on the kind of item you are creating. Most feed items are text-based (e.g., news stories and blog entries), in which case you would use the `TextSyndicationContent` type. However, the data of your item might be a link to binary data, in which case you would use the `UriSyndicationContent` type. Use the `XmlSyndicationContent` type if your content data is formatted as XML.

The next issue of interest is whether to use the `Content` property at all. Because the `Content` object model is modeled on Atom, when you format your feed as an Atom feed, you can use the `Content` property as-is and you're done.

The `Summary` property, which is a `TextSyndicationContent` type, is useful when you want to show a snippet of your feed's content. The `Summary` property is serialized to a `<summary/>` element in Atom-formatted feeds. Note that feed validators (such as the one located at *http://www.feedvalidator.org/*) will not function properly if the `<content/>` element and the `<summary/>` element contain the same data.

If you are formatting your feed as RSS, set the `Content` property to a `TextSyndicationContent` object. The text of the `Content` property will be used to generate the `<description/>` element, as RSS allows you to use the `<description/>` element as the entire entry. This is the case only if the `Summary` property is null. If the `Summary` property is not null, the `<description/>` will contain the text from the `Summary` property and the `Content` property will be serialized as an `<atom:content/>` element inside the RSS item.

For our event log feed example, let's leave the `Summary` property null so that when you format the feed as RSS its value will be used to generate a complete `<description/>`. Example 6-2 shows the code.

Example 6-2. Defining and populating a List of SyndicationItem

```
List<SyndicationItem> items = new List<SyndicationItem>();
feed.Items = items;

foreach (EventLogEntry e in el.Entries)
{
    items.Add(new SyndicationItem
    {
        Title = new TextSyndicationContent(String.Format
```

```
("{0}:{1}:{2}", e.Source, e.Category, e.EntryType.ToString())),
        Content = new TextSyndicationContent(e.Message),
        PublishDate = new DateTimeOffset(e.TimeGenerated),
        LastUpdatedTime = new DateTimeOffset(e.TimeGenerated),
        Id = "urn:uuid:" + e.Index.ToString()


    });

}
```

In this code, the `SyndicationFeed.Items` property is initially null, so we have to create an object that is `IEnumerable<SyndicationItem>` (the type of the `Items` property) and set the `Items` property to that object. For convenience, this code uses the generic `List` type.

The rest of the code is pretty simple; it just enumerates over each `EventLogEntry` in the `EventLog.Entries` collection and creates a new `SyndicationItem` object for each entry. The example uses the machine name, the source, and the category as the `Title`, and uses the data inside the `EventLogEntry` for the `Content` of each item.

To create each `SyndicationItem`, you'll use the new syntax introduced with .NET 3.5 for inline object instantiation; to allow the resource to be retrieved again, you'll use the `EventLogEntry.Index` property for the `Id` property, which is the unique index value of the entry.

It is important to note that the `LastUpdatedTime` and the `PublishDate` are of type `Date TimeOffset`. `DateTimeOffset` is a new type in .NET 3.5 that makes it easier to work with exact dates and times, as well as timezones. To use this type, simply create new objects and pass in the `DateTime` from the `EventLogEntry.TimeGenerated` property.

 The basic idea behind using `DateTimeOffset` versus `DateTime` (besides the fact that you'll continue to use `DateTime` for APIs that require it) is that `DateTimeOffset` is of higher fidelity and represents an exact point in time in a way that is not specific to timezones. So, you would use `Date Time` to represent whole dates, or times that must be the same across multiple timezones (e.g., when referring to a TV show that starts at 10:00 a.m. regardless of timezone).

At this point, we have written code to initialize the `SyndicationFeed` object for the event log feed and filled it with data. Now it's time to turn that object into formatted XML.

Formatters

Recall that `SyndicationFeed` is not format-specific. Instead of requiring `Syndication Feed` to know how to format its data, `System.ServiceModel.Syndication` uses another object to do the formatting—one that derives from `SyndicationFeedFormatter`. As I mentioned earlier, because `SyndicationFeed` supports two formats—RSS 2.0 and Atom

1.0—there are two `SyndicationFeedFormatter`-derived classes: `Rss20FeedFormatter` and `Atom10FeedFormatter`.

This makes it possible to write code that conditionally formats a feed either as RSS or as Atom using the same `SyndicationFeed` object. The code in Example 6-3 creates an XML instance of both formats using the same `SyndicationFeed` instance.

Example 6-3. Formatting a feed with SyndicationFeed

```
SyndicationFeedFormatter formatter = new Atom10FeedFormatter(feed);
XmlWriter xw = XmlWriter.Create("eventlog.atom");
formatter.WriteTo(xw);
xw.Close();
formatter = new Rss20FeedFormatter(feed);
xw = XmlWriter.Create("eventlog.rss");
formatter.WriteTo(xw);
xw.Close();
```

`WriteTo` is the only public method on `SyndicationFeedFormatter` that is useful for writing feeds, and all it takes is an `XmlWriter`. Most of the time, however, the feed will be created during serialization in the WCF return call; this happens because both `Rss20FeedFormatter` and `Atom10FeedFormatter` implement `IXmlSerializable`.

Example 6-4 shows the Atom- and RSS-formatted XML, just so that you can get a feel for what the formats look like in case you're seeing them for the first time.

Example 6-4. Feed XML formatted as Atom and as RSS

```
<?xml version="1.0" encoding="utf-8"?>
<feed xmlns="http://www.w3.org/2005/Atom">
    <title type="text">JON-PC Application EventLog Feed</title>
    <subtitle type="text">A feed of data from the EventLog</subtitle>
    <id>urn:uuid:a0051924-dddb-4e3a-b340-c5ded7782b2d</id>
    <updated>2008-02-25T00:25:52Z</updated>
    <author>
        <name>JON-PC</name>
    </author>
    <entry>
        <id>urn:uuid:496b3acf-2168-4f27-8dca-6895f79c8446</id>
        <title type="text">EventLogTest:(2):Error</title>
        <published>2008-02-24T16:25:52-08:00</published>
        <updated>2008-02-24T16:25:52-08:00</updated>
        <content type="text">Testing Event Log API</content>
    </entry>
    <entry>
        <id>urn:uuid:dc0ccdfe-7ce0-49b4-acc7-702baa3d861c</id>
        <title type="text">EventLogTest:(2):Error</title>
        <published>2008-02-24T16:25:52-08:00</published>
        <updated>2008-02-24T16:25:52-08:00</updated>
        <content type="text">Testing Event Log API - again</content>
    </entry>
    <entry>
        <id>urn:uuid:468d86a1-6aae-411f-ae4a-4b675a5e11fb</id>
        <title type="text">EventLogTest:(2):Error</title>
```

```
            <published>2008-02-24T16:25:52-08:00</published>
            <updated>2008-02-24T16:25:52-08:00</updated>
            <content type="text">Testing Event Log API - yet again</content>
        </entry>
</feed>

<?xml version="1.0" encoding="utf-8"?>
<rss xmlns:a10="http://www.w3.org/2005/Atom" version="2.0">
    <channel>
        <title>JON-PC Application EventLog Feed</title>
        <description>A feed of data from the EventLog</description>
        <a10:author>
            <a10:name>JON-PC</a10:name>
        </a10:author>
        <a10:id>urn:uuid:a0051924-dddb-4e3a-b340-c5ded7782b2d</a10:id>
        <item>
            <guid isPermaLink="false">urn:uuid:496b3acf-
2168-4f27-8dca-6895f79c8446</guid>
            <title>EventLogTest:(2):Error</title>
            <description>Testing Event Log API</description>
            <pubDate>Sun, 24 Feb 2008 16:25:52 -0800</pubDate>
            <a10:updated>2008-02-24T16:25:52-08:00</a10:updated>
        </item>
        <item>
            <guid isPermaLink="false">urn:uuid:dc0ccdfe-
7ce0-49b4-acc7-702baa3d861c</guid>
            <title>EventLogTest:(2):Error</title>
            <description>Testing Event Log API - again</description>
            <pubDate>Sun, 24 Feb 2008 16:25:52 -0800</pubDate>
            <a10:updated>2008-02-24T16:25:52-08:00</a10:updated>
        </item>
        <item>
            <guid isPermaLink="false">urn:uuid:468d86a1-6aae-
411f-ae4a-4b675a5e11fb</guid>
            <title>EventLogTest:(2):Error</title>
            <description>Testing Event Log API - yet again</description>
            <pubDate>Sun, 24 Feb 2008 16:25:52 -0800</pubDate>
            <a10:updated>2008-02-24T16:25:52-08:00</a10:updated>
        </item>
    </channel>
</rss>
```

The last bit of code in Example 6-4 is interesting, although it probably does not represent what you'll be doing with `SyndicationFeed` or `SyndicationFeedFormatter` most of
the time. Typically, you'll be using these two classes in the context of a service, instead
of using `SyndicationFeedFormatter.WriteTo`.

Two additional feed formatters are `Rss20FeedFormatter<T>` and `Atom10FeedFormatter<T>`. These are generic types, where T is a class that must derive from `SyndicationFeed`. This extensibility point allows third parties (e.g., you or ISVs) to build new `SyndicationFeed`-derived types, and still have the formatters you want. You would use this primarily when you are reading a feed, rather than writing one out. When you're reading a feed, the `SyndicationFeed` is created using a factory method, so you must pass the type information to the infrastructure (we'll examine this in Chapter 7 when we discuss consuming feeds in the context of Silverlight, which has the same object model as the desktop CLR).

Exposing a Feed on a Live URI

Now that we've constructed the basic infrastructure for feed serialization, let's build a simple WCF service that exposes this feed data using both RSS and Atom.

I'll make the point again that for the most part people seem to be moving toward Atom as the format of choice for most feeds. Therefore, there isn't really any compelling reason to use RSS unless you must support feed reader client(s) that can consume only RSS. I'm showing both formats here just to emphasize the separation in WCF between the data (`SyndicationFeed`) and the formatting (`SyndicationFeedFormatter`).

Also, you may see examples of methods that return `SyndicationFeed Formatter` as the return type, and conditionally (often based on a query string parameter) return either the `Atom10FeedFormatter` or the `Rss20Feed Formatter`. If you choose to follow those examples, make sure you add the `ServiceKnownTypes` attribute to your service `Type` for both of the derived types. I am not in favor of this, since I'm not in favor of using a query string to differentiate between different formats.

Example 6-5 shows the `ServiceContract` declaration.

Example 6-5. ServiceContract for the EventLogFeed

```
[ServiceContract]
public interface IEventLogFeed
{
    [OperationContract]
    [WebGet(UriTemplate = "/{log}/feed.rss")]
    Rss20FeedFormatter GetRSS(string log);
    [OperationContract]
    [WebGet(UriTemplate = "/{log}/feed.atom")]
    Atom10FeedFormatter GetAtom(string log);
}
```

Note that you do not have to specify special feed attributes; you only have to specify `WebGetAttribute`, which enables the WCF routing mechanism to route `GET` requests to these methods. The feed functionality is built on top of the WCF 3.5 Web Programming Model. This code also uses the `UriTemplateAttribute` to create different URIs, which can retrieve any Event Log by name, and the URI (*feed.atom* versus *feed.rss*) indicates the format of the response.

The implementation of the service is simple; a private method creates the `Syndication Feed` object, and then wraps that object in the appropriate formatter. When the formatter is returned, the WCF infrastructure serializes the formatter to the appropriate feed type, as shown in Example 6-6.

Example 6-6. EventLogFeed implementation

```
public class EventLogFeed : IEventLogFeed
{

    public Rss20FeedFormatter GetRSS(string log)
    {
        SyndicationFeed feed = GetFeed(log);
        Rss20FeedFormatter formatter = new Rss20FeedFormatter(feed);
        return formatter;
    }

    public Atom10FeedFormatter GetAtom(string log)
    {
        SyndicationFeed feed = GetFeed(log);
        Atom10FeedFormatter formatter = new Atom10FeedFormatter(feed);
        return formatter;
    }
}
```

You can then host this service in any of the many WCF hosting options, either in code with a `WebServiceHost` or with an *.svc* file inside ASP.NET/ IIS. The base URI of the service will prefix the `UriTemplate`s, so your URIs will look something like *http://local host/EventLogFeed/<Application>/feed.atom* or *http://localhost/EventLogFeed/<Appli cation>/feed.rss* (with *<Application>* replaced by any valid event log name).

It should now be clear that once you've decided which format(s) to support and what your URI design is going to be (e.g., what templates you are going to put into the `UriTemplate`s), the major work consists of simply fitting your data into the `Syndication Feed` object model. The WCF infrastructure really takes care of the rest.

Feed Validation

WCF doesn't support feed validation; it serializes whatever data you set `Syndication Feed` and `SyndicationItem` objects in to XML, even if you don't set data that most feed readers require. In general, you will probably want to generate feeds that most readers will be able to deal with effectively. In many ways, HTML and feeds have a lot in common, in that different feed generators can generate slightly different data and different readers display the data differently.

Of course, both RSS (*http://feedvalidator.org/docs/rss2.html*) and Atom (*http://tools.ietf .org/html/rfc4287*) are standards, so you can create validators for them. Rather than writing my own, I like to use the validator from *http://www.feedvalidator.org/*, written by Mark Pilgrim and Sam Ruby. After downloading this validator, all you have to do is install the Python runtime (*http://www.python.org/*). The feed validator website has detailed instructions on how to do this and how to run the validator locally.

When you run the validator against your Atom feed URI, you get the following errors/ warnings:

```
line 1, column 0: Missing atom:link with rel="self"
line 1, column 749: Two entries with the same value for atom:updated (2 occurrences)
```

Both lines are just warnings (you know this from looking at the *http://www.feedvalidator .org/docs* page, which lists all the errors and warnings). The second warning indicates there is an error in the feed generator logic and that the updated element isn't really the same time for more than one entry. However, in this case, the entries actually do have the same updated time, so you can safely ignore that warning.

The first warning is more important, however, as it indicates something that is often a problem for feed readers. Although not required by the Atom specification, it is pretty useful to have an `atom:link` element under your feed element with the `rel` (relation) attribute set to `"self"` and the `href` attribute set to the feed's own URI. Without that URI inside the feed, a reader will have to store the base URI of the feed externally from the feed itself. In other words, the `link` element with `rel="self"` is a self-referencing link to the document, and it's pretty useful to have that inside the document for future use, which is why it's recommended.

It turns out that adding this type of link is pretty easy, and you can do it in a fairly generic way using WCF. When the `SyndicationFeed` object is created, add a `Syndica tionLink` object to the `SyndicationFeed.Links` collection. `SyndicationLink` itself has a static factory method for creating this particular type of link, as well as alternate and media enclosure links, which are two other useful types of link elements. You can create the same type of `SyndicationLink` object with the `SyndicationLink` constructor, but these overloads are useful and they make your code easier to understand in terms of what links are being created. Table 6-3 lists the `SyndicationLink` factory methods.

Table 6-3. SyndicationLink factory methods

Method	Description
CreateSelfLink	Creates a link element with rel="self" based on a URI object. An overload has a string parameter that turns into the type attribute delineating the media/MIME type.
CreateAlternateLink	Creates a link element with rel="alternate". This represents another URI that contains the same data as the feed, but in a different media format (typically HTML). It also has an overload, which takes a URI and the media type.
CreateMediaEnclosureLink	Creates a link element with rel="enclosure". This kind of link points a related item to an entry. Typically, this is a binary piece of data (an image, or an *.mp3*, or other audio file) relating to the entry. This method has three parameters: a URI for the link, the media

Method	Description
	type (required), and the length (which isn't required, but which the Atom specification recommends to prevent readers from automatically downloading large linked items).

So, using this method and the `WebOperationContext.Current` object, you can fill this link dynamically with the URI of the feed being requested. Specifically, you can use `WebOperationContext.Current.IncomingRequest.UriTemplateMatch.RequestUri` to get the current URI of the request, which allows you to avoid having to hardcode the URI of the feed into your code or configuration:

```
//the Uri being requested
Uri u = WebOperationContext.Current.IncomingRequest.UriTemplateMatch.RequestUri;
//use the factory method to create a self link
feed.Links.Add(SyndicationLink.CreateSelfLink(u));
```

Now the **feed** element of the Atom feed looks like Example 6-7.

Example 6-7. Atom feed example

```
<feed xmlns="http://www.w3.org/2005/Atom">
    <title type="text">JON-PC application EventLog Feed</title>
    <subtitle type="text">A feed of data from the EventLog</subtitle>
    <id>urn:uuid:4a4e2bb6-82a1-472a-a1fe-209880c77712</id>
    <updated>2008-02-26T21:09:16Z</updated>
    <author>
        <name>JON-PC</name>
    </author>
    <link rel="self" href="http://localhost/EventLogFeed/application/feed.atom"/>
    <!-- Other elements removed for brevity-->
</feed>
```

Notice that the link element now points to the URI of the feed document itself, fixing the missing link warning. Although you still might receive the duplicate date warning, if some of your entries do actually have the same updated time it's really not a concern, and your Atom feed is now valid.

Another way to deal with missing self link warnings is to set the **BaseUri** property of **SyndicationFeed**. The **BaseUri** property, despite its important-sounding name, isn't set by default, although if you do set it, it must match the URI of the document itself. When you set the **BaseUri** property of **SyndicationFeed**, the formatters will add an `xml:base` attribute to the feed or channel elements with the value of that URI. Again, `WebOperationContext` comes in handy here:

```
//the Uri being requested
Uri u = WebOperationContext.Current.IncomingRequest.UriTemplateMatch.RequestUri;
feed.BaseUri = u;
```

Setting the `xml:base` attribute at the feed level allows all the other URIs in the context of the feed to be relative to the value of `xml:base`, so you can (but are not required to) change your self-referencing link like this:

```
feed.Links.Add(SyndicationLink.CreateSelfLink(new Uri("", UriKind.Relative)));
```

This changes the link element with `rel="self"` to look like this:

```
<link rel="self" href=""/>
```

This is a valid, relative, self-referencing URI.

> SyndicationItem and SyndicationLink also have a BaseUri property you can use in exactly the same way to set the xml:base attribute on their generated elements.

This takes care of fixing up your Atom feed, but the feed validator has some problems when it comes to the RSS feed. When you run the feed validator against your RSS feed, you get the following:

```
line 1, column 0: Avoid Namespace Prefix: a10
line 1, column 1142: Missing channel element: link
line 1, column 1142: Missing atom:link with rel="self"
```

The first warning will be difficult to fix. A namespace prefix is being used because Atom elements are being embedded inside the RSS XML (e.g., there is an `xmlns:a10="http://www.w3.org/2005/Atom"` attribute on the `rss` root element). The validator warns you about this because many feed readers have trouble dealing with prefixes for XML namespace URIs. This is a common problem; although the WCF's serialized XML is certainly valid XML, all you can do to fix this is to rewrite the `Rss20FeedFormatter`.

This is not an ideal solution, however, because (in my opinion) improperly dealing with XML namespace prefixes is the feed reader's problem and not mine (at least that's the tack I'd like to take, but realistically it's not always possible to blame the other party). Not dealing with XML namespace prefixes is one of my bad-code pet peeves, and generally it happens because someone has embedded an `XPath` statement into the code with an expected namespace prefix, and that's just bad programming, so I feel justified in ignoring this warning.

The second warning isn't just a warning, but rather a true error, because the RSS 2.0 specification requires a `link` element as a child of the `channel` element. The link element is supposed to point to the HTML representation of the feed. This is a slight problem if you don't actually have an HTML representation of your feed. Although it would be possible to build a WCF operation that returns HTML, it would be more likely (and more logical) that the URI to an HTML representation of your feed would be an ASP.NET page on the same website as your feed service. This is one of the advantages of being able to host WCF endpoints inside an ASP.NET application.

> If you are using RSS and you don't have an HTML representation of your RSS feed, it's fine to put the RSS feed URI in as the alternate link. I'm mainly showing you the flexibility of the programming model by using the feed validator as an example "reader."

If you assume there is an ASP.NET page with the same path (except for the file extension), use the following code to set the alternate link (which is also Atom-compliant since the `Atom10FeedFormatter` will serialize it into an `atom:link`):

```
//assume aspx page with same name
string aspxUri = u.AbsoluteUri.Replace(u.AbsoluteUri.Contains
(".atom")?"atom":"rss","aspx");
Uri nu = new Uri(aspxUri);
//create the alternate link
feed.Links.Add(SyndicationLink.CreateAlternateLink(nu, "text/html"));
```

To make this work, you do have to add a little conditional code that depends on the *.atom* or *.rss* extension being on the URI. Having those extensions on the URI is my convention, not WCF's, so you might have to change this line depending on which URI convention you are using. Example 6-8 shows the resultant RSS.

Example 6-8. RSS example feed

```
<rss version="2.0" xmlns:a10="http://www.w3.org/2005/Atom">
    <channel>
        <title>JON-PC application EventLog Feed</title>
        <link>http://localhost/EventLogFeed/application/feed.aspx</link>
        <description>A feed of data from the EventLog</description>
        <a10:author>
            <a10:name>JON-PC</a10:name>
        </a10:author>
        <a10:id>urn:uuid:faf27956-48aa-436a-8906-e2381af139ac</a10:id>
        <a10:link rel="self" href="http://localhost/
EventLogFeed/application/feed.rss"/>
    </channel>
    <!-- Rest omitted for clarity-->
</rss>
```

Now the alternate link error will go away, as well as the warning about not having an `atom:link` with `rel="self"`. Perhaps you, like I, will find it a little odd that the feed validator is looking for an Atom element when validating an RSS feed, but this just points out that extending RSS with Atom elements isn't unique to WCF.

Adding Links to a Feed

So far, you've seen how to use `SyndicationFeed` to build up the data for your feed, how to use a `SyndicationFeedFormatter` to get WCF to turn the feed data into the appropriate XML format, and how to use WCF to set up the endpoints with a URI that you can retrieve using an HTTP `GET` request (which will allow you to retrieve the WCF endpoint from a feed reader, including most modern browsers). Now we'll discuss the data of the feed, specifically, how to use `SyndicationItem` to build up your item/entry data.

Table 6-2 enumerates all of the properties of `SyndicationItem`, so there's no need to cover them again. However, I do want to discuss a few important issues you need to consider when generating feed item data. For the purposes of this discussion, let's change the example we have been developing in this chapter from an event log feed generator to one that emulates a blog or news story feed. The feed validator we developed for the original example treats the event log feed as valid even though it isn't what most people would consider "traditional" feed data. We're switching the example, not because the earlier example was wrong in any way, but because the issues I want to discuss regarding SyndicationItem don't come up when syndicating that kind of data, and blog data is the easiest example with which to illustrate those issues.

When creating SyndicationItem instances for a feed that consists of blog entries, news stories, or similar data, there are a couple of properties you need to set carefully. Missing on the SyndicationItem instances we created earlier, for instance, was any sort of link property. As with SyndicationFeed, we can fix this in a couple of ways.

Most feed readers will look under the entry element (again, I am using Atom 1.0 terminology) for a link element that has no relationship attribute. The href attribute of the link element can be absolute or relative to the xml:base attribute of either the feed itself or the entry (since the entry can have its own xml:base). The feed reader assumes that this URI is the human-readable representation of the entry. Most readers create a hyperlink that allows the user to click and follow the link to the specific entry.

 One of the constructors to SyndicationItem takes a URI as a parameter and will create a link with rel="alternate". This works for most readers as well. Also, the Atom specification requires this kind of link if you are not setting the Content property (and therefore, there will be no content element inside the entry element).

If you plan to create other links inside your entry (for alternate formats for example), I recommend setting the xml:base by setting the SyndicationItem.BaseUri property. Then the links you add can be relative to that. If you are not adding multiple links, you can just add the entry's link, as shown in Example 6-9.

Example 6-9. Creating SyndicationItem links

```
SyndicationItem item = null;
SyndicationLink theLink = null;
for(int i=0;i<10;i++)
{
    item = new SyndicationItem
    {
        Title = new TextSyndicationContent("Blog entry #" + i.ToString()),
        Content = new TextSyndicationContent("This is the content
         of the blog entry numbered " + i.ToString()),
        PublishDate = DateTimeOffset.Now,
        LastUpdatedTime = DateTimeOffset.Now,
        Id = "urn:uuid:" + Guid.NewGuid().ToString()
    };
    theLink = new SyndicationLink(CreateLinkForItem(item));
    item.Links.Add(theLink);
```

```
    items.Add(item);

}
```

In this example, you are just dummying up the entries, but the main point of this code is to illustrate the creation of a "main" link for each entry. The code calls another method to accomplish this by running an algorithm on the item itself to generate the right URI for the link.

How this is implemented is not part of any specification; readers don't care what the URI is, as long as they can follow it. A typical convention today is to use the year/month/date/title as the link because it makes a nice URI (and the elegance of URIs does matter in this world). Example 6-10 shows the `CreateLinkForItem` method implemented to do just that.

Example 6-10. CreateLinkForItem method

```
private static Uri CreateLinkForItem(SyndicationItem item)
{
    string theUri = String.Format("/{0}/{1}/{2}/{3}",
        item.PublishDate.Year,
        item.PublishDate.Month,
        item.PublishDate.Day,
        item.Title.Text);
    return new Uri(theUri, UriKind.Relative);
}
```

Again, this is just an example of one kind of URI that you can create for the main link of your entry. You might also use `SyndicationLink.CreateMediaEnclosureLink` or `SyndicationLink.CreateAlternateLink`, as an entry can have as many links as necessary.

When implementing a feed, you should be keenly aware of your scalability requirements. If you are building a feed that might be called often (of course, the definition of *often* can vary wildly), you'll want to seriously consider using caching techniques. Chapter 11 discusses caching, from both the IIS/ASP.NET point of view and the HTTP point of view (using a conditional `GET`). Please read Chapter 11 before you implement a feed so that you understand caching sufficiently.

Summary

In this chapter, you've seen how the WCF 3.5 Web Programming Model includes important extensions on top of the basic programming model to include support for creating feeds. You may or may not decide to create feeds for your applications that are not traditional feed sources (such as blogs or news sites), but you should consider doing so since feeds are a fairly well supported way to expose data where the end user, through a feed reader or an application, can find out when your data is updated.

SyndicationFeed abstracts away your need to specify a particular feed format, with SyndicationItem providing the functionality necessary to round out your feed documents. With the SyndicationFeed/SyndicationFeedFormatter split, you can wait until the last possible moment to turn your SyndicationFeed into the format you desire. We also discussed how WCF supports both the RSS 2.0 and Atom 1.0 specifications through the Rss20FeedFormatter and Atom10FeedFormatter classes.

CHAPTER 7

Programming Ajax and Silverlight Clients

An Ajax application is a web browser-based application that relies heavily on JavaScript and web services for its functionality. The idea is to bring some of the richness of desktop clients built directly on operating systems to applications built inside a web browser.

 Ajax used to stand for *Asynchronous JavaScript and XML*. However, the industry has decided that *Ajax* is no longer an acronym, and instead is now a word. It's kind of odd how that happens, but it makes sense in this case because most Ajax applications today use JavaScript, and fewer and fewer use XML, as I'll explain later in the chapter.

Gone are the days when browsers simply made HTTP requests and displayed the resulting web pages. Nowadays, modern browsers support the use of client-side code that allows users to access functions within a web page without having to make additional requests to the server. This code may be JavaScript, or it may be a more sophisticated browser plug-in written in some other language. Applications that use plug-ins are often called *rich Internet applications*, or RIAs. The calls back to the web server are normally used to get data, which then can be used to update the HTML displayed in the browser, via the browser's API (usually referred to as the HTML *Document Object Model*, or DOM). These applications are generally user-friendly, as the page in the browser can change and respond to UI requests without having to be refreshed in its entirety, which otherwise could lead to frustrated users.

 Ajax applications are not really new (my friend and colleague, John Lam, was helping people build them as long ago as 1998), and Outlook Web Access was arguably the first commercial Ajax application.

WCF 3.5's Web Programming Model supports this model. In fact, Ajax clients might be the most ubiquitous type of REST client, and in this chapter you'll see how you can use the WCF Web Programming Model to implement a variety of Ajax clients.

WCF Web Services and Ajax

Since WCF web endpoints are opened via HTTP, you can call them from JavaScript inside a browser without any modification on the service side. The endpoints provide URI-accessible functionality, so accessing them from an Ajax application is simply a matter of making the right calls using JavaScript (or whatever Ajax library you might be using).

For example, you can call the biology service that you wrote in Chapter 2 from an Ajax page without making changes to the service itself. All you have to do is change the URI of the endpoint so that it will listen on the port your website is exposed on.

Example 7-1 shows the code for a simple HTML page that uses drop-down menus (select elements in HTML) to select the hierarchical data returned from the afore-mentioned biology service. Calling the service is just a matter of getting the URIs correct for each request, and then parsing the XML that is returned. To create this page, start by adding the HTML shown in Example 7-1 to a web project inside Visual Studio, and then code away.

Example 7-1. A simple HTML page with drop-down lists for hierarchical data returned from the biology service

```
<!DOCTYPE html PUBLIC "-//W3C//DTD XHTML 1.0 Transitional//EN"
 "http://www.w3.org/TR/xhtml1/DTD/xhtml1-transitional.dtd">
<html xmlns="http://www.w3.org/1999/xhtml">
<head>
    <title>Using WCF Service from "AJAX"</title>
    <script type="text/javascript">
    function getXmlHttp()
    {
        var xmlHttp;
        try {
            xmlHttp = new XMLHttpRequest();
        } catch (e) {
            try {
                xmlHttp = new ActiveXObject("Msxml2.XMLHTTP");
            } catch (e) {
                try {
                    xmlHttp = new ActiveXObject("Microsoft.XMLHTTP");
                } catch (e) {
                    alert("This sample only works in browsers with AJAX support");
                    return false;
                }
            }
        }
        return xmlHttp;
    }
```

```
var serviceURI =  "http://localhost/BioService/";
function getDomains(){

    var xmlHttp = getXmlHttp();


    xmlHttp.onreadystatechange=function(){
        if(xmlHttp.readyState == 4){
            var doc = xmlHttp.responseXML;
            var nodes  = doc.selectNodes("//Domain");
            var select = document.getElementById("domains");
            var opt = null;
            var name = null;
            var uri = null;
            for(var i=0;i<nodes.length;i++)
            {
                    name = nodes[i].selectSingleNode("Name").text;
                    uri = nodes[i].selectSingleNode("Uri").text;
                    opt = new Option(name,uri,false);
                    select.options[select.options.length] = opt;
            }
        }
    }

    xmlHttp.open("GET", serviceURI, true);
    xmlHttp.setRequestHeader("Content-type", "application/xml");
    xmlHttp.send();

 }

function selectDomain(el)
{
    var domainUri = serviceURI  + el[el.selectedIndex].value;
     var xmlHttp = getXmlHttp();


    xmlHttp.onreadystatechange=function(){
        if(xmlHttp.readyState == 4){
            var doc = xmlHttp.responseXML;
            var nodes  = doc.selectNodes("//Kingdom");
            var select = document.getElementById("Kingdoms");
            var opt = null;
            var name = null;
            var uri = null;
            select.options.length = 0;
            for(var i=0;i<nodes.length;i++)
            {
                    name = nodes[i].selectSingleNode("Name").text;
                    uri = nodes[i].selectSingleNode("Uri").text;
                    opt = new Option(name,uri,false);
                    select.options[select.options.length] = opt;
            }
        }
    }
```

```
                xmlHttp.open("GET", domainUri, true);
                xmlHttp.setRequestHeader("Content-type", "application/xml");
                xmlHttp.send();

        }
        </script>

</head>
<body onload="getDomains()">
        <h1>Life classification</h1>
        <p>
        Domain:<select id="domains" onchange="selectDomain(this)"></select>
        </p>
        <p>
        Kingdom:<select id="kingdoms"></select>
        </p>
        <p>
        Phylum:<select id="phylum"></select>
        </p>
        <p>
        Class:<select id="class"></select>
        </p>
        <p>
        Order:<select id="order"></select>
        </p>
        <p>
        Family:<select id="family"></select>
        </p>
        <p>
        Genus:<select id="genus"></select>
        </p>
        <p>
        Species:<select id="species"></select>
        </p>
</body>
</html>
```

The code given in Example 7-1 isn't complex, and is similar to the code you might see inside a typical Ajax page when the service returns XML. Reading through the example, you can see that the code required to call a WCF web endpoint is no different from what you might write to call an exposed endpoint using HTTP.

When this page is loaded, the `getDomains` JavaScript function will call the root URI of the service, which will return the list of biological domains as XML. The function parses the XML and uses it to populate an option element per Domain inside of the HTML select element.

When the user selects a Domain, another function makes the call to the Kingdom URI, concatenating the URI of Kingdom to the root URI. The `selectDomains` function then populates the `select` for Kingdom dynamically, based on the result of the call to the Kingdom URI.

Figures 7-1 and 7-2 show views of typical user interactions with this fairly simple page.

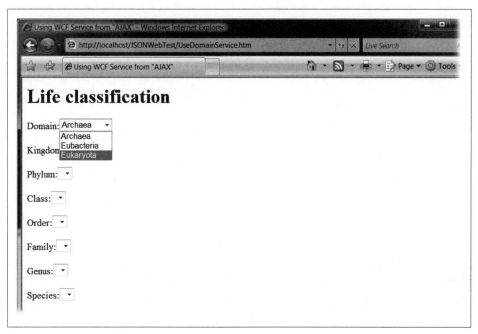

Figure 7-1. Selecting a domain

This example isn't really exciting, but it is here to reinforce the notion that WCF web endpoints are general-purpose REST endpoints and can be called by any REST-enabled client, including JavaScript in a browser.

The JavaScript code is also pretty mundane, and you could improve it by encapsulating the XMLHttpRequest in a JavaScript object model. Many such libraries are available for you to download and use, and they're easy to use against a WCF service as well. However, most of these libraries have moved away from XML parsing to JavaScript Object Notation (JSON) serialization as the preferred format for passing data between services and Ajax clients.

JSON

The industry has moved to JSON for many reasons, including:

- JSON has smaller packets because the JSON format is smaller than XML
- JSON has a more natural programming mode for Ajax clients
- Parsing JSON is more efficient than parsing XML

Another reason (one that is often left unsaid) is that no one really likes to program against XML APIs in the browser because of the general lack of XML API support (the lack of updates to the XML APIs in browsers is probably a direct result of the popularity of JSON).

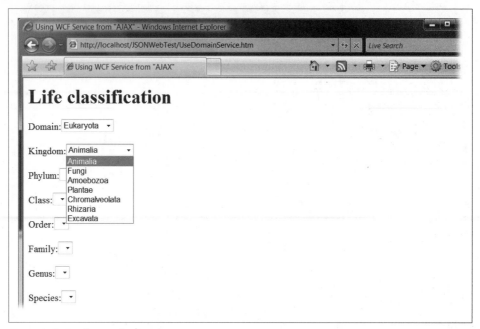

Figure 7-2. Displaying the Kingdom

Example 7-2 shows the getDomains function from Example 7-1, rewritten to use JSON-serialized responses (we'll look at the service code in a moment).

Example 7-2. A simple HTML page after service is ported to use JSON-serialized responses

```
<!DOCTYPE html PUBLIC "-//W3C//DTD XHTML 1.0
 Transitional//EN" "http://www.w3.org/TR/xhtml1/DTD/xhtml1-transitional.dtd">
<html xmlns="http://www.w3.org/1999/xhtml">
<head>
    <title>Using WCF Service from "AJAX"</title>
    <script type="text/javascript">
    window.onload = function()
    {
        getDomains();
    }
    function getXmlHttp()
    {
        var xmlHttp;
        try {
            xmlHttp = new XMLHttpRequest();
        } catch (e) {
            try {
                xmlHttp = new ActiveXObject("Msxml2.XMLHTTP");
            } catch (e) {
                try {
                    xmlHttp = new ActiveXObject("Microsoft.XMLHTTP");
                } catch (e) {
```

```
                    alert("This sample only works in browsers with AJAX support");
                    return false;
                }
            }
        }
    }
    return xmlHttp;
}
var serviceURI =  "http://localhost/BioService/";
function getDomains(){
    var xmlHttp = getXmlHttp();
    xmlHttp.onreadystatechange=function(){
        if(xmlHttp.readyState == 4){
            var result = (eval(xmlHttp.responseText));
            var domain  = null;
            var select = document.getElementById("domains");
            var opt = null;
            var name = null;
            var uri = null;
            for(var i=0;i<result.length;i++)
            {       domain = result[i];
                    name = domain.Name;
                    uri = domain.Uri;
                    opt = new Option(name,uri,false);
                    select.options[select.options.length] = opt;
            }
        }
    }
    xmlHttp.open("GET", serviceURI + "json", true);
    xmlHttp.setRequestHeader("Accept", "application/json");
    xmlHttp.send(null);
}
function selectDomain(el)
{
    var domainUri = serviceURI  + el[el.selectedIndex].value + "/json";
    var xmlHttp = getXmlHttp();
    xmlHttp.onreadystatechange=function(){
        if(xmlHttp.readyState == 4){
            var result = (eval(xmlHttp.responseText));
            var kingdom = null;
            var select = document.getElementById("kingdoms");
            var opt = null;
            var name = null;
            var uri = null;
            for(var i=0;i<result.length;i++)
            {
                    kingdom = result[i];
                    name = kingdom.Name;
                    uri = kingdom.Uri;
                    opt = new Option(name,uri,false);
                    select.options[select.options.length] = opt;
            }
        }
    }
    xmlHttp.open("GET", domainUri, true);
    xmlHttp.setRequestHeader("Accept", "application/json");
```

```
                xmlHttp.send(null);
        }
        </script>
</head>
<body>
        <h1>Life classification</h1>
        <p>
        Domain:<select id="domains" onchange="selectDomain(this)"></select>
        </p>
        <p>
        Kingdom:<select id="kingdoms"></select>
        </p>
          <p>
        Phylum:<select></select>
        </p>
        <p>
        Class:<select></select>
        </p>
        <p>
        Order:<select></select>
        </p>
        <p>
        Family:<select></select>
        </p>
        <p>
        Genus:<select></select>
        </p>
        <p>
        Species:<select></select>
        </p>
</body>
</html>
```

It is true that the code in Example 7-2 isn't smaller than the code in Example 7-1, but
the code in Example 7-2 is much cleaner. Instead of parsing the response XML DOM,
you can just use the JavaScript `eval` function to parse the return into a full-fledged
JavaScript object (in this case, an array of objects that each have a `Name` and `Uri` property). Programming against objects is generally preferable to programming against XML
(in my experience, most people feel this way), unless there is a big performance hit.

It's often useful to look at the network packets moving between a user agent and a
service. Doing so can increase your understanding of how interactions work, and this
information can be invaluable when debugging. Many tools are available to do this; I
prefer the Web Development Helper from *http://www.nikhilk.net/*. If you are using
Firefox as your browser, Firebug does pretty much the same thing.

Figure 7-3 shows the results of using the Web Development Helper, and it's easy to see
that JSON is the performance winner. The size of the JSON request is half the size of
the XML request, and the response time is also half.

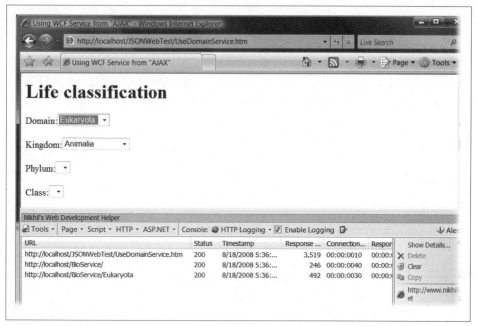

Figure 7-3. JSON size versus XML size using the Web Development Helper

When a page first loads, the browser makes two requests. The first is for the HTML itself and the second is a call (made by the XMLHttpObject) for the list of Domains (Figure 7-4).

If you click on the second line in the trace box, a Detail dialog box will appear, and you can then click the Response tab to see the response data, encoded as a JavaScript object by default. Figure 7-5 shows the expanded response data in its entirety.

Figure 7-6 shows the same data, but this time in a text view (which you can select from the Viewer drop-down list). This view shows the actual JSON data as returned from the server.

JSON-Enabling a Service Endpoint

How do you program a service endpoint to return JSON instead of XML? One way is to use the WebGet.ResponseFormat property to change a single method at a time. The other way is to use the WebScriptBehavior to modify the whole endpoint. We'll look at both of these techniques in this section.

One approach is to use the ResponseFormat property of the WebGet attribute. This property specifies the format that the serializer will use when deserializing incoming messages and serializing outgoing messages. The default value for this property is

Figure 7-4. Web Development Helper in browser

`WebMessageFormat.Xml`, which instructs the serializer to turn your objects into XML. This is the setting that we've seen up to this point.

If you specify `WebMessageFormat.Json` for the `ResponseFormat` property, the serializer will serialize objects into JSON format (you can set the `ResponseFormat` and `RequestFormat` separately, but in general you'll want them to be the same). Later in this chapter, I'll show you how you can have one operation/method return JSON or XML conditionally.

Example 7-3 shows the methods that are called for the top two resources (the root resource, represented by the URI /, and the Domain resource, represented by the URI /{Domain}) in the biological taxonomy service hierarchy, modified to return JSON for different URIs.

Example 7-3. XML and JSON responses

```
//XML responses
[OperationContract]
[WebGet(UriTemplate = "/",ResponseFormat=WebMessageFormat.Xml)]
DomainList GetRoot();
[OperationContract]
[WebGet(UriTemplate = "/{Domain}", ResponseFormat = WebMessageFormat.Xml)]
KingdomList GetDomain(string Domain);
//JSON responses
[OperationContract]
[WebGet(UriTemplate = "/json", ResponseFormat = WebMessageFormat.Json)]
```

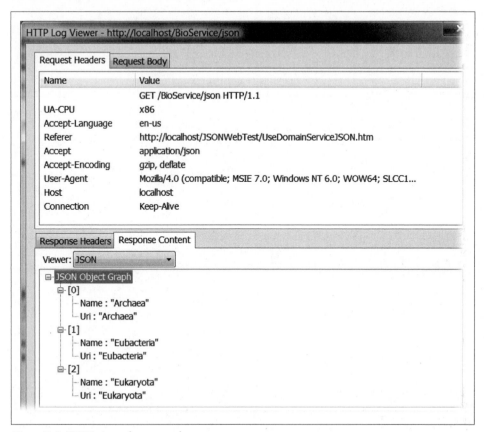

Figure 7-5. JSON view of response data

```
DomainList GetRootJSON();
[OperationContract]
[WebGet(UriTemplate = "/{Domain}/json", ResponseFormat = WebMessageFormat.Json)]
KingdomList GetDomainJSON(string Domain);
```

Example 7-3 contains the addition of two methods to the service contract definition (GetRootJSON and GetDomainJSON). These methods have the same return type and parameters as the methods that return XML (GetRoot and GetDomain). To satisfy the CLR compiler, each method must have a different name because the return values and parameters are the same. The method names are irrelevant to WCF, because the WCF web dispatcher cares only about the UriTemplate value associated with each method. The two methods that return JSON include a new path segment on the end of each UriTemplate: "/json". This allows the user agent to get JSON-encoded responses by adding "/json" to the end of the requested URI, or to get XML by leaving "/json" off the requested URI.

Figure 7-6. Raw JSON response data

In .NET 3.5 SP1, the `UriTemplate` parsing mechanism has been modified to support URIs with special characters between template parameters inside a path segment.

A URI such as *http://localhost/BioService/Domain.json* could be parsed using a `UriTemplate` definition such as `/{Domain}.{format}`. This could allow you to parse out the format automatically and then return JSON or XML. Later in this chapter, we'll discuss when it is possible to return JSON or XML dynamically from the same method.

Any type that can be serialized as XML can also be serialized into JSON, with no additional effort on your part. WCF 3.5 includes a `DataContractJsonSerializer` that performs this "magic." To make the service work overall, however, we have to add another class-level method for each of the operations, but since each method is returning the same types as the XML versions, we only have to delegate to those versions:

```
public DomainList GetRootJSON()
{
    return GetRoot();
}

public KingdomList GetDomainJSON(string Domain)
{
    return GetDomain(Domain);
}
```

If you want to return only JSON from an endpoint, you could use `WebScriptEnabling Behavior` to make all the operations on the endpoint use JSON as the request and response format. `WebScriptEnablingBehavior` is an `EndpointBehavior` that works by automatically modifying all the operations on the configured endpoint to use `WebMessageFormat.Json` for both the request and the response. This is useful if you want all of your operations to return (and accept) JSON. It is also useful if you want endpoints on one host to use XML and endpoints on another host to use JSON, since you can enable the behavior through configuration, requiring no changes to your code.

 If you are hosting in IIS, you can use `WebScriptServiceHostFactory` as the value of the `Factory` attribute in your *.svc* file to further simplify the configuration of a JSON endpoint. It will automatically configure the `WebScriptEnablingBehavior` for you.

To enable `WebScriptEnablingBehavior`, add the code in Example 7-4 to *Web.config.*

Example 7-4. Configuring WebScriptEnablingBehavior

```
<behaviors>
    <endpointBehaviors>
        <behavior name="JSONOnly">
            <enableWebScript/>
        </behavior>
    </endpointBehaviors>
</behaviors>
<services>
    <service name="JSONService">
        <endpoint address="/JSON" behaviorC
onfiguration="JSONOnly" binding="webHttpBinding" contract="TheContract"/>
    </service>
```

Because `WebScriptEnablingBehavior` derives from `WebHttpBehavior`, you don't need to add both `WebHttpBehavior` and `WebScriptEnablingBehavior` separately; you get a two-for-one effect when adding `WebScriptEnablingBehavior`. `WebScriptEnablingBehavior` is the name of the class and `enableWebScript` is the element name for adding this behavior via the configuration file.

```
WebServiceHost sh =
    new WebServiceHost(typeof(Service));
Type t = typeof(Service);
Binding b = new WebHttpBinding();
string uri = "http://localhost/webtest/";
ServiceEndpoint se = sh.AddServiceEndpoint(t,b, uri);
se.Behaviors.Add(new WebScriptEnablingBehavior());
sh.Open();
```

`WebScriptEnablingBehavior` does have one fairly big restriction: the contracts on the endpoint configured with this behavior can't use `UriTemplate` to customize the URI-to-method dispatching infrastructure built into WCF 3.5. Instead of the URI customization enabled by using the `UriTemplate` property on `WebGet` and `WebInvoke`, the default URI-to-method dispatching rules will apply. The default rules are that the URI will include the endpoint of the service plus the name of the method. Inputs to a method with a `WebGetAttribute` will have to be query string parameters (with the query string variable names matching the parameter names). When using `WebInvoke` instead of `WebGet`, the same URI and query string rules apply, although the last parameter of the method marked with `WebInvoke` can still be a complex type (i.e., the deserialized version of the body of the HTTP request).

This restriction might not dissuade you from using `WebScriptEnablingBehavior` if your clients will be using ASP.NET Ajax, because `WebScriptEnablingBehavior` will generate a JavaScript proxy that you can use in the JavaScript environment of a browser running the ASP.NET Ajax client runtime. This means that a developer using ASP.NET Ajax in her browser-based application won't have to use the `XmlHttpRequest` object directly and will have a strongly typed JavaScript object model with which to work against your service.

> An extra benefit of this proxy integration is that Visual Studio 2008 is aware of this proxy class and will give you IntelliSense inside your Java-Script code as well.

ASP.NET Ajax

ASP.NET Ajax is a Microsoft runtime and set of tools that enable developers to build Ajax-based applications in ASP.NET more quickly and easily than if they built raw Ajax applications using JavaScript. It includes a cross-browser JavaScript client (which you can use without using ASP.NET), as well as ASP.NET server-side functionality to help typical ASP.NET developers jumpstart their use of Ajax.

> For this section, we will build out the infrastructure of an ASP.NET web application manually, bit by bit, so that you can see how the pieces fit together. Note, however, that Visual Studio 2008 has templates for an Ajax-enabled WCF service, as well as for an Ajax web form, so feel free to use these templates after you have a grasp of what they do.

Let's start by building a service endpoint that can be called by an ASP.NET Ajax client. For consistency, let's continue to use the biological taxonomy service we created in Chapter 3 (the one that returns resources from the biological taxonomy service as a read-only RESTful service) so that we can contrast the handwritten JavaScript *.html* page with the ASP.NET Ajax-enabled version. I have an ASP.NET web application named *JSONWebTest* already added to my local IIS, so we'll build on top of that pre-existing project.

First, you need a contract that is compatible with `WebScriptEnablingBehavior`. In this case, we'll keep our original non-`WebScriptEnablingBehavior` contract separate (so we can have a more "pure" RESTful endpoint for non-ASP.NET Ajax clients) and we'll add a special one for `WebScriptEnablingBehavior`.

Instead of creating a separate interface (which you will probably never reuse, since the contract is specialized for this particular ASP.NET application), we'll implement the contract as a class. Example 7-5 includes the code for the service contract for the BioWrapper endpoint and also includes implementations of two of its methods (Get Root and GetDomain) rolled into one.

Example 7-5. Service contract for BioWrapper, including implementation of two methods

```
[ServiceContract(Namespace="")]
public class BioWrapper
{
    [OperationContract()]
    [WebGet()]
    public DomainList GetRoot()
    {
        BioTaxService realImpl = new BioTaxService();
        return realImpl.GetRoot();
    }
    [OperationContract()]
    [WebGet()]
    public KingdomList GetDomain(string Domain)
    {
        BioTaxService realImpl = new BioTaxService();
        return realImpl.GetDomain(Domain);
    }
    //other methods excluded for clarity

}
```

To keep things simple, Example 7-5 shows only the top two levels of the BioWrapper service hierarchy. As you can see, the code does not make use of the UriTemplate property of the WebGet attribute. If it did, WCF would throw the following exception:

> Endpoints using 'UriTemplate' cannot be used with 'System.ServiceModel.Descrip tion.WebScriptEnablingBehavior'.

This is about as straightforward an exception as you'll ever get.

UriTemplate Customization and WebScriptEnablingBehavior

Why doesn't WCF allow UriTemplate customization with WebScriptEnablingBehavior? The underlying ASP.NET Ajax proxy code was already written before WCF came out with the UriTemplate mechanism in .NET 3.5, and supporting UriTemplate customization would have meant changing the underlying Java-Script proxy model. This is annoying, but shouldn't be problematic, since the proxy class hides so much of the functionality anyway.

If you want to have a JSON endpoint that will expose UriTemplate to toolkits other than ASP.NET Ajax, you'll have to wrap the UriTemplate-specific functionality with a new contract that doesn't use UriTemplate specialization.

To get the endpoint up and running, one option is to use a typical WCF *.svc* file, put it into your virtual directory, and point the Service attribute at the new BioWrapper type. You can then put a service entry into the `System.ServiceModel` configuration element inside the *web.config* file with a link to an endpoint behavior element that uses the `enableWebScript` element (this is the same configuration you saw in the previous section).

Instead of adding that configuration, however, we can take advantage of the fact that .NET 3.5 includes a new `ServiceHostFactory`-derived type that will automatically configure the service and its endpoint to use that particular configuration. Here are the contents of the *.svc* file:

```
<% @ServiceHost
Factory="System.ServiceModel.Activation.WebScriptServiceHostFactory"
Service="BioWrapper"  %>
```

Pointing the `WebScriptServiceHostFactory` at the `BioWrapper` service type allows it to create an instance of the `WebScriptServiceHost` based on the `BioWrapper` type. `WebScriptServiceHost` is similar to the `WebServiceHost` we discussed in Chapter 5. `WebScriptServiceHost` automatically configures this service with an endpoint using the `WebHttpBinding` and applying the `WebScriptEnablingBehavior` to that endpoint. This saves us from having to configure the service in the *web.config* file.

In order to call this service from a browser using the automatically generated proxy, add the ASP.NET Ajax JavaScript runtime to the browser's JavaScript environment. In this case, we are using an ASP.NET *.aspx* page on the server to generate the browser resource, so add the appropriate ASP.NET server-side controls to the *.aspx* file. Most of the time, we think about ASP.NET server-side controls as generating viewable HTML, but they can also generate JavaScript and hidden HTML elements such as the `script` element.

The ASP.NET page requires a `form` element with the `runat="Server"` attribute. This is necessary for setting up the server environment for the other ASP.NET controls that we will add. This element is generally added automatically for you when you create a new *.aspx* file using Visual Studio. The `form` element requires a `ScriptManager` element (also with the `runat="Server"` attribute). The `ScriptManager` control generates the JavaScript and script elements, which cause the browser to request the necessary JavaScript files from the server, which loads the ASP.NET Ajax client runtime.

The `ScriptManager` allows us to add another server-side control to the page: `ServiceReference`. `ServiceReference` injects another script element into the ASP.NET Ajax-enabled page. The script element creates another request to the server for a JavaScript file, which contains a JavaScript client "class" that extends the ASP.NET Ajax client proxy class for calling services (which is a JavaScript "class" named `System.Net.WebServiceProxy`). This new class will be automatically generated based on the .NET metadata of the service (this is in some ways like the automatic proxy generation that many languages have for SOAP-based services using WSDL, except the proxy is generated dynamically at runtime).

The URI for the JavaScript file is added by WebScriptEnablingBehavior. This Web ScriptEnablingBehavior adds an additional endpoint to the underlying service endpoint. The additional endpoint responds when an HTTP GET request is made to the service endpoint that has the additional "/js" path segment added to the URI (or "/jsdebug" when a debug build is used).

In our case, the JavaScript proxy's URI will be *http://localhost/JSONWebTest/BioWrap perService.svc/js* (or *http://localhost/JSONWebTest/BioWrapperService.svc/jsdebug* for debug builds).

Example 7-6 shows the markup for an *.aspx* page that puts these features to work.

Example 7-6. ASP.NET Ajax page using autogenerated WCF JSON proxy

```
<!DOCTYPE html PUBLIC "-//W3C//DTD XHTML 1.0
 Transitional//EN" "http://www.w3.org/TR/xhtml1/DTD/xhtml1-transitional.dtd">
<html xmlns="http://www.w3.org/1999/xhtml">
<head>
    <title>Using WCF Service from ASP.NET AJAX</title>

</head>
<body>
<form runat="server">
<asp:ScriptManager runat="server" id="_scriptMan">
<Services>
<asp:ServiceReference Path="~/BioWrapperService.svc" />
</Services>
</asp:ScriptManager>
    <h1>Life classification</h1>
    <p>
    Domain:<select id="domains" onchange="selectDomain(this)"></select>
    </p>
    <p>
    Kingdom:<select id="kingdoms"></select>
    </p>
      <p>
    Phylum:<select></select>
    </p>
    <p>
    Class:<select></select>
    </p>
    <p>
    Order:<select></select>
    </p>
    <p>
    Family:<select></select>
    </p>
    <p>
    Genus:<select></select>
    </p>
    <p>
    Species:<select></select>
    </p>
    </form>
```

```
</body>
</html>
```

We can now modify the JavaScript code to integrate with ASP.NET Ajax. First, modify the `window.onload` functionality in a method named `pageLoad`. This is a special method known by ASP.NET Ajax that will be called after all the ASP.NET Ajax context is loaded into the browser. Next, use the syntax of the JavaScript proxy generated by `WebScriptEnablingBehavior`. Figure 7-7 shows a screenshot of that object in the Web Development Helper.

It's not necessary to dive into the code in detail, but clearly there is a class named `BioWrapper`, which exposes a number of properties and methods. The two methods we are most interested in are the `GetRoot` and `GetDomain` methods that correspond to the methods on our service. The syntax to get the list of domains is `BioWrapper.GetRoot`.

 Be careful: the class name will also be prefixed by the namespace URI of the `ServiceContract`. In this case, I explicitly set the namespace to an empty string, which is why the code doesn't need that namespace. The default namespace is `tempuri.org`, so if I hadn't set the namespace to an empty string, the JavaScript code would use `tempuri.org.BioWrapper Service`. For RESTful service purposes, the namespace is irrelevant, so setting it to an empty string is probably a good practice.

The proxy is inherently asynchronous, so we will specify the JavaScript function that we want called when the initial call completes. The natural parameters to the method would come before the function parameter, but since this particular "method" doesn't have any parameters, the function call comes first:

```
function pageLoad()
{
    BioWrapper.GetRoot(domainsDone);
}
```

Next, implement the `domainsDone` method, shown in Example 7-7, which will be called after the `GetRoot` asynchronous call completes. This method takes one parameter, which is the result of the asynchronous call. Note that you can also pass a JavaScript object as a `context` object to the initial call, which can then be passed to the `done` call. This is useful because the `domainsDone` call isn't done in the context of the JavaScript `this` reference (as in Example 7-3).

Example 7-7. domainsDone function (JavaScript)

```
function domainsDone(result)
{
    var domain  = null;
    var select = document.getElementById("domains");
    var opt = null;
    var name = null;
    var uri = null;
    for(var i=0;i<result.length;i++)
```

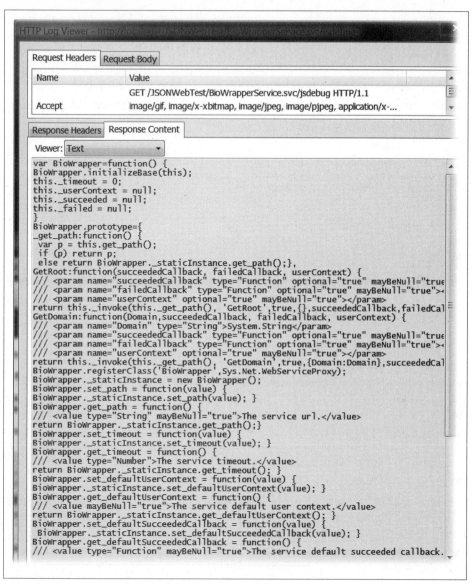

Figure 7-7. WebScriptEnablingBehavior JavaScript proxy

```
{       domain = result[i];
        name = domain.Name;
        uri = domain.Uri;
        opt = new Option(name,uri,false);
        select.options[select.options.length] = opt;
    }
}
```

The differences between this function and the earlier, non-ASP.NET Ajax version are that this one doesn't call the XmlHttpRequest object (because the generated proxy takes care of that) and that it doesn't parse the response into JSON using eval (because the infrastructure has already done it). The rest of the JavaScript code follows in Example 7-8; I modified it from the earlier version in the same way I modified the code in Examples7-2 and 7-3 by removing the explicit XmlHttpRequest and eval calls.

Example 7-8. selectDomain function (Javascript)

```
function selectDomain(el)
{
    var domain = el[el.selectedIndex].value;
    BioWrapper.GetDomain(domain,kingdomDone);

}
function kingdomDone(result)
{
    var kingdom = null;
    var select = document.getElementById("kingdoms");
    var opt = null;
    var name = null;
    var uri = null;
    for(var i=0;i<result.length;i++)
    {
        kingdom = result[i];
        name = kingdom.Name;
        uri = kingdom.Uri;
        opt = new Option(name,uri,false);
        select.options[select.options.length] = opt;
    }
}
```

It is also interesting to look at the calls the browser made to the server during this interaction. In Figure 7-8 you can see the calls the browser makes when the page first loads.

The last two URLs in Figure 7-8 (in the Web Development Helper pane) are the requests to load the debug version of the proxy and the call to the service endpoint itself, this time to the GetRoot method. This call is made in response to the code inside the page Load client-side function. Now look at Figure 7-9, which is the page displayed after a Domain is selected from the first drop-down list.

You can see that the proxy automatically adds the parameter from the call to GetDomain as a query string parameter. The advantage of the WebScriptEnablingBehavior is that when you customize your ServiceContract explicitly for ASP.NET Ajax clients, the programming model the clients must use is much simplified.

Example 7-9 pulls the ASP.NET markup and code together into one sample.

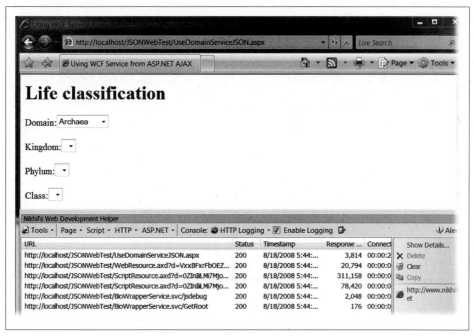

Figure 7-8. ASP.NET Ajax page loading

Example 7-9. Full ASP.NET markup and code

```
<!DOCTYPE html PUBLIC "-//W3C//DTD XHTML 1.0
 Transitional//EN" "http://www.w3.org/TR/xhtml1/DTD/xhtml1-transitional.dtd">
<html xmlns="http://www.w3.org/1999/xhtml">
<head>
    <title>Using WCF Service from ASP.NET AJAX</title>
    <script type="text/javascript">
function pageLoad()
{
    BioWrapper.GetRoot(domainsDone);
}
function domainsDone(result)
{
    var domain  = null;
    var select = document.getElementById("domains");
    var opt = null;
    var name = null;
    var uri = null;
    for(var i=0;i<result.length;i++)
    {       domain = result[i];
            name = domain.Name;
            uri = domain.Uri;
            opt = new Option(name,uri,false);
            select.options[select.options.length] = opt;
    }
}
function  selectDomain(el)
```

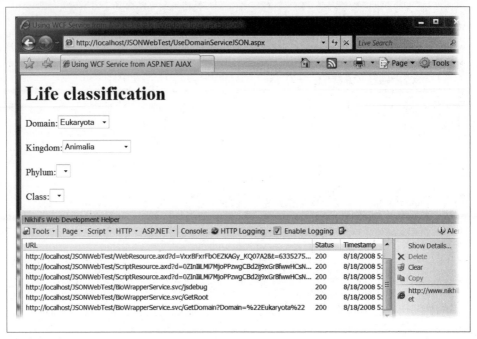

Figure 7-9. GetDomain client-side call

```
{
    var domain = el[el.selectedIndex].value;
    BioWrapper.GetDomain(domain,kingdomDone);


}
function kingdomDone(result)
{
    var kingdom = null;
    var select = document.getElementById("kingdoms");
    var opt = null;
    var name = null;
    var uri = null;
    for(var i=0;i<result.length;i++)
    {
        kingdom = result[i];
        name = kingdom.Name;
        uri = kingdom.Uri;
        opt = new Option(name,uri,false);
        select.options[select.options.length] = opt;
    }
}
    </script>

</head>
<body>
<form runat="server">
<asp:ScriptManager runat="server" id="_scriptMan">
```

```
<Services>
<asp:ServiceReference Path="~/BioWrapperService.svc" />
</Services>
</asp:ScriptManager>
    <h1>Life classification</h1>
    <p>
    Domain:<select id="domains" onchange="selectDomain(this)"></select>
    </p>
    <p>
    Kingdom:<select id="kingdoms"></select>
    </p>
      <p>
    Phylum:<select></select>
    </p>
    <p>
    Class:<select></select>
    </p>
    <p>
    Order:<select></select>
    </p>
    <p>
    Family:<select></select>
    </p>
    <p>
    Genus:<select></select>
    </p>
    <p>
    Species:<select></select>
    </p>
    </form>
</body>
</html>
```

Silverlight 1.0

Silverlight 1.0 is a cross-browser, cross-platform web browser plug-in that allows you to build interactive applications inside a browser. Silverlight 1.0 is targeted mainly at media display (e.g., videos and images), along with the ability to use JavaScript to interact with the plug-in to enable dynamic applications that can respond to user input.

In essence, Silverlight 1.0 is really an Ajax programming environment, since it doesn't have any executable language. Silverlight 1.0 pages are pure XML (specifically, they are formatted using an XML dialect known as XAML, which stands for *eXtensible Application Markup Language*).

You use WCF RESTful and JSON services with Silverlight 1.0 in much the same way as you would with ASP.NET Ajax. The difference in using Silverlight 1.0 is that instead of interacting with the HTML DOM, Silverlight 1.0 JavaScript code interacts with the Silverlight 1.0 plug-in.

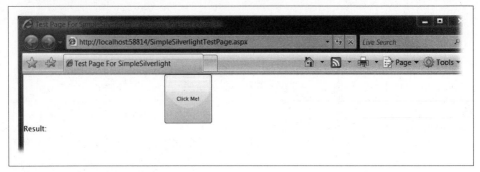

Figure 7-10. A simple Silverlight page

Silverlight 2.0

The more interesting runtime to look at is Silverlight 2.0. Unlike Silverlight 1.0, which is really an Ajax programming environment, Silverlight 2.0 is actually a cross-platform version of the CLR (a subset of the CLR, but with the same programming model and ideas).

Silverlight 2.0 is also a more complete development experience in terms of common programming paradigms such as controls and data binding (unlike Silverlight 1.0, which is geared more toward media playback). Because of this, and because you can write Silverlight 2.0 code in your favorite .NET language, it is a much friendlier environment for calling services.

As in Silverlight 1.0, calling services with Silverlight 2.0 is always asynchronous to prevent the browser's UI from being locked while a service call is being made. For reading from RESTful services (there are actually more facilities for calling SOAP services from Silverlight 2.0), the typical pattern is to use the `WebClient` class, call either the `DownloadStringAsync` or `OpenReadAsync` method, and set up the appropriate delegate, which will be called when the `async` call is completed.

The `WebClient` class in Silverlight 2.0 uses the underlying browser functionality (à la `XmlHttpRequest` from JSON). It allows you to make HTTP requests, although there are some restrictions in terms of its interaction with the full HTTP stack. I'll point these out as we go along.

First, let's use a simple example that isolates `WebClient`. We will then revisit the biological Domains sample and build a Silverlight application with a little more functionality. For this example, I have created a simple Silverlight application by using the Silverlight project template with an associated Web Application project. I added a `Button` to the *Page.xaml* file for invoking the code that uses `WebClient` and a `Text Block` to hold the result (see Figure 7-10).

The following code will run when a user clicks on the button:

```
private void _getData_Click(object sender, RoutedEventArgs e)
{
```

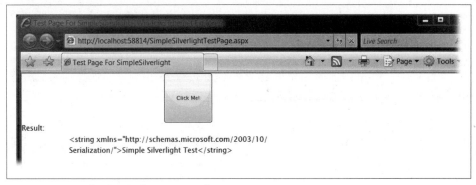

Figure 7-11. Result of WebClient async call

```
    WebClient wc = new WebClient();
    wc.DownloadStringCompleted +=delegate
(object o,DownloadStringCompletedEventArgs args)
    {
        _result.Text = args.Result;

    };
    wc.DownloadStringAsync(new Uri(_uri));
}
```

You can see that the `WebClient` programming model is fairly simple. You create a new instance of `WebClient`, register for the `Completed` event that is appropriate for the `Begin` call you are going to make, and then pass a URI to the `Begin` call. This code uses the `DownloadStringAsync Begin` call, which makes an HTTP `GET` request to the URI passed to it, and when the server or service returns the resource at that URI, the `WebClient` fires the delegate associated with the `Completed` event. The `Completed` event passes in an `EventArgs` type, which contains information about the request; most importantly, it holds onto the result of the call on the aptly named `Result` property.

This example employs a simple WCF `WebGet`-enabled service endpoint on the server that returns a string when called. Here is that service:

```
    public class SimpleService : ISimpleService
    {

        public string Simple()
        {
            Thread.Sleep(2000);
            return "Simple Silverlight Test";
        }


    }
```

There is a `Thread.Sleep` in the code so that when you click the button on the Silverlight page, the UI remains responsive. This is why the `WebClient` API is asynchronous only. Figure 7-11 shows the page that is displayed when you click the button.

Table 7-1 lays out the rest of the WebClient API. Although DownloadStringAsync was useful in this simple case, we will use the OpenReadAsync method throughout the rest of this chapter to get a Stream as the return value, since a Stream is somewhat more useful when you're trying to parse the format of most resources. All of the WebClient methods have a Progress event as well, which allows you to create UI effects such as progress bars when downloading or uploading large resources.

Table 7-1. WebClient API

Method	Completed event	Progress event	Comment
DownloadStringAsync	DownloadStringCompleted	DownloadStringProgressChanged	Useful for simple cases
OpenReadAsync	OpenReadCompleted	OpenReadProgressChanged	Useful for read-only REST calls
OpenWriteAsync	OpenWriteCompleted	OpenWriteProgressChanged	Useful in simple POST scenarios
UploadStringAsync	UploadStringCompleted	UploadStringProgressChanged	Useful in simple POST scenarios

Parsing XML in Silverlight 2.0

Once you get past the simple cases, you'll need to parse the result of a WebClient call into something useful, which will generally be XML, but might be JSON. In this section, we'll look at the different ways you can program against XML inside Silverlight.

For the rest of the examples in this section we'll use the biological taxonomy service when parsing service results. For this, we will set up another Silverlight application with an associated Web Application project, although the Silverlight application will be invoking the already-existing service endpoint (again, running on the same host and port as the Web Application project; we'll discuss cross-domain access later in this chapter).

There are three basic ways to parse XML in Silverlight 2.0: via XmlReader, XDocument (LinqToXml), or XmlSerialization. For these examples, I've created a Silverlight page with buttons for each of these options. The event handlers for these buttons use the WebClient.OpenReadAsync method to make the appropriate service call, and use different forms of parsing the results in the delegate method associated with the OpenReadCompleted event.

In all cases, we'll parse the results into a list of objects that can be data-bound to a `ListBox` control in the Silverlight XAML. We will also use a few LINQ queries in the code to further simplify the programming (taking advantage of the fact that Silverlight 2.0 is CLR implementation). We will bind the result of the top of the resource tree to one `ListBox` (the list of Domains), and we will bind the result of the second level of the hierarchy (the Kingdoms) to another `ListBox`.

We will use this same page later in this chapter when we discuss how to parse JSON and feed formats, so there are tabs in the page for that functionality. You can see this page in Figure 7-12 (please remember that this book is about REST programming with WCF, and not about how to make a pleasing design with Silverlight; I'm not an accomplished UI expert by any means).

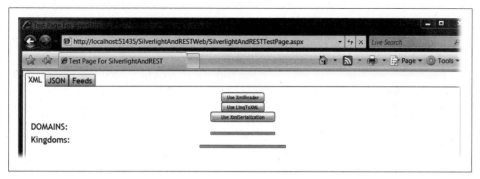

Figure 7-12. Silverlight page for testing different response formats

The code samples from this book are available at *http://www.rest-ful.net/book*, so we won't discuss all of this code in detail here; instead, we will focus only on the pieces that are relevant to our current topic.

Here is the code that is invoked whenever you click one of the buttons:

```
private void DoRest()
{
    _domainsListBox.DataContext = null;
    _kingdomsListBox.DataContext = null;
    WebClient c = new WebClient();
    c.OpenReadCompleted += DomainComplete;
    c.OpenReadAsync(new Uri(_baseUri));
}
```

The preceding code simply uses a URI to make a `GET` request using the `WebClient` class. The `DomainComplete` method will be called when the result is available, and we can carry out different types of XML parsing inside that method.

Before getting into the details of this parsing, let me remind you of the format of the resources. Figure 7-13 shows the top-level XML of the list of Domains, and Figure 7-14 shows the result from the second level: a list of Kingdoms from a specific

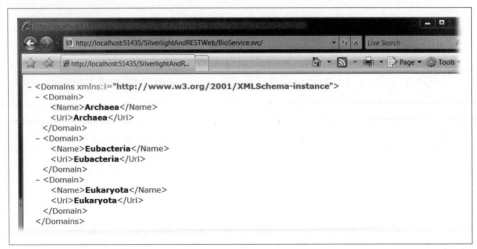

Figure 7-13. Domains XML

Domain. These are here as a reference for you to understand what the code in the following sections is parsing.

Each button causes a flag to be set in the Silverlight page so that code inside the `Domain Complete` method will know which kind of parsing to perform. Example 7-10 shows the `DomainComplete` method in full.

Example 7-10. DomainComplete method

```
void DomainComplete(object sender,
    OpenReadCompletedEventArgs e)
{
    Stream streamResult = e.Result;

    switch (_currentMode)
    {
        case Mode.XmlReader:
            WriteDomainsXmlReader(streamResult);
            break;
        case Mode.LinqToXML:
            WriteDomainsLinqToXML(streamResult);
            break;
        case Mode.XMlSerializer:
            WriteDomainsXmlSerializer(streamResult);
            break;
        default:
            break;
    }

}
```

Figure 7-14. Kingdoms XML

When you click a button, the `ListBox` will be displayed with the list of Domains. That list is exactly the same no matter which kind of parsing you use; Figure 7-15 shows what the page looks like after you click any of those buttons.

If you were to click on a Domain in the `ListBox` and then click the name of the Domain, the page would respond by going back to the service to get the list of Kingdoms for that Domain (in the XAML, there is a `HyperlinkButton` inside each `ListItem` in the `List Box`). When you click a Domain, you will see a page that looks similar to the one shown in Figure 7-16. The event handler for getting the Kingdoms for a particular Domain will use the same form of XML parsing as the first call.

Now that we have set up the basic operation of the sample, let's examine the different parsing methods.

Using XmlReader

Probably the most straightforward way to read XML in Silverlight is to use the familiar `XmlReader`. For the most part, the `XmlReader` works the same in Silverlight as it does in

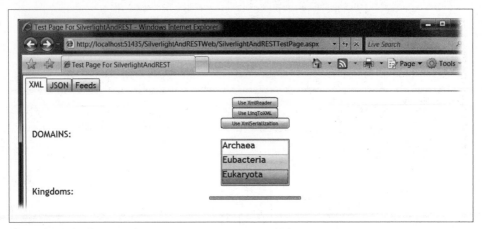

Figure 7-15. Domains result

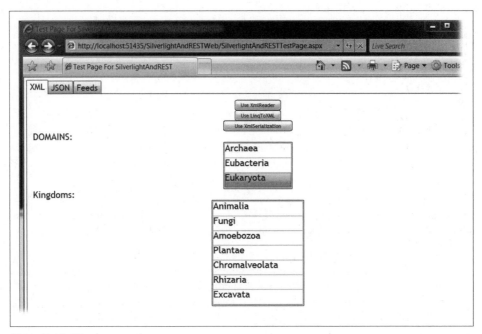

Figure 7-16. Kingdoms result

the regular CLR. Example 7-11 shows the code that will parse the result from the call to the "root" of the resource tree (this is the code that is called in the `DomainComplete` method when you click the `XmlReader` button).

Example 7-11. Parsing the result from the call to the root of the resource tree

```
private void WriteDomainsXmlReader(Stream streamResult)
{
    //create the collection for data binding
    List<BindingClass> bindingContext =
        new List<BindingClass>();
    string uri = null;
    //parse the result stream to an XmlReader
    using (XmlReader xr = XmlReader.Create(streamResult))
    {
        xr.MoveToContent();
        xr.Read();//Move past Domains
        while (xr.Read())
        {
            //pull the Uri result
            if (xr.Name == "Uri" &&
                xr.NodeType == XmlNodeType.Element)
            {
                //read out the value of the Uri element
                uri = xr.ReadElementContentAsString();
                //add a new Binding class
                bindingContext.Add(new BindingClass { Text = uri });
            }
        }
    }
    //give the collection to the ListBox for data binding
    _domainsListBox.DataContext = bindingContext;
}
```

The code is pretty straightforward, following one typical pattern of XmlReader usage, which is to call XmlReader.Read a number of times based on the format of the XML being parsed. In this case, we are currently viewing the Domain elements, so we can just check to see whether the element name is Uri and that the current node isn't the end element. Once we find each Uri element, we can read the value using ReadElement ContentAsString and use that value to create a new object to add to the list for data binding against the ListBox. The ListBox will then automatically redraw itself with the appropriate data.

Using XDocument

Another facility Silverlight 2.0 offers for parsing XML is LinqToXml. The LinqToXml API centers on the XDocument type as the container for the XML stream, and allows you to use the LINQ query syntax in your code to derive a set from the XML document itself. The following code will parse the Domain XML resource using LinqToXml.

> To use LinqToXml in Silverlight 2.0 you need to add a reference to the *System.Xml.Linq.dll* assembly in your project.

```
private void WriteDomainsLinqToXML(Stream streamResult)
{
    XDocument xd =
        XDocument.Load(XmlReader.Create(streamResult));
    var results = from uris in xd.Descendants("Uri")
                    select new BindingClass { Text = uris.Value };

    _domainsListBox.DataContext = results;
}
```

You can see that this code is significantly more compact than the XmlReader version. This code loads the XML result into an XDocument instance using XDocument.Load. You can then use a LINQ query to get all of the descendant nodes of the document element named Uri in the XML by using XDocument.Descendants. This code uses LINQ to create a new set of BindingClass objects, using the value of the Uri element to set the Text property of the newly created BindingClass instances. Again, this collection is given to the ListBox, which will automatically update the UI based on this new data.

Using XmlSerialization

The XmlSerialization API in Silverlight 2.0 is similar to the same API in the "regular" CLR: it allows you to serialize an object into XML, or to serialize XML into a live object. Here is the code from the Silverlight page that uses the XmlSerializer:

```
private void WriteDomainsXmlSerializer(Stream streamResult)
{
    Domains domains = (Domains)_domainSerializer.Deserialize(streamResult);
    var results = from domain in domains.Domain
                    select new BindingClass { Text = domain.Uri };
    _domainsListBox.DataContext = results;

}
```

This code uses LINQ to build the list of objects for the ListBox to bind to. Note that, as in the "regular" CLR, XmlSerializer.Deserialize returns an object that must be cast into the type that fits the shape of the incoming XML stream. How, then, did I get this type definition (in this case, a class named Domains for the collection of Domain objects), since the RESTful service doesn't have any metadata from which such a definition could be generated (à la WSDL from a SOAP service endpoint)?

I went through a few manual but very easy steps. First, I used the browser to invoke the service, and then I entered a View Source command in the browser to get the XML text, which I copied into an XML file inside Visual Studio 2008. Visual Studio provides an XML menu when you are editing an XML file, and from that menu I selected Create Schema. Visual Studio then generated an XSD schema file for this XML. Next, I used the *XSD.exe* command-line tool against the XSD to generate the class (using the /c command-line switch).

In order to use the `XmlSerializer` object in Silverlight 2.0 you need to add a reference to the *System.Xml.Serialization.dll* assembly in your Silverlight project.

XML parsing wrap-up

You are now familiar with the three basic options for parsing raw XML results in Silverlight 2.0. You should pick whichever of those options is most comfortable for you as a programmer, although I tend to prefer the `LinqToXml` approach since it generally results in the most compact code.

Parsing JSON in Silverlight 2.0

Another format you may run into when programming using Silverlight 2.0 is JSON. Many services are intended for use from multiple web clients. Earlier in the chapter we discussed the advantage of using JSON as your resource format when building REST services, and these apply just as much to a Silverlight application.

 In order to use the `JsonObject` in Silverlight 2.0 you need to add a reference to the *System.Json.dll.assembly* in your project.

In Silverlight 2.0, there is a JSON serialization/deserialization layer centered on a class named, appropriately, `JsonObject`. Unlike the JSON usage we saw earlier with Java-Script clients, this is a weakly typed object model, because Silverlight 2.0 code is compiled instead of interpreted. For parsing JSON, we can set up a different tab in the Silverlight page, but the functionality is exactly the same as the XML parsing tab: when you click the Use Json button, the code uses `WebClient` to call to a RESTful endpoint using an HTTP `GET`, and on the return, the stream is JSON-encoded. The code will then parse the JSON stream using `JsonObject.Load`. In this case, `JsonObject.Load` returns a `JsonArray` object that holds onto an array of Domain objects, since this is the format of the returned resource (in other cases, `JsonObject.Load` may return only a single `JsonObject`). Example 7-12 shows the three methods that, working together, provide this functionality.

Example 7-12. Silverlight event handler code

```
//event handler for JSON button
private void _domainJSON_Click(object sender, RoutedEventArgs e)
{

    HyperlinkButton button = sender as HyperlinkButton;
    TextBlock text = button.Content as TextBlock;
    string domain = text.Text;
    ProcessDomainJSON(domain);
```

```
}
//WebClient call for JSON
private void ProcessDomainJSON(string domain)
{
    WebClient c = new WebClient();
    c.OpenReadCompleted += DomainCompleteJson;
    c.OpenReadAsync(new Uri(_baseUri + domain + "/json"));
}
//Complete event handler for JSON
void DomainCompleteJson(object sender,
    OpenReadCompletedEventArgs e)
{
    Stream streamResult = e.Result;
    JsonArray json = (JsonArray)JsonObject.Load(streamResult);
    var result = from j in json
                 select new BindingClass { Text = j["Uri"] };
    _domainsListBoxJSON.DataContext = result;
}
```

Again, LINQ provides a fair amount of help in taking the result set and turning it into
the list of objects against which the ListBox control can data-bind.

Consuming Feeds in Silverlight 2.0

As discussed in Chapter 6, web feeds are quickly becoming a popular way to expose
various types of data (not just blogs). In that chapter, we wrote a service using WCF
that exposes the data from a computer's event log using a RESTful API approach. If
you look at the Silverlight example in Figure 7-17, which admittedly is a very simple
UI, the Silverlight code will consume the event log feed when you click the button on
the third tab.

Since feeds are such a ubiquitous and well-known XML format, instead of parsing feed
data using one of the three XML parsing approaches, Silverlight 2.0 uses the same feed
object model as WCF does in the "regular" CLR. This model is based on the
SyndicationFeed class. Example 7-13 shows the code that supports the third tab of the
page.

Example 7-13. Parsing feed data in Silverlight

```
//event handler for button
private void _feed_Click(object sender, RoutedEventArgs e)
{
    WebClient c = new WebClient();
    c.OpenReadCompleted += FeedComplete;
    c.OpenReadAsync(new Uri(_feedUri));
}
//called when feed is delivered
void FeedComplete(object sender,
OpenReadCompletedEventArgs e)
{
    Stream streamResult = e.Result;
    XmlReader xr = XmlReader.Create(streamResult);
```

Figure 7-17. Silverlight Feeds tab after button is clicked

```
    SyndicationFeed feed =
        SyndicationFeed.Load(xr);
    var result = from item in feed.Items
                 select new BindingClass
                 {
                     Text =
                     ((TextSyndicationContent)item.Content).Text
                 };
    _feedListBox.DataContext = result;
}
```

The same basic object model for `SyndicationFeed` exists for Silverlight 2.0 (see Chapter 6 for more information about the `SyndicationFeed` API).

OpenWriteAsync in Silverlight 2.0

The `WebClient` API in Silverlight 2.0 also includes the ability to send `POST` data to HTTP endpoints. Unfortunately, to support multiple browser plug-in models, the `WebClient` doesn't allow you to change the HTTP method. Using Silverlight 2.0 against a RESTful service that implements more than just the `GET` and `POST` parts of the uniform interface is problematic. This means that, to support Silverlight 2.0 clients fully, you will have to deal with the other parts of the uniform interface (PUT and DELETE) through POST (à la a SOAP service).

Cross-Domain Security in Silverlight 2.0

One consideration when using web-based applications is cross-domain security. It can be dangerous for clients whose pages came from one domain to call into a service from another domain.

Silverlight 2.0 will look for either a *clientaccesspolicy.xml* or a *crossdomain.xml* file at the root of your website's virtual directory. (Silverlight 2.0 supports a subset of the *crossdomain.xml* schema). Here is a *clientaccesspolicy.xml* file that enables access from all client domains to all services in your virtual directory:

```xml
<?xml version="1.0" encoding="utf-8"?>
<access-policy>
  <cross-domain-access>
    <policy>
      <allow-from http-request-headers="*">
        <domain uri="*"/>
      </allow-from>
      <grant-to>
        <resource path="/" include-subpaths="true"/>
      </grant-to>
    </policy>
  </cross-domain-access>
</access-policy>
```

Adding restrictions to the domain element or resource elements can restrict the access of Silverlight 2.0 clients to your services.

For the *crossdomain.xml* file, Silverlight 2.0 will respond correctly to the file only if it allows full access from any domain:

```xml
<?xml version="1.0"?>
<!DOCTYPE cross-domain-policy SYSTEM
  "http://www.macromedia.com/xml/dtds/cross-domain-policy.dtd">
<cross-domain-policy>
  <allow-http-request-headers-from domain="*" headers="*"/>
</cross-domain-policy>
```

Again, Silverlight 2.0 was in beta at the time of this writing, so please verify these settings with the current Silverlight 2.0 documentation.

Returning JSON and XML Conditionally with a Single Method

In this chapter, you've seen the power of JSON from an Ajax programming point of view. WCF provides a nice model for returning either JSON or XML from a particular method on your RESTful service class, but there isn't an easy way to make a method return either JSON or XML conditionally.

Generally, you'd like to return JSON or XML based on one of two constructs. Clients send an Accept HTTP header when making requests of your RESTful endpoints. It would be nice to be able to return JSON when the Accept header value is "application/json" and XML when the Accept header value is "text/xml". Another thing to consider is supporting different URIs for each resource format (e.g., *http://server/Resource* for the XML version and *http://server/Resource/json* for a JSON-encoded resource). WCF actually supports the latter fairly well because it is easy to add another method to your `ServiceContract` and specify the same `UriTemplate` value as the XML resource URI, but with "/json" concatenated at the end. This is what we did for the biological taxonomy service used earlier in this chapter. This requires a bit of hand-coding, but in the end it is fairly easy to build because the JSON version of your method can just call the XML version, making the JSON version a shim that is necessary for the WCF web infrastructure. Supporting this approach was actually necessary for the examples in this chapter since you can't change the Accept header of the Silverlight 2.0 `WebClient` object.

Supporting the former approach is possible in WCF, but it will require a bit more heavy lifting on your part when you write the code for your methods. To return JSON or XML based on the Accept header, you have to write your methods in WCF to return the `System.ServiceModel.Channels.Message` type as your return parameter. For `WebInvokeAttribute` methods, the HTTP body parameter will have to be `Message`. Note that you can still use `UriTemplate` even when you are using this generic message serialization functionality.

A special message property is added during the execution of a web request in WCF (when using the `WebHttpBehavior`) that tells the underlying serialization infrastructure whether to use `DataContractSerializer`, `XmlSerializer`, or `DataContractJsonSerializer` for the message. This special message property is `WebBody FormatMessageProperty`. The `WebBodyFormatMessageProperty` has a property named `Format`, which is an enumeration value of type `WebContentFormat`. The values of this enumeration are given in Table 7-2.

Table 7-2. WebContentFormat values

Value	Description
Default	The message formatter can't be determined
Xml	The message will be formatted using XML
Json	The message will be formatted using JSON
Raw	The message will be treated as a raw stream (used when the type of the parameter is `Stream`)

When strongly typed messages (i.e., not `System.ServiceModel.Channels.Message`) are used, the value of this `WebContentFormat` is configured for both the parameters and the return values of each operation as the `ServiceHost` is opening its communication infrastructure. This property becomes read-only and can't be changed dynamically at runtime.

On the other hand, when using Message as the input and output type for your methods, you can set this property dynamically based on whatever condition you like. The code in Example 7-14 is a rewrite of the two methods that relate to the top two resources in the biological taxonomy service hierarchy, using Message as the return value. Note that we can still use the strongly typed objects to create the message; you just need to create a WCF Message object by passing in the object to the Message.CreateMessage factory method.

Example 7-14. Using Message as the return value

```
//"loosely" typed top-level method
public Message GetRoot()
{
    DomainList list = new DomainList();
    string[] domains = new string[] { "Archaea", "Eubacteria", "Eukaryota" };
    foreach (string domain in domains)
    {
        list.Add(new Domain { Name = domain, Uri = domain });

    }
    Message ret = CreateMessage(list);
    return ret;
}
//"loosely" typed method to get Kingdoms
public Message GetDomain(string Domain)
{
    KingdomList list = new KingdomList();
    switch (Domain)
    {
        case "Eukaryota":
            string[] kingdoms = new string[] { "Animalia", "Fungi",
    "Amoebozoa", "Plantae", "Chromalveolata", "Rhizaria", "Excavata" };
            list.AddRange((from s in kingdoms
                            select new Kingdom { Name = s, Uri = s }));
            break;
        default:
            break;
    }
    Message ret = CreateMessage(list);
    return ret;
}
//method to create Message object
Message CreateMessage(object msg)
{
    //find the right serializer
    XmlObjectSerializer serializer = SetSerializer(msg);
    //create the message
    Message ret = Message.CreateMessage(MessageVersion.None,
                            "*",
                                        msg, serializer);
    return ret;

}
//method that looks at the accept header to
```

```
//determine the right serializer
XmlObjectSerializer SetSerializer(object msg)
{
    XmlObjectSerializer ret = null;
    if (WebOperationContext.Current.IncomingRequest.Accept == "application/json")
    {
        //set up the right formatter for the message
        WebBodyFormatMessageProperty formatter =
            new WebBodyFormatMessageProperty(WebContentFormat.Json);
        OperationContext.Current.OutgoingMessageProperties.Add(
            WebBodyFormatMessageProperty.Name,
            formatter);
        //set the right content-type header
        WebOperationContext.Current.OutgoingResponse.ContentType = "application/json";
        //create the right serializer
        ret = new DataContractJsonSerializer(msg.GetType());
    }
    else
    {
        //create the normal XML serializer
        ret = new DataContractSerializer(msg.GetType());
    }
    return ret;
}
```

The really important code in Example 7-14 is in the last method, `SetSerializer`, which is a method we can use to dynamically determine, based on the value of the incoming Accept header, which serializer to use for the outgoing message.

> We can't simply set this message property on the `OperationContext.Current.OutgoingMessageProperties` because when a strongly typed message is used, the WCF serialization infrastructure is statically created to do either JSON or XML for a particular operation, and won't respond correctly on a case-by-case basis based on this value being in the `Message`. When the loosely typed `Message` type is used, however, all of the serialization is done based on the `Message` itself, without regard for how the operation was set up.

Summary

In this chapter, we looked at how the Web Programming Model in WCF 3.5 extends its reach to multiple clients. The ability to use WCF RESTful services from Ajax is one level of that reach, but the ability to deal with the JSON serialization format helps to extend that reach even further, since so many programming environments provide support for calling services that return and accept JSON.

We also looked at how the `WebScriptEnablingBehavior` element tightly integrates WCF services and the ASP.NET Ajax programming environment. Finally, the RIA environment of Silverlight brings a whole new dimension to web programming, and the WCF RESTful services (including feed support) built into the Silverlight 2.0 programming model make building interactive web applications even easier.

CHAPTER 8

Securing REST Endpoints

Security is always an important consideration when you're building any kind of system. This is certainly true when you're building services, perhaps more so because of the nature of exposing endpoints that could be called using a variety of toolkits and protocols. Those who favor SOAP services (specifically the WS-* set of specifications) tend to look down upon the security of RESTful services. In truth, though, enterprises have much more experience managing security for web applications than they do for SOAP service endpoints. Because RESTful services are just HTTP endpoints, all of the security techniques (HTTPS, certificates, etc.) that have been used for years with web applications are the same techniques we use for REST. Although it is certainly true that REST services don't support end-to-end security over multiple protocols (as the suite of WS-Security-related protocols allows), in the end are you really going to need that?

In this chapter, we'll look at the out-of-the-box capabilities that WCF 3.5 provides for building secure services with REST. First, we'll discuss how to authenticate users of your WCF web endpoints, and then I'll delve into the several ways available to authorize users once they've been authenticated.

Authenticating: Self-Hosted Endpoints

The security of an endpoint is set using properties of `WebHttpBinding`. Before we dive into the security functionality `WebHttpBinding`, it's important to digress for a moment and consider hosting. For the purposes of this chapter, it's useful to divide the options for hosting endpoints into two categories: self-hosting and managed hosting (see Chapter 5 for more information).

The distinction between the two is important because in managed hosting (inside IIS) the configuration of `WebHttpBinding` endpoints is determined by the security settings of IIS and ASP.NET. In the self-hosting case, most if not all of the security settings will be controlled by your code and your application configuration file. For now, we will focus on `WebHttpBinding`'s security from a self-hosting point of view. Later in this chapter we'll contrast it with what happens in IIS managed hosting.

Here is a simple RESTful service that helps to illustrate how security with WebHttpBinding works. Example 8-1 shows the code for a service that generates a string that reports current authentication information.

Example 8-1. SecureService

```
[ServiceContract(Namespace = "")]
public class SecureService
{
[OperationContract]
[WebGet(UriTemplate = "/")]
public string AuthType()
{
    ServiceSecurityContext securityCtx;
    securityCtx = OperationContext.Current.ServiceSecurityContext;
    string authType = "No security context";
    if (securityCtx != null)
    {
        if (securityCtx.IsAnonymous)
            authType = "Anonymous";
        else
            authType = securityCtx.PrimaryIdentity.Name;

    }
    return authType;

}
}
```

Example 8-1 is a pretty simple service definition, with just one method that listens for HTTP GET requests and returns a string. Since the service's UriTemplate value is \, it will respond only to GET requests at the root of the URI (i.e., at the address of the endpoint). Inside this method is some code that generates a string based on the current authentication information.

This implementation will work inside any code executing in the context of a WCF service (not just a REST service) because it is using WCF's ServiceSecurityContext class. The code accesses it through the ServiceSecurityContext.Current static property, which always returns the correct instance for the currently executing request, assuming the client has been authenticated. To get this service endpoint up and running you need to fire up a WebServiceHost instance and add an endpoint using WebHttpBinding. This is shown in Example 8-2.

Example 8-2. Hosting and adding an endpoint for SecureService

```
WebServiceHost sh = new WebServiceHost(typeof(SecureService));
string uri = "http://win2008/wcfrestsecoiis/";
WebHttpBinding wb = new WebHttpBinding();
sh.AddServiceEndpoint(typeof(SecureService),wb,uri);
sh.Open();
Console.WriteLine("Service running");
Console.ReadLine();
```

When you make a request of this endpoint (using a browser in this case), you get the result shown in Figure 8-1.

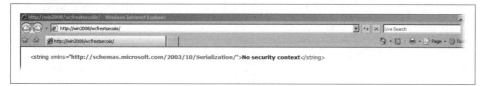

Figure 8-1. No security context by default with WebHttpBinding

The result shown in Figure 8-1 indicates that, by default, `WebHttpBinding` has no security configured. So the question then becomes, "How can I configure security, and what effect will that have on the execution of my service?" The answer is the `Security` property of `WebHttpBinding`, which we'll discuss next.

Setting Endpoint Security: WebHttpBinding.Security's Mode Property

The security of an endpoint is set by the aptly named `Security` property of `WebHttp Binding`. The `Security` property is of a type named `WebHttpSecurity` and is used to determine the security mode required by the binding and the type of client credential it requires. Table 8-1 lists `WebHttpSecurity`'s properties and their use.

Table 8-1. WebHttpSecurity properties

Property	Type	Description
Mode	WebHttpSecurityMode	Determines the security mode required by the binding
Transport	HttpTransportSecurity	Determines the type of client credential required by the binding

I'll discuss the `Mode` property first, and the `Transport` property a bit later in this chapter. Table 8-2 shows the three levels of security that can you can specify using the `WebHttpSecurityMode` enumeration (`WebHttpSecurity` is a new type for WCF 3.5).

Table 8-2. WebHttpSecurityMode enumeration values

Value	Description
None	The endpoint will not require any sort of security (this is the default)
Transport	The endpoint will require SSL (i.e., the address of the endpoint must start with *https*)
TransportCredentialOnly	The endpoint will require a client to authenticate itself, but will not require SSL

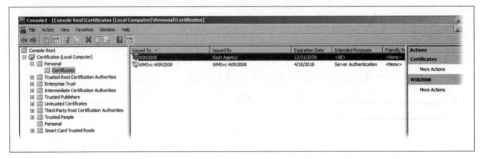

Figure 8-2. The certificate MMC

It is clear that an endpoint using `WebHttpBinding` has no security configured, since the default value of `WebHttpSecurityMode` is `None`, which is why there is no `ServerSecurity Context` when the service is invoked.

When the `Mode` property is set to `WebHttpSecurityMode.Transport`, the binding will require that the address of the endpoint start with *https*. As a logical corollary, in order to use SSL, you will have to configure a valid certificate on the machine on which the endpoint is running.

SSL stands for Secure Sockets Layer. SSL has been superseded by another standard called Transport Layer Security (TLS). In this book I use the terms interchangeably, and refer to SSL specifically for two reasons: first, the configuration in IIS still refers to SSL even though newer clients technically will use TLS instead of SSL when connecting, and second, SSL is the more familiar term.

SSL is a well-known and well-tested protocol for securing the confidentiality of messages and, by so doing, also reducing the opportunity for certain types of security attacks, such as the *replay* attack (whereby the attacker tries to replay the request of the original sender). Although some attacks against SSL might be successful (isn't that true of all types of security?), SSL has become the de facto standard for secure conversations.

In order to use SSL you'll need a certificate, and you'll need to configure your web server to use that certificate.

On my machine, which happens to be running Windows Server 2008 and IIS7, I've configured a certificate that can be used for SSL. You can see this certificate in the certificate console shown in Figure 8-2. This discussion would be almost identical if I were running Windows Server 2003 with IIS6, apart from some differences in the screenshots.

For ease of configuration in this example, I'm using a self-issued certificate instead of a "real" certificate from one of the many SSL certificate vendors.

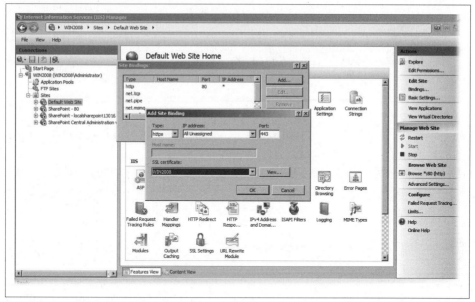

Figure 8-3. The IIS HTTPS configuration

This certificate is installed inside the Personal store of the Computer account's store. Interestingly, to make `WebHttpBinding` able to use an address using HTTPS, you need to use the IIS Manager tool to enable a binding at the *Http.sys* level for HTTPS (I could use *NetSh.exe*, but I generally prefer a GUI tool).

In the IIS Manager, create a binding for HTTPS (which defaults to port 443); you can see this in Figure 8-3.

To get to the screen shown in Figure 8-3, select Default Web Site in the tree view, and then click on Bindings in the upper-right corner. When the Site Bindings dialog box is displayed, click Add, select https from the Type list, and select the correct certificate from the SSL certificate combo box. Now that this reservation has been made, you can start using SSL with the `WebHttpBinding` endpoint.

To make this happen, set `HttpWebSecurityMode` on the `WebHttpBinding.Security` property to `Transport`. You then change the scheme of the endpoint's address to https. Note that if you make only one of these changes without making the other, WCF will validate the endpoint configuration and will produce an error when it tries to open the endpoint. WCF assumes that if you want Transport security you must have intended to use "https" instead of "http". It also assumes that if you are using "https" in your address, you intended to use `HttpWebSecurityMode.Transport`.

Here is the changed code (it also contains a call to `Process.Start` with the URI to make an Internet Explorer window come up automatically and request the URI—just a small timesaver):

```
WebServiceHost sh = new WebServiceHost(typeof(SecureService));
string uri = "https://win2008/wcfrestsecoiis/";
WebHttpBinding wb = new WebHttpBinding();
wb.Security.Mode = WebHttpSecurityMode.Transport;
sh.AddServiceEndpoint(typeof(SecureService),wb,uri);
sh.Open();
Console.WriteLine("Service running");
Process.Start(uri);
Console.ReadLine();
```

When you start the service, you will see a screen similar to the one shown in Figure 8-4.

Figure 8-4. HTTPS-enabled REST endpoint with WCF

Not only does "https" appear in the address bar of the browser, indicating that the connection is secured using SSL, the output also shows the string "Anonymous" instead of "No Security Context." This means there is a `ServerSecurityContext` object available to the code running inside of IIS. When you make any configuration of an endpoint with WCF that requires security (and this endpoint now requires that https be used), the `ServerSecurityContext` becomes available. Also notice that no authentication is occurring; any client can still make calls to the endpoint, and now the client can rest assured that all the calls it makes to this service are encrypted and safe from prying eyes. You can also think of SSL as the client authenticating the service, because the SSL certificate must be a valid certificate and must be used by the site it was issued to. As long as we trust the issuer of the certificate, we implicitly trust the site itself (this is why I feel comfortable entering my credit card information when I am shopping at Amazon.com, for example).

 You can configure a WCF service contract definition so that the contract will be used only with Transport-level security (such as SSL) by setting the `ProtectionLevel` property on the `ServiceContractAttribute`. You can set this to `ProtectionLevel.EncryptAndSign` to enforce and validate that your contract is being used with SSL when used with the `WebHttp Binding` object. If the `Mode` property isn't set to `Transport`, WCF will throw an exception when the endpoint attempts to open. This feature isn't limited to the `WebHttpBinding` object; it's a universal feature in WCF.

Setting Authentication Requirements: WebHttpBinding's Transport Property

SSL makes the user agent feel better since it can be assured that the service is what it says it is. The service might want to feel better as well, though, by identifying each client and forcing it to authenticate before allowing it to use the service.

This is where the `WebHttpBinding.Security.Transport` property comes into play. `WebHttpBinding.Security.Transport` is of a type named `HttpTransportSecurity`, which, interestingly, isn't new for .NET 3.5, but is the same type used in .NET 3.0 to configure transport security on other HTTP-based bindings.

Table 8-3 lists the `HttpTransportSecurity` properties.

Table 8-3. HttpTransportSecurity properties

Property	Type	Description
ClientCredentialType	HttpClientCredentialType	Determines which type of client authentication will be required
ProxyCredentialType	HttpProxyCredentialType	Determines which type of authentication will be used against a proxy server (used only from a WCF client)
Realm	String	Used with Basic and Digest authentication to indicate the scope of the authentication to the client

In most situations you're likely to encounter, you really only need to be concerned about the `ClientCredentialType` property. That's because the `ProxyCredentialType` property relates to client-side proxy configuration, and the `Realm` property is generally not explicitly set. Table 8-4 lists the potential values for `ClientCredentialType` (which is of type `HttpClientCredentialType`).

Table 8-4. HttpClientCredentialType enumeration

Value	Description
None	No client authentication is required (the default)
Basic	The client is required to authenticate using the HTTP-based Basic authentication protocol (RFC 2617)
Digest	The client is required to authenticate using the HTTP-based Digest authentication protocol (RFC 2617)
Ntlm	The client is required to authenticate using the NTLM authentication protocol (Windows authentication)
Windows	The client is required to authenticate using Kerberos (NTLM will be the fallback protocol if Kerberos can't be used)
Certificate	The client is required to present a valid certificate to the server when authenticating

As you can see, the `ServiceSecurityContext.PrimaryIdentity.Name` showed the authenticated user as "Anonymous" because the default value of `HttpClientCredentialType.None` was used for the `ClientCredentialType` property.

Let's start at the bottom of this enumeration and go through each possibility for the client credential (other than None). Note that these are the same options that are generally available for client authentication inside IIS. So, if you are familiar with these possibilities from experience with web applications, you can be assured that the options are exactly the same.

 When the WebHttpSecurity.TransportOnlyCredential option is selected, the client is forced to authenticate, but the service is not authenticated by the client (i.e., there is no SSL). In this mode, if you were to use a URI with HTTPS, WCF would throw an exception on opening. Except for Certificate authentication, all the other HttpClientCredentialType options are available for use.

Certificate authentication

One option for authenticating the client with a WebHttpBinding-based service is to require the client to submit a certificate of its own when using SSL. Again, note that SSL is required for this option; you cannot use client certificates for authentication without using SSL, so HttpClientCredentialType.Certificate isn't compatible with WebHttpSecurity.TransportCredentialOnly. You can enable this option by setting the Transport property to HttpClientCredentialType.Certificate:

```
WebServiceHost sh = new WebServiceHost(typeof(SecureService));
string uri = "https://win2008/wcfrestsecoiis/";
WebHttpBinding wb = new WebHttpBinding();
wb.Security.Mode = WebHttpSecurityMode.Transport;
wb.Security.Transport.ClientCredentialType = HttpClientCredentialType.Certificate;
sh.AddServiceEndpoint(typeof(SecureService), wb, uri);
sh.Open();
Console.WriteLine("Service running");
Process.Start(uri);
Console.ReadLine();
```

In this mode, the client is required to send a certificate when making an HTTP request to this service endpoint. We'll look at the client code for doing this in a moment.

The advantage of client certificates is that you can be fairly confident that the client is who she says she is, since only that client should have the certificate (of course, this depends on the client not losing her computer or leaving it open for someone to steal the certificate).

The disadvantage of client certificates is that if you have more than a handful of clients, generating and distributing the client certificates is a big job. Again, this is just like using certificates for client authentication for websites; it works well in some situations but not so well in others.

Here's an example of a WCF REST client calling the service endpoint using Certificate authentication:

```
Uri uri =
    new Uri("https://win2008/wcfrestsecoiis/");
WebChannelFactory<SecureService>
    cf = new WebChannelFactory<SecureService>(uri);
WebHttpBinding wb =
    cf.Endpoint.Binding as WebHttpBinding;
wb.Security.Transport.ClientCredentialType
    = HttpClientCredentialType.Certificate;
wb.Security.Mode =
    WebHttpSecurityMode.Transport;
cf.Credentials.ClientCertificate.SetCertificate(
StoreLocation.LocalMachine,
StoreName.My,
X509FindType.FindByThumbprint,
"930b54bb7e5a70ce11c1cef7d2ad9e5e557a3366");
SecureService service = cf.CreateChannel();
string auth = service.AuthType();
Console.WriteLine(auth);
```

Windows authentication

Under the covers, Windows and NTLM are different, but in most respects they behave similarly when it comes to authentication and RESTful services with WCF.

The one major difference may concern authorization because with Kerberos it is possible to do constrained delegation, allowing a token to make more than one network hop and still be valid. See the current documentation on constrained delegation and Kerberos for more information.

Note that IIS 7.0 doesn't enable Kerberos by default. To enable it, add the following code to your application *Host.config* file (either at the global level or inside your particular location):

```
<windowsAuthentication enabled="true">
    <providers>
        <clear />
        <!-- the first element isn't here by default-->
        <add value="Negotiate"/>
        <add value="NTLM" />

    </providers>
</windowsAuthentication>
```

NTLM authentication

If all of your clients will be running Windows and your RESTful services will be exposed only inside your enterprise, NTLM might be a viable option for client authentication. Setting this option is fairly easy (for the rest of the examples in the chapter using the ClientCredentialType property I'll show you only a snippet of code that actually sets the property):

Figure 8-5. NTLM client authentication

```
WebHttpBinding wb = new WebHttpBinding();
wb.Security.Mode = WebHttpSecurityMode.TransportCredentialOnly;
wb.Security.Transport.ClientCredentialType = HttpClientCredentialType.Ntlm;
```

Remember that the `Mode` doesn't have to be `Transport` for NTLM to work. In fact, the NTLM protocol is inherently secure, although only the authentication is secure; once the authentication takes place, all the traffic from the client to the service is not encrypted unless `Transport` is used as the `Mode`.

You can see the response to the call in Figure 8-5.

In this case, the authentication is happening automatically because the browser is configured to send the proper credentials when an HTTP status of 401 is sent back to the browser, where the type of authentication requested is NTLM (this is the default).

Here is the WCF client code to call this service using NTLM authentication:

```
Uri uri =
    new Uri("https://win2008/wcfrestsecoiis/");
WebChannelFactory<SecureService>
    cf = new WebChannelFactory<SecureService>(uri);
WebHttpBinding wb =
    cf.Endpoint.Binding as WebHttpBinding;
wb.Security.Transport.ClientCredentialType =
    HttpClientCredentialType.Ntlm;
wb.Security.Mode =
    WebHttpSecurityMode.Transport;
SecureService service = cf.CreateChannel();
string auth = service.AuthType();
Console.WriteLine(auth);
```

Notice that this code doesn't require any credentials to be explicitly passed; it will use the current user's token to authenticate. You can provide an alternative Windows credential by setting the `ChannelFactory`'s `Credential.WindowsUser` property explicitly.

Digest authentication

Digest authentication is similar to Basic authentication, which is discussed next (in fact, the client code is exactly the same). Digest authentication uses a more secure method of embedding authentication information in the HTTP request than Basic does.

Despite this fact, Digest authentication is used less often than Basic because it requires the web server to belong to a domain, which isn't always possible or practical. Also, the extra security provided by Digest authentication over Basic authentication isn't usually enough to make it a more popular option. In addition, most of the time when we are worried about protecting client credentials, we turn to SSL. In the end, then, Digest provides little in terms of actual security over Basic. For these reasons, I've limited the discussion of Digest authentication to just these points.

Basic authentication

Basic authentication is a well-known and popular HTTP standard. Like NTLM and Digest, Basic authentication is a challenge-response authentication protocol whereby the server will issue a 401 back to the client and ask the client to present credentials.

In the case of Basic authentication, the credential is a base64-encoded copy of the username and password. Although it isn't required, it's a best practice to always use SSL with Basic authentication to avoid having your user's password stolen from the clear text packets containing this base64-encoded string:

```
WebHttpBinding wb = new WebHttpBinding();
wb.Security.Mode = WebHttpSecurityMode.TransportCredentialOnly;
wb.Security.Transport.ClientCredentialType = HttpClientCredentialType.Basic;
```

When this endpoint is hit with a browser, the browser presents a username and password dialog box for the user to enter her credentials. Here is the WCF code for calling a service using Basic authentication:

```
Uri uri =
    new Uri("https://win2008/wcfrestsecoiis/");
WebChannelFactory<SecureService>
    cf = new WebChannelFactory<SecureService>(uri);
WebHttpBinding wb =
    cf.Endpoint.Binding as WebHttpBinding;
wb.Security.Transport.ClientCredentialType =
    HttpClientCredentialType.Basic;
wb.Security.Mode =
    WebHttpSecurityMode.Transport;
cf.Credentials.UserName.UserName = "administrator";
cf.Credentials.UserName.Password = "P2ssw0rd";
SecureService service = cf.CreateChannel();
string auth = service.AuthType();
Console.WriteLine(auth);
```

Authenticating: Managed Hosting Endpoints

Everything you've seen so far in this chapter has applied to self-hosting. However, it would behave exactly the same if we had used the managed hosting of IIS. The settings would be the same, although with IIS you are more likely to be using the *web.config* file to make these configuration changes than doing your configuration in code.

When hosting an endpoint inside IIS, you have to be acutely aware that the WCF settings must match precisely (i.e., they don't conflict) with those in *web.config*, and vice versa. In reality you have to be concerned with more than just your local *web.config*; you have to be aware of the settings all the way up to the IIS website level and ensure that they are consistent.

For example, if you are hosting inside a virtual directory, you can't disable Basic authentication at the virtual directory level and then try to use `HttpClientSecurity Type.Basic` as your *.svc* file configuration.

The `Mode` setting is another setting to watch out for. If the virtual directory inside which your service is running isn't configured correctly for SSL, using `Transport` as the value of `Mode` will cause an exception. Conversely, if you have the virtual directory configured to require SSL and then you try to use `TransportClientCredentialOnly` as the value for the `Mode` property, you'll get this error:

```
Could not find a base address that matches scheme http
  for the endpoint with binding WebHttpBinding. Registered base
  address schemes are [https].
```

This is one of the many things that must be consistent between your IIS settings and the WCF settings for your service.

Authorizing Endpoints

Once you've sorted out authentication (figuring out how to tell which client is connecting), the next step is often to figure out authorization (what the client can and cannot do inside your services).

This is another topic where the WCF Web Programming Model doesn't deviate much from that of any other WCF service. The options for specifying what a client can do inside your RESTful service are almost the same as those for specifying what a client can do with a SOAP-based web service in WCF.

Authorization with Impersonation

One way to provide authorization in WCF is to impersonate the client. When you impersonate the client, you are essentially delegating the job of authorization down one layer.

For example, if you are implementing the `POST` part of the uniform interface on a resource, you might be using `System.Data.SqlClient.SqlConnection` and friends to insert a new record into a SQL Server database. If you impersonate the incoming client and the client doesn't have permissions to insert records into that table, an exception will be thrown at the database level. You can choose to let this exception bubble back to the client, or you can choose to catch the exception and return a more generic error. The idea here is that it will be the responsibility of the system you are interacting with to provide role-based security.

In WCF, you have two options when using impersonation. One option is to explicitly impersonate an incoming client using `ServiceSecurityContext` and its `WindowsIdentity` property:

```
ServiceSecurityContext securityCtx;
securityCtx = OperationContext.Current.ServiceSecurityContext;
securityCtx.WindowsIdentity.Impersonate();
```

You can also get `WindowsIdentity` by using `System.Threading.Thread.Current Principal.Identity` (although this requires an explicit case to `WindowsIdentity`).

The other way to do impersonation in WCF is to do it implicitly by using `OperationBehaviorAttribute` on your service implementation, as shown in Example 8-3.

Example 8-3. Impersonating with OperationBehaviorAttribute

```
[OperationContract]
[WebGet(UriTemplate = "/")]
[OperationBehavior(Impersonation
        = ImpersonationOption.Required)]//this causes impersonation to
//happen automatically
public string AuthType()
{
    ServiceSecurityContext securityCtx;
    securityCtx = OperationContext.Current.ServiceSecurityContext;
    string authType = "No security context";
    if (securityCtx != null)
    {
        if (securityCtx.IsAnonymous)
            authType = "Anonymous";
        else
        {

            authType = securityCtx.PrimaryIdentity.Name;
        }

    }
    return authType;

}
```

Role-Based Authorization

Another way to implement authorization with WCF is to restrict access to operations to certain users or groups. You can do this either by using the `PrincipalPermissionAttribute` on your service methods (which will enforce this automatically at the operation level) or by using `ServiceAuthorizationManager` with WCF. We'll discuss these options in the next two sections.

Using the PrincipalPermissionAttribute

The values of the `PrincipalPermissionAttribute` can be explicitly defined as Windows users and/or groups, or you can use Authorization Manager AzMan or even an ASP.NET membership provider. The former may require less work if you are already using Windows authentication (although maintaining the same values across different deployments might complicate the usage); the latter is more flexible since you can scope roles by application (rather than globally, based on Windows local or Domain groups).

 AzMan is a role-based framework that you can download and install for free from Microsoft. It can be used in many different types of applications including ASP.NET and WCF.

Instead of using the attribute, you can use the `Thread.IsInRole` API to evaluate a user's permissions dynamically. Using code inside your methods can also give you finer-grained permission control than what you get with `PrincipalPermissionAttribute` (which is applied at the operation level, so it's fairly coarse-grained).

Example 8-4 shows code that uses `PrincipalPermissionAttribute`.

Example 8-4. Using PrincipalPermissionAttribute

```
[OperationContract]
[WebGet(UriTemplate = "/")]
[OperationBehavior(Impersonation
        = ImpersonationOption.Required)]
 [PrincipalPermission(SecurityAction.PermitOnly,
     Role="Administrators")]
public string AuthType()
{}
```

Example 8-5 shows code that implements `IsInRole`.

Example 8-5. Using IsInRole

```
[OperationContract]
[WebGet(UriTemplate = "/")]
[OperationBehavior(Impersonation
        = ImpersonationOption.Required)]
public string AuthType()
{
    if (Thread.CurrentPrincipal.IsInRole("Administrators"))
    {//omitted for clarity
    }
}
```

The ServiceAuthorizationManager class

Alternatively, you can provide role-based authorization to your WCF services by using a `ServiceAuthorizationManager`-derived class. `ServiceAuthorizationManager` is a class you can plug into the WCF infrastructure on a particular ServiceHost (even WebServiceHost) instance through the ServiceAuthorizationBehavior service behavior. ServiceAuthorizationManager is called once for every message the service instance is going to process. It returns a Boolean value based on whether the particular ServiceAuthorizationManager instance decides the caller should be allowed to perform the operation. Returning false means the caller will be rejected; returning true allows the caller in through the rest of the WCF stack.

The advantage of using ServiceAuthorizationManager instead of PrincipalPermissionAttribute or IsInRole is that ServiceAuthorizationManager determines whether a user can perform a particular operation before the deserialization or method invocation on the service instance occurs. Why allow a method to be invoked if you are just going to end up rejecting it because the user isn't in the right group?

Another advantage of ServiceAuthorizationManager, since it is configured via Service AuthorizationBehavior, is that you are separating the business logic of your service from your authorization logic (since using PrincipalPermissionAttribute or IsInRole has embedded your authorization logic inside your service code). This allows you to change the authorization without having to recompile your service code.

The only notable issue in this area that is different for REST services versus SOAP services is that many of the examples you will see will use the incoming Action header as part of the logic inside ServiceAuthorizationManager. Since REST services aren't based on an Action header (in fact, the Action header will always be null when using WCF and REST), you'll want to use the URI being invoked along with the HTTP method to make your determination. Example 8-6 includes ServiceAuthorizationManager, which extracts the URI and method from the incoming context.

Example 8-6. Using ServiceAuthorizationManager

```
public class RESTServiceAuthorizationManager :
    ServiceAuthorizationManager
{
    protected override bool CheckAccessCore(OperationContext operationContext)
    {
        Message msg = operationContext.RequestContext.RequestMessage;

        string uri = msg.Properties.Via.AbsoluteUri;
        HttpRequestMessageProperty http = null;
        http = msg.Properties[HttpRequestMessageProperty.Name]
            as HttpRequestMessageProperty;
        Console.WriteLine("CheckAccessCore");
        Console.WriteLine("Resource: {0} part of uniform interface: {1}",
            uri, http.Method);
        return base.CheckAccessCore(operationContext);
    }
}
```

This clearly isn't a full implementation of `ServiceAuthorizationManager`, since the example doesn't actually return `true` or `false` based on the incoming claims. To fill out the implementation you'd need to determine what heuristic you want to use to determine access control for your particular application.

Summary

In this chapter, we discussed the basics of security with WCF and its Web Programming Model. First, we looked at how to secure the communications of your RESTful services by using SSL (setting the `WebHttpBinding.Security.Mode` property to `WebHttpSecurity.Transport`). Using SSL takes care of one of the biggest issues with securing web endpoints: making sure the communication between a client and a service is confidential.

Next we examined the built-in options for providing authentication. `WebHttpBinding` supports all of the different security settings that IIS supports: Anonymous (i.e., `HttpClientCredentialType.None`), Basic, Digest, NTLM, Windows, and Certificate. Which authentication you select will depend on the scope of what you are trying to accomplish with your RESTful endpoint. Basic authentication has the widest reach because more clients support it than any other credential type. Windows authentication probably has the smallest reach, but it is a useful and convenient authentication mode when you build services to be exposed only inside your enterprise.

Finally, we discussed how to perform authorization, which allows you to control which users can do what inside your service. WCF has some built-in options for accomplishing authorization based on the authenticated user's identity or role. Another choice is to use impersonation to push the authorization decisions down the stack to the resources being accessed by your service. Perhaps the best choice for authorization is to use a custom `ServiceAuthorizationManager` to put the authorization logic higher in the WCF call stack. This is more efficient and provides more extensibility since the authorization logic isn't built into your code.

CHAPTER 9

Using Workflow to Deliver REST Services

WCF in .NET 3.0 provided a way for you to use and expose services using your favorite .NET language. Also part of .NET 3.0, Windows Workflow Foundation (WF) provided a way to use a declarative language to create model-driven, reactive programs. Both frameworks shipped in the same vehicle (.NET 3.0), but neither had any OOTB integration with the other. Using them together in .NET 3.0 applications required a fair amount of repetitive manual coding.

Along with the Web Programming Model, .NET 3.5 brings a layer of integration between WCF and WF in the form of a pair of WF activities to model the processes of sending and receiving messages into workflows using WCF. .NET 3.5 also provides a hosting environment that allows you to stand up a service endpoint using a workflow in a way that is similar to how you can stand up a service endpoint using code. No explicit integration between the Web Programming Model and WF was included in this release, but it is still possible to use these two new frameworks together.

In this chapter, we'll look at how to consume REST endpoints using WF. We'll also examine how to create stateless and long-running stateful workflows to expose REST endpoints. As I discuss these options, I will raise the issue of whether melding the well-understood advantages of statelessness on the server in a REST service with the potential long-running nature of WF is a good idea. For the purposes of this chapter, I will assume that you already have some knowledge of WF, so we will focus on using WCF and WF together.

Consuming REST Services from WF

If you are using WF to build application logic, it is fairly common to consume services from your workflows. Both REST and SOAP services are quickly becoming the de facto way to expose functionality today. So, consuming services from workflows is just a side effect of using WF, since any code you write today most likely consumes services.

Of course, some logic is more appropriate for a workflow framework and some logic is more appropriate to write in raw source code. As an example for this chapter, I'll stick with business logic that is "classic workflow": document approval. In this chapter we'll add a modern twist: making the document types blog entries.

You can imagine that some commercial bloggers might benefit from a workflow system around their blog posts; I know I could use a grammar and spell-check before I submit a live blog post. Later in this chapter we'll discuss sending REST messages from WF using SendActivity. In preparation for that, we'll create a simple client application that hosts a workflow called the "checklist of things to do before you post" workflow. We will examine the implementation of the full approval scenario in the discussion of ReceiveActivity toward the end of the chapter. Since this book is about REST and not WF, we won't spend much time on the workflow features being used, other than discussing the features surrounding SendActivity itself.

The SendActivity Instance

One of the two activities added in .NET 3.5 is SendActivity. From a WCF developer's point of view, SendActivity can be viewed as the workflow equivalent of an instance of ChannelFactory. SendActivity acts as a WCF client for workflow instances, and will use whatever address and binding have been configured for that particular SendActivity instance.

First, you must have a WCF service contract to use as the basis for your SendActivity. Example 9-1 contains the contract we will use. See Chapter 10 for more information about creating client-side contracts for use with WebHttpBinding.

Example 9-1. WCF service contract for blog editing

```
namespace BlogCheckListContracts
{
    [ServiceContract(Namespace="")]
    public interface IBlogAPI
    {
        [OperationContract]
        [WebInvoke(UriTemplate="/blog",Method="POST")]
        Atom10ItemFormatter AddEntry(Atom10ItemFormatter entry);
        [OperationContract]
        [WebGet(UriTemplate = "/blog")]
        Atom10FeedFormatter GetBlog();
        //rest of the members omitted for clarity
    }
}
```

In this case, we'll use a SequentialWorkflow to implement my logic. You can see the workflow in Figure 9-1. The logic of the workflow is apparent in its model.

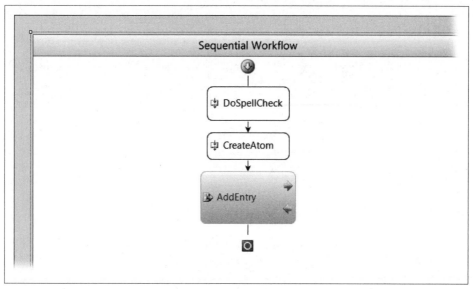

Figure 9-1. Client "checklist" workflow

 People often ask me why I would use WF when anything that I can accomplish in WF could be written using just code. My typical answer is that I think WF is a powerful model for some (perhaps many) use cases because of the visibility it provides, both at development time and at runtime. For instance, notice that I didn't have to spend much time explaining what this workflow does, as Figure 9-1 explains it well. In fact, while I was writing this chapter, I asked my 15-year-old son (who is not a developer) to look at the figure, and with no background knowledge of WF he was able to discern the functionality of the workflow. Using WF to explain application logic to a 15-year-old is probably a stretch, but I think it illustrates the power of WF's visibility-encouraging modeling.

The workflow first checks the blog entry for any spelling errors. If there are errors, the UI will notify the user and allow him to fix the errors. Then the workflow creates an Atom entry, and finally it executes the last and most important activity in the workflow: the `AddEntry` activity. This instance of `SendActivity` will call the RESTful endpoint that implements the service function of the `IBlogAPI` contract (the code for the `IBlogAPI` contract is included with the code samples for this book).

You can add a `SendActivity` instance to your workflow by dragging it from the Toolbox and dropping it onto your workflow design surface in the appropriate area. To configure it, double-click on it in the Designer (or go to the Property Grid and modify all the required properties). When you double-click on `SendActivity`, the Choose Operation dialog box will appear (see Figure 9-2).

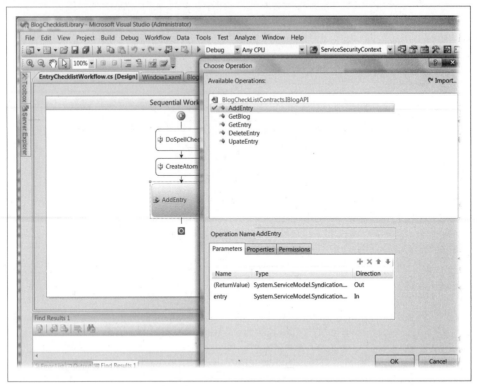

Figure 9-2. The SendActivity Choose Operation dialog box

In this dialog box, you can click the Import button in the upper-right corner to browse for the contract definition you want to associate with this `SendActivity`. Once you've selected `IBlogAPI`, you can select `AddEntry` as the operation you want this `SendActivity` to use when calling the service. Note that the `IBlogAPI` contract definition must be in the same project as the workflow, or in an assembly that is referenced in the workflow project.

When you select `AddEntry` and click OK on the Choose Operation dialog box, two new properties will be added to the `SendActivity` instance in the Properties window. `SendActivity`'s Designer dynamically adds these properties, and they represent the request and response messages this operation will accept and return. You can data-bind these properties to properties on other activities in your workflow, or to properties on the workflow type itself. In this example, we'll add a new property of type `Atom10ItemFormatter` to the workflow definition. We can then use the WF activity binding syntax to bind the input and output parameters of the `AddEntry` operation to that property. You can see this configuration in Figure 9-3.

The other property to note in Figure 9-3 is the `ChannelToken` property of `SendActivity`. `ChannelToken` is an identifier that the WCF/WF integration in WF 3.5 uses to determine

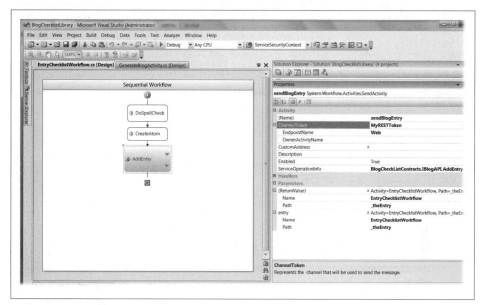

Figure 9-3. SendActivity properties

what client endpoint configuration to use for a particular `SendActivity`. The first time a particular `ChannelToken` is encountered inside a particular `WorkflowRuntime`, `SendActivity` will create a new `ChannelFactory`. Any further `SendActivity` in a particular workflow instance can reuse the same channel by using the same `ChannelToken` identifier. The `OwnerActivity` property allows a `ChannelToken` to be scoped as a child activity inside of a composite Activity, which facilitates advanced scenarios when there are multiple `SendActivity` instances inside a workflow, and one set of activities is sharing the same channel instance while another set of activities is using the same configuration but another channel instance.

The basic upshot of `ChannelToken` is that multiple `SendActivity` instances can reuse the same channel, thereby sharing things such as a common session.

A more important property of `ChannelToken` is the `EndpointName` property. The `Endpoint Name` property must correspond to either a client endpoint entry in the application configuration file or a named `ServiceEndpoint` instance inside a `WorkflowRuntime`-level service known as the `ChannelManagerService`. Note that the `ChannelManagerService` isn't added to the `WorkflowRuntime` by default, but you can explicitly add it and avoid having to rely on configuration file entries for your `SendActivity` configuration.

 Just to avoid confusion, the concept of a `WorkflowRuntime` service is different from the notion of a REST service. The `WorkflowRuntime` in WF delegates most of its functionality to objects known as services.

If you want SendActivity to read its configuration from the application configuration file, you simply specify the appropriate value on the name attribute in the client endpoint configuration (i.e., the value must match the EndpointName property on the ChannelToken). Example 9-2 shows the code used to do this.

Example 9-2. Workflow service configuration file

```xml
<?xml version="1.0" encoding="utf-8" ?>
<configuration>
  <system.serviceModel>
    <client>
      <endpoint name="Web"
                address="http://localhost/BlogWorkflowWeb/blogengine.svc"
                binding="webHttpBinding"
                behaviorConfiguration="webBehavior"
                contract="BlogCheckListContracts.IBlogAPI"/>
    </client>
    <behaviors>
      <endpointBehaviors>
        <behavior name="webBehavior">
          <webHttp/>
        </behavior>
      </endpointBehaviors>
    </behaviors>
  </system.serviceModel>
</configuration>
```

The important thing here is that the WCF client endpoint configuration stays exactly the same; the SendActivity doesn't require any new syntax or entries.

If you want to use the ChannelManagerService to manage the endpoints, the code would look like that shown in Example 9-3.

Example 9-3. Using ChannelManagerService to manage endpoints

```csharp
//create the workflow runtime
WorkflowRuntime wr = new WorkflowRuntime();
List<ServiceEndpoint> listOfEndpoints
    = new List<ServiceEndpoint>();
//create the endpoint
WebHttpBinding b = new WebHttpBinding();
string uri = "http://localhost/BlogWorkflowWeb/blogengine.svc";
ContractDescription cd =
    ContractDescription.GetContract(typeof(IBlogAPI));
ServiceEndpoint webServiceEndpoint =
    new ServiceEndpoint(cd, b, new EndpointAddress(uri));
webServiceEndpoint.Behaviors.Add(new WebHttpBehavior());
//make sure to name it correctly
webServiceEndpoint.Name = "Web";
listOfEndpoints.Add(webServiceEndpoint);
ChannelManagerService cms =
    new ChannelManagerService(listOfEndpoints);
wr.AddService(cms);
wr.StartRuntime();
```

No matter how the `SendActivity` gets its channel (either from the configuration file or from the `ChannelManagerService`), it will call the service just like any other WCF client. Because we are using the WCF 3.5 attributes on the contract and specifying the `WebHttpBinding` along with the `WebHttpBehavior` when configuring the client endpoint, the WCF client channel infrastructure uses the correct URI and correct method when invoking the service endpoint.

I should also point out that you can combine the two approaches, in which case the `SendActivity` will first ask the `ChannelManagerService` for the correct named endpoint configuration, and if the `ChannelManagerService` doesn't have it available, the `SendActivity` will try to find the named endpoint in the configuration file. If `SendActivity` finds the configuration in the configuration file, that information will be cached in the `ChannelManagerService` for future use.

The ReceiveActivity Instance

WCF 3.5 also includes an activity named `ReceiveActivity`. In Chapters 2 and 3, we discussed how to use WCF to expose instances of a .NET class as a WCF service by using attributes, configuration, and the `WebServiceHost`. In WCF 3.5, the same attributes, configuration, and `WorkflowServiceHost` (in conjunction with the `ReceiveActivity`), can do the same thing with a workflow definition: expose instances of it as a WCF service.

Conceptually, there's no difference between hosting code as a service and hosting workflow as a service, but there are some unique design decisions to consider when implementing a service using WF. The first and arguably most important issue is what to do with a message that comes into the service endpoint. There has to be some way for the WCF infrastructure to determine whether it is supposed to create a new workflow instance for the message or route it to an existing instance. If the message is to be routed to an existing instance, how should the runtime determine what that instance is?

Both of these issues exist when you're writing certain types of code with WCF as well. When you're writing a code-based service with WCF, one of the decisions you have to make is what your `InstanceContextMode` will be. If `InstanceContextMode` is left as the default (`InstanceContextMode.PerSession`), a new instance of your service type is created "per session," and as long as that session is active, your instance is also active and additional messages from the same client will be routed to the same object instance.

`InstanceContextMode.PerCall` is a stateless mode in which a new object is created per message, and that instance is discarded after each operation (similar to the ASP.NET page lifetime mode). `PerCall` is typically considered to be the most scalable mode, since each call can safely be routed to any machine in your farm (assuming you are doing load balancing), because `PerCall` forces you to stick with a stateless programming model.

Although people typically think of WF as being a stateful way to write programs (and to be honest, WF is somewhat geared toward that idea), you can actually write a WF program to be stateless. Because one of the underlying tenets of REST is to keep the server stateless, we will first create a workflow-based WCF service that is stateless. Then we'll create one that is stateful, after which we'll discuss the issues that may arise when taking this approach.

Stateless Workflow Services

To get your feet wet with Workflow Services, let's use a simple example that allows us to implement a service with a single operation using a workflow. I'll admit that this example is somewhat contrived, since it is unlikely you'd ever have a service with a single operation, but it's a good idea to start small here so that you can get the basics of Workflow Services before we work on a workflow that implements a more realistic contract.

For consistency, we'll use the contract we used in the workflow as a client example from earlier in this chapter. We will implement the `IBlogAPI.GetBlog` method in the workflow.

`ReceiveActivity` (like `SendActivity`) has a `ServiceOperationInfo` property that has to be associated with a particular service contract and operation. Instead of using the contract and operation, as `SendActivity` does, `ReceiveActivity` is going to implement it. It's clear that this property is essential to `ReceiveActivity`'s functionality because immediately after you drag it onto a workflow design surface from the Toolbox, it shows you that it's unhappy (indicated by a red dot with a white bang character inside it) because it hasn't been associated with a contract and operation.

To make `ReceiveActivity` happy, you can either double-click on it or go to the `ServiceOperationInfo` property to configure the contract and operation, at which point the Choose Operation dialog box will appear (this is the same dialog box you use to configure `SendActivity`). Click Import to browse the references in the workflow project. You are looking for the contract to implement with this activity (remember that each `ReceiveActivity` implements only one method on the service).

> The upper-right corner of the Choose Operation dialog box contains an Add Contract button. In my opinion, you should never click this button. When you click this button, you create a contract that you cannot reuse without first going through a metadata (i.e., WSDL) generation process. This would be a disaster, especially for RESTful service contracts. Furthermore, there are no facilities for adding the `WebGet`/`WebInvoke` attributes to this "contract." This generally is a button to avoid.

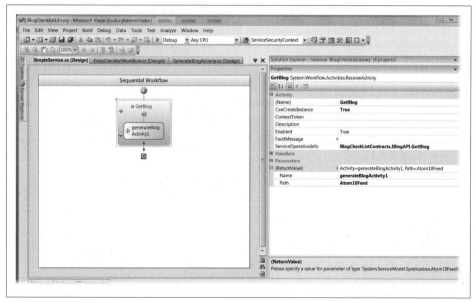

Figure 9-4. IBlogAPI.GetBlog ReceiveActivity

For this example, choose the `IBlogAPI` contract and the `GetBlog` operation. The parameters to the method become parameters on the `ReceiveActivity` and you can databind those properties to other activities in your workflow.

One other property to note on `ReceiveActivity` is the `CanCreateInstance` property. This is a Boolean value that tells the WCF/WF infrastructure when to create a new workflow instance. For this particular `ReceiveActivity`, set `CanCreateInstance` to `true`; we are building a stateless service and this will create a new instance whenever a new message is received for this operation. Figure 9-4 shows the configured `ReceiveActivity`.

You can see that the `(ReturnValue)` property is bound to a property on a child activity of `ReceiveActivity`. Both `SendActivity` and `ReceiveActivity` are composite activities, which means that child activities can be placed inside those activities and they will execute before either the `SendActivity` or `ReceiveActivity` is complete. Generally, the child activities are the actual implementations of the operation on the server side, and in this case the `GenerateBlogActivity` is equivalent to the code inside a service operation method implementation.

We now have a workflow (note that this is a `SequentialWorkflow`) that can be deployed as a service. Depending on your hosting environment, you have a few different options for deploying the workflow.

If you are self-hosting, you must use the `WorkflowServiceHost` type to create an environment where incoming messages are routed from the endpoint to workflow instances instead of objects. In Chapter 2 we discussed how custom `ServiceHost`-derived types can be extremely useful, and how the REST support in WCF 3.5 somewhat centers around the `WebServiceHost` (and `WebServiceHostFactory`). `WorkflowServiceHost` is similar in functionality because it replaces the object invocation infrastructure in the WCF channel stack on the server side with an implementation that will invoke workflow instances instead of class instances.

If you are hosting inside IIS, you still need a file in the virtual directory as the mechanism to get your service loaded into the IIS hosting environment. As with a REST-based service, `WebServiceHostFactory` uses a `WorkflowServiceFactory`. For this scenario, we'll host inside IIS, so the *.svc* file looks like this:

```
<%@ ServiceHost
Service="BlogChecklistLibrary.SimpleService"
Factory="System.ServiceModel.Activation.WorkflowServiceHostFactory" %>
```

 I again feel obligated to point out a WF feature. The `WorkflowService Host` will take a pure XAML file as the parameter to its constructor. This means that not only can you drop an *.xoml* file inside a virtual directory to get a Workflow Service, but also you can use an *.svc* file and point the `Service` attribute in the `ServiceHost` directive to an *.xoml* file. Also, when self-hosting you can pass an `XmlReader` to the `WorkflowService Host` constructor, so there are many different ways, depending on your application's needs, to create a workflow service from XAML.

Of course, this type of `ServiceHostFactory` doesn't automatically add an endpoint (as `WebServiceHostFactory` will), so we will have to place a service configuration inside the *web.config* file:

```
<services>
  <service name="BlogChecklistLibrary.SimpleService">
    <endpoint address="" binding="webHttpBinding"
     contract="BlogCheckListContracts.IBlogAPI"/>
  </service>
</services>
```

After setting these two necessary pieces of the IIS hosting infrastructure, we should be able to hit this endpoint with a browser (since it is implementing the `GET` part of the uniform interface). When you do hit the endpoint via a browser, however, you will get a surprise (shown in Figure 9-5).

At the start of this section, I mentioned that it is more common to think about a workflow as a long-running stateful service than as a short-running stateless one. It appears that implementation of `WorkflowServiceHost` thinks this way as well. `WorkflowService Host` expects a *context channel* to be configured on this binding. A WCF 3.5 context channel determines which workflow instance should get an incoming message when that message is not intended for creating a new workflow.

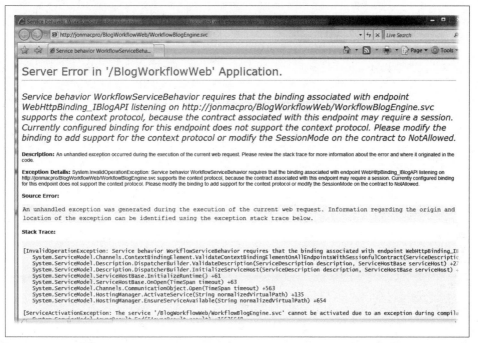

Figure 9-5. WorkflowServiceHost expects a session

So, is our only hope to add a context channel to the binding to make this exception go away? No. In fact, we can do something much simpler to fix this issue: on the `IBlogAPI` contract, simply declare that sessions are not allowed by setting the `ServiceContractAttribute.SessionMode` property to `SessionMode.NotAllowed`:

```
[ServiceContract(Namespace="",
    SessionMode=SessionMode.NotAllowed)]
public interface IBlogAPI
{}
```

`WorkflowServiceHost` is now happy and the browser can successfully make a request for this endpoint (see Figure 9-6).

To recap, getting a workflow up and running as the implementation of a stateless service contract requires the following steps:

1. Modify the contract to specify `SessionMode.NotAllowed`.

2. Add the `ReceiveActivity` into a workflow and set `CanCreateInstance` to `true`.

3. Set the `ServiceOperationInfo` on the newly added `ReceiveActivity` to the correct operation on the contract.

4. Put activities inside `ReceiveActivity` to "implement" the operation.

5. Bind the input and output parameters of the operation to appropriate fields or properties.

Figure 9-6. Workflow service returning a feed via REST

6. Use `WorkflowServiceHost` with the appropriate binding and behavior (in the REST-ful case this will be `WebHttpBinding` and `WebHttpBehavior`).

7. In the IIS hosting case, add an *.svc* file that specifies `WorkflowServiceHostFactory` and points to the workflow type (or to the *.xoml* file in the case of a XAML-activated workflow).

8. Invoke the service.

To implement a more complex contract (e.g., one with more than one operation), you must repeat steps 2 through 5 modifying the name and potentially the parameters.

There is, of course, one more complicating factor: the workflow execution model.

The simple example shown up to this point uses a `SequentialWorkflow` model to implement the service, and since there was only one operation, a `SequentialWorkflow` model made sense. However, to implement something that could activate a workflow instance based on multiple operations, the `StateMachineWorkflow` is probably a more useful model.

Selecting the workflow model for your service implementation is really outside the scope of this chapter and book, but this rule of thumb can probably help you: if your contract requires a particular order for invoking operations, the SequentialWorkflow model is probably the one for you. If there isn't an order to operation invocation (or if multiple operations can be invoked at certain times during the execution of your service), the StateMachineWorkflow model is probably the better of the two OOTB "root" models.

In the StateMachineWorkflow model, multiple "events" can be listening at the same time. Each "event" is really the invocation of an operation on a service (implemented using ReceiveActivity). To more effectively illustrate this point, let's implement the entire uniform interface on the "blog" resource (this doesn't implement the whole Atom Publishing Protocol; it's just a sample of a custom "blog" API). The new contract is shown in Example 9-4.

Example 9-4. The new contract

```
public interface IBlogAPI
{
    [OperationContract]
    [WebInvoke(UriTemplate = "/blog")]
    Atom10ItemFormatter AddEntry(Atom10ItemFormatter entry);
    [OperationContract]
    [WebGet(UriTemplate = "/blog")]
    Atom10FeedFormatter GetBlog();
    [OperationContract]
    [WebGet(UriTemplate = "/blog/{id}")]
    Atom10ItemFormatter GetEntry(string id);
    [OperationContract]
    [WebInvoke(UriTemplate = "/blog/{id}", Method = "DELETE")]
    Atom10ItemFormatter DeleteEntry(string id);
    [OperationContract]
    [WebInvoke(UriTemplate = "/blog/{id}", Method = "PUT")]
    Atom10ItemFormatter UpateEntry(string id, Atom10ItemFormatter entry);
}
```

Figure 9-7 shows the StateMachineWorkflow implementation of this contract (which is still stateless).

The key to making this implementation stateless is setting the CanCreateInstance property on all of the ReceiveActivity instances in this workflow to true. You can't see this from the StateMachine designer, since it shows only the EventDrivenActivity instances. The ReceiveActivity instances are the first activities inside each EventDrivenActivity instance. Figure 9-8 shows the GetBlogEvent "implementation" to see inside one of the EventDrivenActivity instances. This image doesn't include the *web.config* file because it's the same as in Example 9-2 (except for the value of the name attribute).

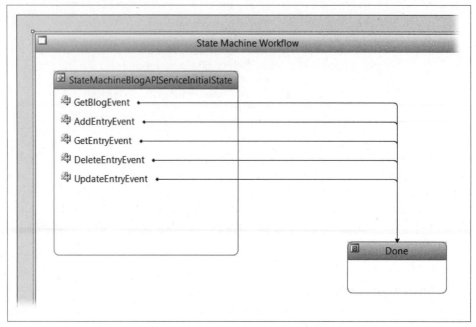

Figure 9-7. StateMachine stateless workflow

At this point, the Workflow Service is just like a code-based service using `InstanceContextMode.PerCall`. Because all the `ReceiveActivity` instances have their `CanCreateInstance` property set to `true`, every message arriving to this service endpoint causes a new instance of the workflow type to be created (just as a new .NET object is created for each and every call in the `PerCall` case).

The message is routed to the correct `EventDrivenActivity` based on the URI and method, which is also what would happen in a code-based REST service. Once the operation completes (which happens after the activities under `EventDrivenActivity` complete), `StateMachineWorkflow` transitions to the "Done" state, which causes the workflow instance to complete. We could call this the PerCall Workflow Services model.

This is one valid way to use Workflow Services with WCF 3.5's Web Programming Model. I like this model because it allows you to implement services using workflow while maintaining the statelessness of the REST architecture. You can easily scale this service out to multiple web servers with no ill effects, since any state management and concurrency will have been dealt with at the data-store level (assuming the service is backed by a database). See the note on visibility earlier in this chapter for reasons why I think using workflow in general is useful. This usage is just a specialized case of that general concept.

On the other hand, one of the most commonly cited reasons to use WF is that `Work flowRuntime` (when used in conjunction with a persistence service) can provide a

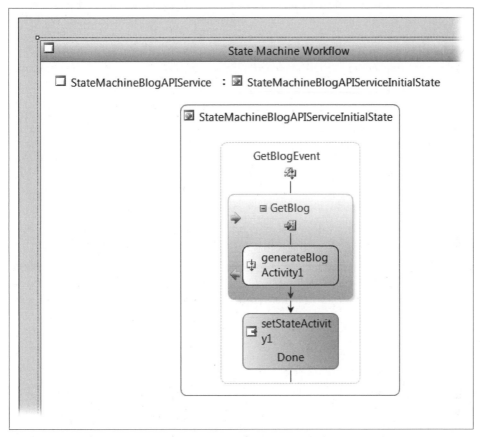

Figure 9-8. GetBlog operation implementation with CanCreateInstance set to true

simplified model to create stateful, long-running services. Of course, you can build this style of workflow service with the WCF/WF integration in 3.5.

Stateful Workflow Services

The first issue you'll face when moving to a stateful service model with Workflow Services and REST concerns how WCF will determine when to create a new instance and when to send a message to an existing instance.

This is where the concept of *context* comes into play in .NET 3.5. Context describes, in general terms, how this problem is solved. Because each particular type of binding or service might decide to manage the actual details in different ways, a general terminology is actually helpful. Having an extra piece of "context" data associated with an incoming message enables the infrastructure to provide an implementation to solve this problem. Let's walk through a basic abstract example.

Imagine a case where a message arrives at a service endpoint implemented by a workflow and there isn't any extra "context" information in the message. The WCF/WF infrastructure determines which operation should be invoked based on this message (it does this using the same mechanism used in a code-based service, so in the RESTful case it will be based on the URI/method). If the `ReceiveActivity` instance that implements the operation has its `CanCreateInstance` set to `true`, a workflow instance is created and the "context" is added back to the response message so that the client can retrieve and store that "context" and use it again for another invocation.

If the `ReceiveActivity` instance that implements the operation has its `CanCreateInstance` set to `false`, a fault will be returned to the client. Also note that as I showed you in the stateless example,you can have multiple activities with `CanCreateInstance` set to `true`, depending on which operation you expect or want to allow a client to call to create the instance of the workflow.

When the client makes another call, it is responsible for sending this "context" back to the endpoint, so the subsequent invocation will be routed to the already-created workflow instance.

The WCF/WF integration doesn't actually dictate what this "context" must be, but the implementation of the context channel in WCF 3.5 uses the `WorkflowInstance.InstanceId` value (the GUID that uniquely identifies each workflow instance) as the context value.

The WCF/WF integration also doesn't dictate the exact storage mechanism in the response message to the initiating operation, but there are two places where the OOTB context channel will store the context: either in a SOAP header (this is not an option if you are building RESTful services) or in the form of an HTTP cookie. The HTTP cookie option will work because we are using HTTP with REST, so clients in a RESTful environment are usually able to reply on subsequent calls with the cookie value (most do it automatically).

Without getting into a deep discussion of the propriety of using cookies with a RESTful design, let's enable this in a Workflow Service exposed using REST.

 This potential discussion includes an argument against cookies with special values in REST because it takes the state out of the two places where clients expect state to be: in the resource itself and in the URI.

The key will be to create a custom binding for your endpoint, one that includes the same binding elements as `WebHttpBinding` and adds the context binding element as well. Here is the XML configuration for such a binding:

```
<customBinding>
  <binding name="WebWithContext">
    <context contextExchangeMechanism="HttpCookie" protectionLevel="None" />
    <textMessageEncoding messageVersion="None" />
```

```
            <httpTransport manualAddressing="true" />
        </binding>
    </customBinding>
```

Recall from Chapter 2 that WebHttpBinding is just a custom binding wrapper that uses HttpTransport and TextMessageEncoder with MessageVersion set to None. Adding in the context binding element enables the context channel to be loaded into this channel stack when the endpoint is opened. In the configuration, the context mechanism is "cookies" so the requirement of having the cookie protected with an encrypted transport (protectionLevel="None") has been turned off.

We must now create a contract that will allow us to build a stateful workflow (we're finally getting to the "document approval" scenario I mentioned at the beginning of the chapter). Create a new service contract that includes approval by using inheritance:

```
[ServiceContract(Namespace = "")]
public interface IBlogApprovalAPI : IBlogAPI
{
    [OperationContract]
    [WebInvoke(UriTemplate = "/blog/{id}/approve",Method="PUT")]
    Atom10ItemFormatter ApproveEntry(string id,Atom10ItemFormatter entry);
}
```

By inheriting from IBlogAPI, your new IBlogApprovalAPI gets all the operations from its base type and allows you to add the ApproveEntry operation. In this case, that approval will use PUT, since it is really modifying the state of an existing resource (the entry). Next, add a literal value onto the end of the UriTemplate to disambiguate ApproveEntry calls from UpdateEntry calls.

Before you implement this service contract using a stateful workflow model, design a protocol that will dictate the order in which the operations can be called. Decide which operation(s) start a workflow, which operation(s) cause a workflow to complete, and which operation(s) can be called multiple times. This information can't be expressed fully in the service contract itself, but it will be embedded in the workflow model based on the workflow design.

In a stateless (InstanceContextMode.PerCall) WCF code-based service (or in the stateless workflow model in the preceding section), a service is always "ready" for any operation to be called. There isn't a particular order for calling operations; all operations can be called at any time, so you don't have to take this issue into consideration in a stateless model.

If you move to a stateful workflow model, you will have to specify the order in which the operations can be called. Which operations creates and which operation closes a workflow instance has to be built into your service contract. The design of the workflow will dictate the order the other operations can be called. This "operation order" information will have to be passed along to clients in the form of documentation.

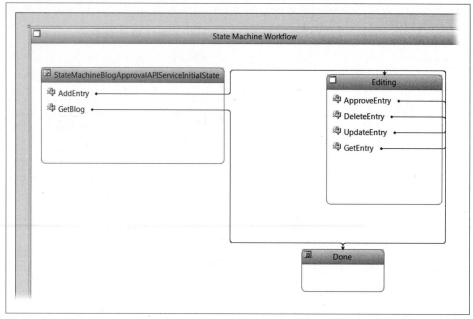

Figure 9-9. Stateful workflow service

Because of the way `ReceiveActivity.CanCreateInstance` works (note the "can" part of that property name) you can have multiple operations create an instance, but the rest of the operations still have to be put into a particular order.

Our example scenario will use the following protocol:

- A call to `GetBlog` or `AddEntry` will result in the creation of a new workflow (i.e., `CanCreateInstance` is set to `true` for those two operations). A call to `GetBlog` will cause an instance to complete, since there is no reason for that call to be stateful, but I want that operation to be implemented on the same endpoint as the rest of my API.

- Calls to either `ApproveEntry` or `DeleteEntry` will cause the workflow to complete (since there will be no more work to do in either case).

- Calls to `UpdateEntry` or `GetEntry` can happen at any time during the lifetime of the workflow.

Figure 9-9 shows the `StateMachineWorkflow` implementation.

The protocol used for this contract is embedded into the design of the workflow and we cannot deviate from it. In some situations, this could be a compelling reason to choose a stateful workflow as the implementation choice for a particular service—in a stateless model, you would have to implement this kind of protocol using code and, potentially, custom status code responses.

The only other issue with this service (and with the concept of a stateful workflow service) is ensuring the client automatically returns cookies. `WebHttpBinding` will do this automatically.

Summary

This chapter covered the possible reasons you might integrate WF workflows into your REST architecture, either as a client or as part of your service implementation. `SendActivity` enables a workflow to become a RESTful client by using `WebHttpBinding` from a WCF client's point of view.

`ReceiveActivity` and `WorkflowServiceHost` make it possible to implement a service contract using a workflow. When doing this you must decide whether you want to have a stateful or stateless workflow service. Using a stateless workflow service is fairly straightforward, whereas implementing a stateful workflow service means a little more design work and ensuring your clients can successfully accept and send cookies to manage the workflow instance context.

CHAPTER 10

Consuming RESTful XML Services Using WCF

One important feature of WCF is that the server and client programming models are symmetrical. Unlike earlier technologies such as ASMX, a WCF service is defined the same way a WCF client is defined (i.e., via `ServiceContract` et al.). There is no notion in WCF of a "service binding"; there are just bindings. Bindings are used on both listening endpoints (the service) and sending endpoints (the client).

WCF 3.5 and its Web Programming Model do not change this fundamental fact concerning WCF. As in all other parts of WCF, the Web Programming Model works on the client in exactly the same way it works on the server. Throughout most of this book, we have focused on how to create RESTful services using WCF, and most of the time we've been using a browser or a raw-HTTP API to consume those services. Using a browser or a raw-HTTP API provides a big advantage to RESTful services in general, but it is sometimes useful to have an abstraction on top of the client programming model. In this chapter we'll explore how to use the WCF Web Programming Model to consume RESTful services.

Defining the Client

Unlike SOAP-based services that often expose metadata (via WSDL or Mex), RESTful services don't have any inherent metadata. This means that creating RESTful clients is generally a manual process.

Many people look at the lack of metadata as one of the big downsides of REST. Others look at the lack of metadata as an upside of REST, since it makes the network boundary explicit. Lack of an explicit boundary when using remote invocation has long been a perceived downside of various RPC systems.

As discussed in Chapter 1, a faction of the RESTful world promotes a metadata format known as Web Application Description Language (WADL). Currently, WCF has no OOTB support for WADL on the service or the client side.

There are a number of ways to create clients in .NET against RESTful services:

- Use `System.Net.Sockets.Socket`, which is a very low-level approach.
- Use `System.Net.WebRequest` and friends, which is an HTTP abstraction layer on top of `System.Net.Sockets.Socket`. The downside of `WebRequest` is that you work with both request and response entity bodies using a stream. There is no strongly typed programming model available for use.
- Create a set of classes that use `System.Net.WebRequest`, which uses either `XmlSerializer` or `DataContractSerializer` to create a more strongly typed model.
- Use the WCF client-side infrastructure.

Each of these options has pros and cons, although the `Socket` options probably have only the advantage of total control. See Appendix B for an example of a strongly typed approach on top of `WebRequest` in the ADO.NET Data Services client-side infrastructure.

In this chapter you will use the WCF web programming infrastructure to build a client against a non-WCF-based RESTful service by building a WCF contract from the ground-up for use on the client-side. If you want to call a WCF-based RESTful service you built yourself, you can just reuse the WCF metadata at the .NET level.

To be honest, I often reuse WCF metadata. In fact, I often reuse the assemblies I create when I build SOAP-based services with WCF between the client and service as well. Especially during development, while the contract is changing often, I find that directly using the .NET metadata is more efficient than going through the metadata generation process.

Everything we discuss in this chapter regarding building clients with WCF will apply if you have direct access to the service contract and data contract types. We'll start with a discussion of how to decompose a RESTful service into a WCF service contract and data contract so that you can invoke it via WCF.

Generating the Contract

Because WCF works exactly the same on both the client and server sides, the first thing you need in order to call a RESTful service using WCF is a contract. To review WCF basics, three things comprise an endpoint: an address, a binding, and a contract. The address will be based on the service endpoint's URI. The binding will likely be `WebHttp Binding` or some custom variation of the parts that make up `WebHttpBinding`. The contract is the part you have to create on the client side to call a random RESTful service.

For this chapter, we will use a particular RESTful service against which to build the WCF contract definition: SQL Server Data Services (SSDS). SSDS is a new cloud-based storage facility that Microsoft has built on top of Windows Server and SQL Server.

> In *RESTful Web Services* (O'Reilly), Leonard Richardson and Sam Ruby use Amazon.com's S3 storage service as a RESTful consumption example. I decided to use the Microsoft example for this book, not to be a Microsoft shill, but because I thought the symmetry of using a similar type of service would be useful if you read both books. Not to be a shill for my publisher, either, but I highly recommend that you read *RESTful Web Services* before you read this book. If you haven't read it, please read it after you read this book. Thanks.

SSDS is one way to store data in the "cloud" on a set of highly scalable and available servers hosted at one of Microsoft's many data centers. Storage is quickly becoming one of those services that are advantageous to outsource to "cloud" providers. This chapter isn't about the concept of using this kind of service; it's just about how to use this particular one.

SSDS offers both SOAP and RESTful endpoints for you to call; the SOAP endpoint exports WSDL, whereas the RESTful endpoint (appropriately) doesn't. Since we're interested in the RESTful endpoint, we need to deconstruct the service and build our WCF contract types. If you understand the concepts of REST regarding URIs and the uniform interface, you'll find that creating the contract is straightforward in most cases. If a service endpoint follows the constraints of REST, creating the client-side metadata is relatively simple. First I'll explain SSDS from a conceptual point of view.

> Since this is a book about REST and not SSDS, I'm going into only enough detail on SSDS to explain how to build a WCF RESTful client against it. If you want more information about SSDS, see *http://www .microsoft.com/sql/dataservices/default.mspx*. Another thing I should note is that SSDS is currently in beta.
>
> If you are interested in learning how to use the `WebRequest` API to interact with SSDS, consult the SSDS documentation, which contains an extensive set of samples on how to do this.

SSDS exposes three core resources: Authorities, Containers, and Entities. An *Authority* is conceptually similar to a database. An Authority has *Containers*, and Containers can be compared to database tables. *Entities* are the raw pieces of data inside Containers, so they can be compared to rows in a table.

The big difference between Containers and database tables is that Containers are just named constructs; they have no predefined schema and they enforce no schema. Entities can have any shape, and any Entity can be stored in any Container. The shape of an Entity and the Container in which it should be stored are constraints that concern the application using SSDS; SSDS itself doesn't care.

An application that uses SSDS will first create one or more Authorities. Inside each Authority it will create one or more Containers, and inside each Container it will store the appropriate Entities. To get data from SSDS an application will ask a particular Authority for a particular Entity from a particular Container. All resources have unique identifiers, so addressability is fairly straightforward.

One interesting part of the SSDS implementation is that each Authority will get its own unique URI based on the hostname rather than on part of the URI path. To scale out and provide load balancing and failover, each Authority gets its own hostname.

For example, if you were to create an Authority with an identifier of "users", your URI would be:

> *https://users.data.beta.mssds.com/v1/*

If you created another Authority with the identifier "foo", that URI would be:

> *https://foo.data.beta.mssds.com/v1/*

Identifiers must be unique only within the scope of a particular authentication context. We'll discuss how to authenticate to SSDS in a moment.

Another interesting thing about creating Authorities is that the "factory" URI (the URI to which to POST a new Authority resource for creation by SSDS) is different from the Authority URI. This makes sense in terms of implementation, since it would be difficult for the SSDS infrastructure to respond to a unique URI based on the hostname without knowing that hostname beforehand. The URI for Authority creation is the "base" SSDS URI:

> *https://data.beta.mssds.com/v1/*

In this version of SSDS, the only parts of the uniform interface available to Authorities are POST and GET. You can probably guess that, to create an Authority using POST, you POST the representation of the Authority to *https://data.beta.mssds.com/v1/*, and to GET the representation of the Authority, you make a GET request to the Authority-specific URI.

You also can create and retrieve Containers, so they also implement only POST and GET. However, you can create, retrieve, modify, and delete Entities, so they implement the entire uniform interface. Table 10-1 lays out the resources of SSDS and which parts of the uniform interface they implement. All of the URI column values are relative; the first row's URI is relative to the "base" SSDS URI of *https://data.beta.mssds.com/v1/*, and all the subsequent rows are relative to an Authority-specific URI.

Table 10-1. SSDS resources and uniform interfaces

URI	Method	Description	Input	Output
/ (the root of the base SSDS URI)	POST	Creates an Authority	Authority	None
/	GET	Retrieves an Authority	N/A	Authority
/	POST	Creates a Container	Container	None
/{containerId}	GET	Retrieves a Container	N/A	Container
/{containerId}	POST	Creates an Entity	Entity	None
/{containerId}/{entityId}	GET	Retrieves an Entity	N/A	Entity
/{containerId}/{entityId}	PUT	Updates an Entity	Entity	None
/{containerId}/{entityId}	DELETE	Deletes an Entity	N/A	N/A

 This table should look pretty familiar to you at this point in the book, and one of the reasons I put this chapter near the end of the book is that when I was learning about REST, the more I understood the creation side of REST the easier it was for me to build clients. This table is something I'd also typically map out when creating a service that had the functionality SSDS has, so I find it useful to use the same techniques to deconstruct an existing service as to consume the service.

Creating the Resource Representations

With our discussion of SSDS under our belts, it's time to create the resource representations. You will need definitions for three resources: the Authority, Container, and Entity. In this section, I'll walk you through how I created the class definitions to represent these resources.

The SSDS documentation provides a sample XML definition for Authority (I assume an actual XML Schema will also be provided at some point, and that therefore you'll be able to skip the following steps, but I'm discussing all the steps here because many RESTful services don't provide schemas of any kind). The XML definition looks like this:

```
<?xml version="1.0" encoding="utf-8"?>
<s:Authority xmlns:s='http://schemas.microsoft.com/sitka/2008/03/'>
  <s:Id>NewAuthorityId</s:Id>
  <s:Version/>
</s:Authority>
```

Notice that the Version element doesn't have a value. This is because when you submit an Authority resource for creation, it must not have the Version element, but when you get back an Authority via a GET request, it does have the Version element with a value.

Place this XML inside an XML file in Visual Studio 2008. Run the Generate Schema command under the XML menu. Visual Studio 2008 will infer an XSD schema that is similar to the one shown in Example 10-1.

Example 10-1. Visual Studio 2008 XSD schema

```
<?xml version="1.0" encoding="utf-8"?>
<xs:schema xmlns:s="http://schemas.microsoft.com/sitka/2008/03/"
 attributeFormDefault="unqualified" elementFormDefault="qualified"
 targetNamespace="http://schemas.microsoft.com/sitka/2008/03/"
 xmlns:xs="http://www.w3.org/2001/XMLSchema">
  <xs:element name="Authority">
    <xs:complexType>
      <xs:sequence>
        <xs:element name="Id" type="xs:string" />
        <xs:element name="Version" type="xs:string"  nillable="true"/>
      </xs:sequence>
    </xs:complexType>
  </xs:element>
</xs:schema>
```

Next, run this XSD definition through the WCF *svcutil.exe* tool. *svcutil.exe* is generally used to create proxy definitions from WSDL, but you can also use it to create .NET class definitions from schemas. Since this particular XSD is compatible with the Data ContractSerializer in WCF, run the following command:

```
svcutil.exe /dconly Authority.xsd /out:Authority.cs
```

The output (in the *Authority.cs* file) is a class that you can use to represent the Authority resource in the code, and it allows you to program against a .NET type rather than using the XML APIs in .NET directly to use this resource. This type will have the appropriate DataContractAttribute and DataMemberAttributes so that the DataContract Serializer in WCF can turn an instance of the class into the appropriate XML, and then turn a resource response from the service into the appropriate object instance.

As mentioned earlier, you can use the XML APIs in .NET along with WebRequest to build your RESTful service clients, but in this case we will use the WCF programming model instead, using these steps:

1. Get the XML definition into Visual Studio 2008.
2. Run the Generate Schema tool in the XML menu.
3. Run *svcutil.exe* on the command line to generate the DataContract type.

At some point, I assume Microsoft will simplify these three steps down to one; in fact, the tools from Microsoft's BizTalk Labs cloud service at *http://labs.biztalk.net* include a Paste as XML Serializable command for Visual Studio that will automate these three steps from XML held on the clipboard.

The generated class is fine, except for one interesting restriction that SSDS has placed on the resource representation. To create an Authority resource, the Version element must be absent. Since the schema element definition for Version has nillable set to true, WCF will generate the follow XML if Version is null on the object being serialized:

```
<?xml version="1.0" encoding="utf-8"?>
<s:Authority xmlns:s='http://schemas.microsoft.com/sitka/2008/03/'
 xmlns:xsi='http://www.w3.org/2001/XMLSchema-instance'>
  <s:Id>newauthorityid</s:Id>
  <s:Version xsi:nil='true'/>
</s:Authority>
```

SSDS doesn't like this XML because it disallows the xsi:nil attribute. So, you'll need to tweak the DataContractAttribute type definition generated by *svcutil.exe*. Do this by changing the DataMemberAttribute.EmitDefaultValue property to false. As a result of that small change, WCF will now generate the following XML if the Version property is not set:

```
<?xml version="1.0" encoding="utf-8"?>
<s:Authority xmlns:s='http://schemas.microsoft.com/sitka/2008/03/'
 xmlns:xsi='http://www.w3.org/2001/XMLSchema-instance'>
  <s:Id>newauthorityid</s:Id>
</s:Authority>
```

Example 10-2 shows the generated class definition.

Example 10-2. The Authority class

```
//------------------------------------------------------------------------------
// <auto-generated>
//     This code was generated by a tool.
//     Runtime Version:2.0.50727.1434
//
//     Changes to this file may cause incorrect behavior and will be lost if
//     the code is regenerated.
// </auto-generated>
//------------------------------------------------------------------------------

[assembly: System.Runtime.Serialization.ContractNamespaceAttribute(
    "http://schemas.microsoft.com/sitka/2008/03/",
    ClrNamespace="schemas.microsoft.com.sitka._2008._03")]

namespace schemas.microsoft.com.sitka._2008._03
{
    using System.Runtime.Serialization;


    [System.Diagnostics.DebuggerStepThroughAttribute()]
    [System.CodeDom.Compiler.GeneratedCodeAttribute("System.Runtime.Serialization",
                                     "3.0.0.0")]
    [System.Runtime.Serialization.DataContractAttribute(Name="Authority",
                    Namespace="http://schemas.microsoft.com/sitka/2008/03/")]
    public partial class Authority : object,
                        System.Runtime.Serialization.IExtensibleDataObject
    {
```

```csharp
        private System.Runtime.Serialization.ExtensionDataObject
                                        extensionDataField;

        private string IdField;

        private string VersionField;

        public System.Runtime.Serialization.ExtensionDataObject ExtensionData
        {
            get
            {
                return this.extensionDataField;
            }
            set
            {
                this.extensionDataField = value;
            }
        }
        [System.Runtime.Serialization.DataMemberAttribute(IsRequired=true,
                                        EmitDefaultValue=false)]
        public string Id
        {
            get
            {
                return this.IdField;
            }
            set
            {
                this.IdField = value;
            }
        }
        //I changed the EmitDefaultValue
        [System.Runtime.Serialization.DataMemberAttribute(IsRequired=false,
                                        EmitDefaultValue=false)]
        public string Version
        {
            get
            {
                return this.VersionField;
            }
            set
            {
                this.VersionField = value;
            }
        }
    }
}
```

In general, it's preferable not to modify a code-generated file, since you will have to re-create the change if you have to regenerate it for some reason. In this case, however, it's a necessary change, and the fact that you are generating the code file manually reduces the chances of a regeneration whacking your changes.

You use the same steps to create the Container class definition. Take the XML from the SSDS documentation, create the XML file, generate the schema, and use *svcutil.exe* to generate the class.

The Entity definition is a bit more difficult. There is no set Entity XML definition from SSDS. The Entity can be any valid XML with the following restrictions:

- The first child element of the document element must be the `Id` element from the SSDS schema.

- The `Version` and `Kind` elements from the SSDS schema can follow `Id`, but they are optional.

- You can place any number of additional child elements after `Id`, but they must be scalar values and you must specify the types using the `xsi:type` attribute. These are referred to in SSDS as *flexible properties*.

- The additional child elements are limited to the following scalar types: `string`, `base64binary`, `decimal`, `boolean`, or `dateTime`.

This variable XML creates a slightly more complex scenario for serialization. One typical option is to use `System.ServiceModel.Channels.Message` to represent this resource. However, this won't work with the WCF Web Programming Model because when you make a creation request for an Entity, you'll be passing the identifiers of both the Authority and the Container as part of the URI. Therefore, you need to use `UriTemplate`, with the first two parameters of your method being the two path segments of the URI. You can use `Message` as a parameter only if it is the only parameter to an operation.

If you were using a preset Entity type and you weren't planning to change it, you could do something like this:

```
[XmlTypeAttribute(AnonymousType = true, Namespace = "")]
[XmlRootAttribute(Namespace = "", IsNullable = false)]
public class MyEntityType
{
    [XmlElementAttribute(Namespace =
                "http://schemas.microsoft.com/sitka/2008/03/")]
    public string Id;
    public Title Title { get; set; }
}
```

Notice that this code uses `XmlSerializer` (you would also specify `XmlFormatterAttribute` on the `ServiceContract` operation to make this work) because `DataContract` won't allow you to add an element from a different namespace. In this case, the Entity will be an XML element with the root element name of `MyEntityType`, and will have one scalar property of a type string named `Title`.

This will work, but is neither generic nor reusable. So, for the Entity resource, we can use a method similar to the way that WCF deals with web feed data (see Chapter 6), creating a .NET class to represent any Entity by having that class implement `IXmlSerializable`. By implementing `IXmlSerializable` you can have tighter control over the XML that is generated or parsed, and you can create a more general-purpose and reusable type that can be used for any Entity, as shown in Example 10-3.

Example 10-3. Entity type using IXmlSerializable

```
public class SSDSEntityFormatter : IXmlSerializable
{

    public string Id { get; set; }
    public string Version { get; set; }
    public string Kind { get; set; }
    public string Name { get; set; }

    string _SSDSNS = "http://schemas.microsoft.com/sitka/2008/03/";
    public IList<SSDSEntityFlexibleProperty> FlexibleProperties { get; set; }
    #region IXmlSerializable Members

    public System.Xml.Schema.XmlSchema GetSchema()
    {
        return null;
    }

    public void ReadXml(XmlReader reader)
    {
        //omitted for clarity
    }

    public void WriteXml(XmlWriter writer)
    {
        writer.WriteAttributeString("xmlns", "xsi", null,
                "http://www.w3.org/2001/XMLSchema-instance");
        writer.WriteAttributeString("xmlns", "xsd", null,
                "http://www.w3.org/2001/XMLSchema");
        writer.WriteElementString("Id", _SSDSNS,this.Id);
        if (this.FlexibleProperties != null)
        {
            foreach (var item in this.FlexibleProperties)
            {
                item.WriteXml(writer);
            }
        }

    }

    #endregion
}
```

The SSDSEntityFlexibleProperty instances in the list of flexible properties do most of the heavy lifting, except for writing out the two standard namespace URIs. There is one SSDSEntityFlexibleProperty derived class for each allowable scalar type, as shown in Example 10-4.

Example 10-4. SSDSEntityFlexibleProperty

```
public  abstract class SSDSEntityFlexibleProperty
{
    public string Name { get; set; }
    protected string XSDType { get; set; }
    protected internal virtual void WriteXml(XmlWriter writer)
    {
        writer.WriteStartElement(this.Name);
        writer.WriteAttributeString(_attr,
                                    _ns,
                                    String.Format("xsd:{0}",this.XSDType));
        writer.WriteString(this.GetValue());
        writer.WriteEndElement();
    }
    protected internal abstract string GetValue();
    private string _ns = "http://www.w3.org/2001/XMLSchema-instance";
    private  string _attr = "type";
}
public class StringProperty : SSDSEntityFlexibleProperty
{
    public string StringValue { get; set; }

    public StringProperty()
    {
        this.XSDType = "string";
    }

    protected internal override string GetValue()
    {
        return this.StringValue;
    }
}
public class Base64Property : SSDSEntityFlexibleProperty
{
    public Base64Property()
    {
        this.XSDType = "base64Binary";
    }
    public byte[] Base64Value { get; set; }
    protected internal override string GetValue()
    {
        return Convert.ToBase64String(this.Base64Value);
    }

}
public class BooleanProperty : SSDSEntityFlexibleProperty
{
    public BooleanProperty()
    {
        this.XSDType = "boolean";
    }
    protected internal override string GetValue()
    {
        return this.BooleanValue.ToString();
    }
}
```

```
        public bool BooleanValue { get; set; }
}
public class DecimalProperty : SSDSEntityFlexibleProperty
{
    public DecimalProperty()
    {
        this.XSDType = "decimal";
    }
    protected internal override string GetValue()
    {
        return this.DecimalValue.ToString();
    }
    public decimal DecimalValue { get; set; }
}
public class DateTimeProperty : SSDSEntityFlexibleProperty
{
    public DateTimeProperty()
    {
        this.XSDType = "dateTime";
    }
    protected internal override string GetValue()
    {
        return this.DateTimeValue.ToString();
    }
    public DateTime DateTimeValue { get; set; }


}
```

Each `SSDSEntityFlexibleProperty` derived type is responsible for returning a string representation of its data, and the base class writes out the XML for the flexible property itself using this string.

There is one additional catch with this implementation. Because of the way `IXmlSerializable` works, the document element name is derived from the name of the implementation type or via a value set with the `XmlRootAttribute`. If you want to have different document element names for Entity resources (which is part of the point of having a generic solution), we need to take the `IXmlSerializable` idea one step further and create a new type derived from the `SSDSEntityFormatter` class, and add the `XmlRootAttribute` to that class. Otherwise, the document element for all of your entities will be `SSDSEntityFormatter`, which probably isn't what you want. Here is one example:

```
[XmlRoot("Testing")]
public class DerivedSSDSEntityFormatter : SSDSEntityFormatter
{
}
```

It isn't difficult to create this class. It's the same pattern used by the `SyndicationFeedFormatter` with the derived `Atom10SyndicationFeedFormatter` and `Rss20SyndicationFeedFormatter`. Each of the derived classes has an `XmlRootAttribute` indicating what the root element name should be. The difference is that you must create a new type for each Entity document element to use this technique, where the derived classes in the syndication API are already set.

This can seem very complex, but the SSDS REST endpoint is a relatively complex endpoint, which is why it is a good example of how to consume a RESTful service. But in general you'll find that many of the resources you work with will be more like the Authority and Container resources than like the Entity resource in terms of complexity.

Creating the ServiceContract

The next step in our quest to build a WCF client for SSDS is to define the ServiceContract type that will use the resource types we just created. There is an interesting dilemma here as well.

Remember the way SSDS works when creating resources: the Authority resource is created at the "base" SSDS URI (*http://data.beta.mSSDS.com*), and the Authority then gets its own URI (*http://authorityid.data.beta.mSSDS.com*). You then do a POST to the Authority-specific host URI to create a Container.

This split forces us to create two different contracts: one for creating the Authority and another for creating Containers and working with Entities. Because two operations would have a method of POST and a UriTemplate of root (/), it is impossible to have both operations on a single service contract interface. Here is the contract for creating Authorities:

```
[ServiceContract]
public interface ICreateAuthority
{
    [WebInvoke(Method="POST",UriTemplate="/")]
    [OperationContract()]
    void CreateAuthority(Authority authority);
}
```

The other contract, shown in Example 10-5, will take care of getting an Authority, creating or getting a Container, and handling the entire uniform interface on the Entity resource.

Example 10-5. Contract for getting an Authority, creating or getting a Container, and handling the entire uniform interface on the Entity resource

```
[ServiceContract]
[ServiceKnownType(typeof(DerivedSSDSEntityFormatter))]
public interface IContainer
{
    //gets an Authority
    [WebGet(UriTemplate = "/")]
    [OperationContract]
    Authority GetAuthority();
    //creates a Container
    [WebInvoke(UriTemplate = "/",Method="POST")]
    [OperationContract]
```

```
Container CreateContainer(Container container);
//gets a Container
[WebGet(UriTemplate="/{containerid}")]
[OperationContract]
Container GetContainer(string containerid);
//Deletes a Container
[WebInvoke(UriTemplate="/{containerid}",Method = "DELETE")]
[OperationContract]
void DeleteContainer(string containerid);
//Creates an Entity
[WebInvoke(UriTemplate = "/{containerid}", Method = "POST")]
[OperationContract]
[XmlSerializerFormat()]
void CreateEntity(string containerid, SSDSEntityFormatter body);
//Gets an Entity
[WebGet(UriTemplate="/{containerid}/{entityid}")]
[OperationContract]
[XmlSerializerFormat()]
SSDSEntityFormatter GetEntity(string containerid, string entityid);
//Deletes an Entity
[WebInvoke(UriTemplate = "/{containerid}/{entityid}", Method = "DELETE")]
[OperationContract]
void DeleteEntity(string containerid, string entityid);
//Updates an Entity
[WebInvoke(UriTemplate = "/{containerid}/{entityid}", Method = "UPDATE")]
[OperationContract]
[XmlSerializerFormat()]
void UpdateEntity(string containerid, string entityid, SSDSEntityFormatter
                                                       body);
}
```

Notice that there is an extra attribute on the interface: ServiceKnownTypeAttribute.
Remember from our discussion of SSDSEntityFormatter that you must create a derived
type for each Entity type. DerivedSSDSEntityFormatter is one of those types.

When it serializes types, WCF needs to know the exact data type being serialized or
deserialized. When using polymorphism (as we are here with the derived type), WCF
requires registration of the potential derived types that might be passed for a particular
base type. This is why you have to put this attribute on the service contract definition.

On the operations that deal with the SSDSEntityFormatter type, you must also specify
that you want WCF to use XmlSerializer by putting XmlSerializerFormatAttribute on
the operation.

Other than these two specializations, this contract is similar to all the other contracts
we've created so far. It uses WebGetAttribute or WebInvokeAttribute as appropriate and
it uses UriTemplate and template syntax to specify how to map the outgoing method
calls to the correct URIs. This thought process is opposite to the one we used when
creating contracts for implementing services. Looking at the contract from this angle
might be a little different, but it is in line with the concept of WCF client/service
symmetry.

Using the Service

At this point, we have all the data types to represent the desired resources. We also have contracts that represent the URIs and parts of the uniform interface that we want to interact with in relation to those resources. Now we can actually use these definitions to interact with the service.

The first step is to create an Authority. To do this, use the `ICreateAuthority` interface and create the client infrastructure. To host a RESTful endpoint, use the `WebService Host` to create a `ChannelListener` in WCF to listen for messages on the service side. `ChannelListener` is referred to as a Channel Manager, a type that can create live channel stacks.

There is another kind of Channel Manager on the client side, known as a `ChannelFactory`. To create client-side channel stacks, use a `ChannelFactory` and inform the `ChannelFactory` of the appropriate binding and URI.

WCF's Web Programming Model includes a type that is the client-side equivalent to `WebServiceHost`, called `WebChannelFactory`. In the same way that `WebServiceHost` configures service endpoints correctly to use a RESTful approach, `WebChannelFactory` modifies each client endpoint (on the client there is only one endpoint per `ChannelManager`, which is one of the few differences between the client and service models).

Example 10-6 shows the helper method (as well as some of the static data from my example), which uses the `WebChannelFactory` and the `ICreateAuthority` interface to call SSDS and create an Authority.

Example 10-6. Creating an SSDS Authority

```
static void CreateAuthority(string authorityId)
{
    WebHttpBinding binding = new WebHttpBinding();
    binding.Security.Mode = WebHttpSecurityMode.TransportCredentialOnly;
    binding.Security.Transport.ClientCredentialType =
                                    HttpClientCredentialType.Basic;
    WebChannelFactory<ICreateAuthority> cf =
        new WebChannelFactory<ICreateAuthority>(binding,
                                        new Uri(ServiceUri));
    cf.Credentials.UserName.UserName = Username;
    cf.Credentials.UserName.Password = Password;
    Authority authority = new Authority { Id = authorityId };
    ICreateAuthority channel = cf.CreateChannel();
    using (new OperationContextScope((IContextChannel)channel))
    {
        OutgoingWebRequestContext ctx =
            WebOperationContext.Current.OutgoingRequest;
        ctx.ContentType = ContentType;
        channel.CreateAuthority(authority);
        IncomingWebResponseContext rctx =
            WebOperationContext.Current.IncomingResponse;
        if (rctx.StatusCode == System.Net.HttpStatusCode.Created)
```

```
                    Console.WriteLine("Authority {0} created!", authorityId);
        }
    }
    static string ContentType = "application/x-ssds+xml";
    static string Username = "getyourown";
    static string Password = "getyourown";
    static string ServiceUri = "http://data.beta.mssds.com/v1/";
    static string AuthorityUri = "http://{0}.data.beta.mssds.com/v1/";
```

From the WCF point of view, the first thing to note here is the generic `WebChannelFac`
`tory`. With the generic `WebChannelFactory`, you can create any channel, where the channel is based on a WCF `ServiceContractAttribute` annotated interface. SSDS does use
Basic authentication, so you must set those properties appropriately (see Chapter 8 for
more information about using security with WCF and REST).

Next, the code creates an instance of `OperationContextScope`. `OperationContextScope`
creates an `OperationContext` around a WCF client call. Because we require the `Out`
`goingWebRequestContext`   object,   we   need   an   `OperationContext`   (since
`WebOperationContext` is built on top of `OperationContext`).

We also require the `OutgoingWebRequestContext` because we have to set the HTTP
Content-Type header. SSDS requires that this header be set to `application/x-ssds`
`+xml`, which is a new media type that was created for SSDS.

To create the Authority, create an instance of the `DataContract`-based type, and then
call `ICreateAuthority.CreateAuthority`.

After that call, use the `IncomingWebResponseContext` to determine the `StatusCode`. If the
call is successful, print out the string "Authority {0} created" with the format string
replaced by the Authority name.

> With most "created" responses, you would expect to receive a Location
> header (see Chapter 11 for more information about the Location
> header).
>
> The SSDS version being programmed against here doesn't return the
> Location header, although the SSDS team has stated that it plans to
> implement this functionality in future beta versions, so by the time SSDS
> is released, I expect that it will be doing this correctly.

Now that the Authority has been created, use the other interface you defined to interact
with it. You can also use that interface to get the Authority. The Authority is particularly
interesting; it's a container for Containers, and Containers are just containers for Entities. It's at the Entity level that things get a little more interesting.

It's best to be methodical, though, so Example 10-7 shows the code to get an Authority,
as there is something interesting about it.

Example 10-7. Getting an Authority

```
private static void GetAuthority(string authority)
{
    WebChannelFactory<IContainer> cf = GetChannelFactory(authority);
    IContainer channel = cf.CreateChannel();
    using (new OperationContextScope((IContextChannel)channel))
    {
        OutgoingWebRequestContext ctx =
                WebOperationContext.Current.OutgoingRequest;
        ctx.Accept = ContentType;
        Authority auth = channel.GetAuthority();
        IncomingWebResponseContext rctx =
                WebOperationContext.Current.IncomingResponse;
        if (rctx.StatusCode == System.Net.HttpStatusCode.OK)
            Console.WriteLine("Authority {0} {1} retrieved!", auth.Id,
                                                    auth.Version);
    }
}
```

Since all of the code in the program, except for the code to create the Authority, will be using the same contract, this code wraps the creation of WebChannelFactory in a helper method, which we'll discuss in a moment. The only other interesting piece in this code occurs where it sets the HTTP Accept header. This header isn't strictly required by SSDS, but it is still a good practice to include it, and some services will require it since those services might return different representations based on its value.

The interesting code is inside the GetChannelFactory method, shown in Example 10-8.

Example 10-8. GetChannelFactory method

```
static WebChannelFactory<IContainer> GetChannelFactory(string authority)
{
    //create the WebHttpBinding, and set its properties
    WebHttpBinding binding = new WebHttpBinding();
    binding.Security.Mode = WebHttpSecurityMode.TransportCredentialOnly;
    binding.Security.Transport.ClientCredentialType =
                                    HttpClientCredentialType.Basic;
    //SSDS sends back chunked responses
    binding.TransferMode = TransferMode.StreamedResponse;
    //Copy the WebHttpBinding into a CustomBinding
    CustomBinding custom = new CustomBinding(binding);
    //Get the encoding element
    WebMessageEncodingBindingElement be =
        custom.Elements.Find<WebMessageEncodingBindingElement>();
    //set the content type mapper
    be.ContentTypeMapper = new SSDSContentTypeMapper();
    //create the URI
    string uri = String.Format(AuthorityUri, authority);
    //create the WebChannelFactory
    WebChannelFactory<IContainer> cf =
        new WebChannelFactory<IContainer>(custom,
                                        new Uri(uri));
    //set the credentials
    cf.Credentials.UserName.UserName = Username;
```

```
cf.Credentials.UserName.Password = Password;
return cf;
```

The first few lines of code in Example 10-8 aren't significantly different from Example 10-6. The one difference is that this code sets the `WebHttpBinding.TransferMode` to `TransferMode.StreamedResponse`, since SSDS is sending back responses using HTTP chunking.

Next, take the `WebHttpBinding` instance you just configured and copy all the binding elements in it into a new Custom Binding object. This is required because you have to change something that isn't exposed directly on `WebHttpBinding`: you need to set the `WebMessageEncodingBindingElement.ContentTypeMapper` property.

`ContentTypeMapper` is of type `WebContentTypeMapper`. The job of `WebContentTypeMapper` is to help the WCF message infrastructure determine the message type. `WebContentTypeMapper` is passed the Content-Type header of an HTTP response, and it returns a `WebContentFormat`-enumerated value. This informs the message-parsing layer how to treat the data in the message. Here are the values of `WebContentFormat`:

```
public enum WebContentFormat
{
    Default,//the format can't be determined
    Xml,//the format of the message is XML
    Json,//the format of the message is Json encoded
    Raw//the format is binary
}
```

The message-encoding layer in WCF needs this information to know how to treat the response message.

The default is to map `application/xml` to `WebContentFormat.Xml`, `application/json` to `Json`, and everything else to `Raw`. Since SSDS always returns `application/x-ssds+xml` we need a custom `WebContentTypeMapper`.

Here is the custom `WebContentTypeMapper` implementation:

```
public class SSDSContentTypeMapper : WebContentTypeMapper
{
    public override WebContentFormat GetMessageFormatForContentType(string
                                                                    contentType)
    {
        return WebContentFormat.Xml;
    }
}
```

The preceding code in the `GetChannelFactory` method has the code that reaches into the `WebHttpBinding` configuration, pulls out the necessary configuration element (`WebMessageEncodingBindingElement`), and modifies the appropriate property (`ContentTypeMapper`).

The only other usage of the `IContainer` service contract that is different from the samples shown so far is the `IContainer.CreateEntity` method. This method is more interesting because it's going to use the `IXmlSerializable` type you created especially to represent the loosely typed Entity resource (see Example 10-9).

Example 10-9. CreateEntity method

```
private static void CreateEntity(string authority, string container, string entity)
{
    WebChannelFactory<IContainer> cf = GetChannelFactory(authority);
    IContainer channel = cf.CreateChannel();
    SSDSEntityFormatter flexEntity = new DerivedSSDSEntityFormatter();
    flexEntity.Name = "Test";
    flexEntity.Id = entity;
    StringProperty property = new StringProperty
    {
        StringValue = "Testing",
        Name = "TestElement"
    };
    List<SSDSEntityFlexibleProperty> props = new
    List<SSDSEntityFlexibleProperty>();
    props.Add(property);
    flexEntity.FlexibleProperties = props;
    using (new OperationContextScope((IContextChannel)channel))
    {
        OutgoingWebRequestContext ctx =
                        WebOperationContext.Current.OutgoingRequest;
        ctx.ContentType = ContentType;
        channel.CreateEntity(container, flexEntity);
        IncomingWebResponseContext rctx =
                        WebOperationContext.Current.IncomingResponse;
        if (rctx.StatusCode == System.Net.HttpStatusCode.Created)
            Console.WriteLine("Entity {0} created!", entity);

    }
}
```

To create an Entity, create an instance of an `SSDSEntityFormatter` class, which is the base class created to wrap the functionality of creating the custom XML instance using `IXmlSerializable`. Create an `IList` collection of `SSDSEntityFlexibleProperty` to which to add the single property.

Here is what the resultant XML looks like:

```
<?xml version="1.0" encoding="utf-8"?>
<Testing xmlns:xsi="http://www.w3.org/2001/XMLSchema-instance"
 xmlns:xsd="http://www.w3.org/2001/XMLSchema">
<Id xmlns="http://schemas.microsoft.com/sitka/2008/03/"
>booktestentity7d0ddc98-b403-4465-9ab5-d3b3777ac26b</Id>
<TestElement xsi:type="xsd:string">Testing</TestElement>
</Testing>
```

This XML fits into the constraints that SSDS puts on Entity XML formats. Figure 10-1 shows the interaction between the client and SSDS.

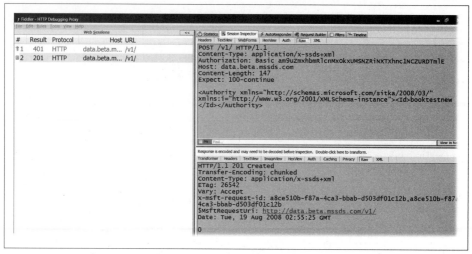

Figure 10-1. Fiddler view of the POST to create an Entity in SSDS

Client Extensibility

One thing you might have noticed while reviewing the code in this chapter is that each of the methods contains some repetitive code. What stood out to me after writing the code in this chapter is that the code inside each method setting the outgoing Content-Type header for all the calls that interact with resources where I need to send a message body (POST and PUT, in this example) was the same.

Although it would be an advantage if the base Web Programming Model included a Content-Type setting, WCF has a nice extensibility model that can wrap up that repetitive functionality into a reusable component.

The first thing you need is a behavior. We've seen behaviors in almost all of the chapters in this book, but the WebHttpBehavior is the main behavior included with the Web Programming Model. Behaviors are objects that change the way a service, operation, or endpoint behaves or executes. In this case, we want to create an endpoint behavior so that we can modify the way the client endpoint behaves when it sends a POST or PUT.

With an endpoint behavior (which is a class that implements the IEndpointBehavior interface), you can add a Message inspector (a class that implements the IClientMessageInspector interface). With a Message inspector in place, you can modify the outgoing Content-Type header when needed.

Example 10-10 shows the behavior.

Example 10-10. ContentTypeBehavior

```
public class ContentTypeBehavior : IEndpointBehavior
{
    public string ContentType { get; set; }
    #region IEndpointBehavior Members
```

```
    public void AddBindingParameters(ServiceEndpoint endpoint,
                         BindingParameterCollection bindingParameters)
    {

    }

    public void ApplyClientBehavior(ServiceEndpoint endpoint,
                                    ClientRuntime clientRuntime)
    {
        ContentTypeMessageInspector mi = null;
        mi = new ContentTypeMessageInspector { ContentType = this.ContentType };
        clientRuntime.MessageInspectors.Add(mi);
    }

    public void ApplyDispatchBehavior(ServiceEndpoint endpoint,
                          EndpointDispatcher endpointDispatcher)
    {

    }

    public void Validate(ServiceEndpoint endpoint)
    {

    }

    #endregion
}
```

Since we plan to use this behavior only on the client side for now, you can just implement the `ApplyClientBehavior` method and add your Message inspector into the client runtime stack. Notice that it contains a string property named `ContentType` so that we can reuse this behavior and Message inspector for other endpoints and media types.

The message inspector code is also fairly simple, as shown in Example 10-11.

Example 10-11. MessageInspector implementation

```
public class ContentTypeMessageInspector : IClientMessageInspector
{
    public string ContentType { get; set; }
    #region IClientMessageInspector Members

    public void AfterReceiveReply(ref Message reply, object correlationState)
    {

    }

    public object BeforeSendRequest(ref Message request, IClientChannel channel)
    {
        HttpRequestMessageProperty prop =
                    request.Properties[HttpRequestMessageProperty.Name] as
                                        HttpRequestMessageProperty;
        if (prop != null && (prop.Method=="POST"||prop.Method=="PUT"))
        {
```

```
            prop.Headers["Content-Type"] = this.ContentType;
        }
        return null;
    }

    #endregion
}
```

In the `BeforeSendRequest` method, you're looking for the `HttpRequestMessageProperty`, and if it is there and the method is correct, you can add the configured media type. The code where we created the `WebChannelFactory` also needs one line of code, but now we can remove the explicit code before each appropriate method call that sets the `ContentType`:

```
//create the WebChannelFactory
WebChannelFactory<IContainer> cf =
    new WebChannelFactory<IContainer>(custom,
                                      new Uri(uri));
cf.Endpoint.Behaviors.Add(new ContentTypeBehavior { ContentType = ContentType });
```

This behavior might not be applicable to every use case, but I put it here as an example of how you might find parts of working with WCF tedious, and when you do, to make sure that you look for an extensibility point because there almost always is one.

Summary

The major point of this chapter is to show you that WCF is symmetrical on the client and server. The same constructs that enable building RESTful services enable building RESTful clients.

You may be more comfortable with the raw `WebRequest` API, which is a fine way to program against RESTful services, but using WCF as the client programming model does have the advantage of having a built-in, strongly typed programming model with rich facilities for URI templates.

CHAPTER 11

Working with HTTP

One of the benefits of programming in the world of REST is the ability to take advantage of the maturity of HTTP and the established infrastructure of the Web. To do this successfully in a programming environment, you need access to the underlying HTTP constructs so that you can modify HTTP headers programmatically and take full advantage of this rich platform.

In this chapter, you will learn how WCF exposes the world of HTTP through its programming model, along with the most common ways you'll likely end up interacting with HTTP.

Programming HTTP with WCF

I introduced the WCF HTTP programming model in Chapter 2. Whenever you are using HTTP with WCF, you can ask for the current `WebOperationContext` object through the `WebOperationContext.Current` static property. The first time you ask for this property, a new instance of the `WebOperationContext` object is created and attached to the current WCF generic `OperationContext` object. On subsequent property accesses, of course, the already-created instance is returned.

> I should reiterate that WCF automatically modifies the HTTP requests and responses based on the `ServiceContract` definition. An operation's `WebGetAttribute` or `WebInvokeAttribute` tell WCF a lot about what to do with HTTP requests and responses. The URI and the HTTP method are completely influenced by that mechanism.
>
> The HTTP context I will discuss in this chapter illustrates how to go beyond that base functionality.

`WebOperationContext` is the WCF wrapper around the HTTP programming model. The `WebOperationContext` object itself (defined in Example 11-1) has no real functionality; it is a wrapper for the four individual context objects that represent the different states of an HTTP request.

Example 11-1. WebOperationContext

```
namespace System.ServiceModel.Web
{
    public class WebOperationContext : IExtension<OperationContext>
    {
        public static WebOperationContext Current { get; }
        public IncomingWebRequestContext IncomingRequest { get; }
        public IncomingWebResponseContext IncomingResponse { get; }
        public OutgoingWebRequestContext OutgoingRequest { get; }
        public OutgoingWebResponseContext OutgoingResponse { get; }

    }
}
```

At all four stages of an HTTP request-response interaction, the appropriate context object is available and you can use it to modify the HTTP environment (see Table 11-1).

Table 11-1. WebOperationContext properties

Property	Actor	Description
OutgoingRequest	Client	The context that enables a client to change the HTTP headers that will be sent to a service
IncomingResponse	Client	Contains the HTTP headers for a response sent to a client from a service
IncomingRequest	Server	Contains the HTTP headers for an incoming request from a client
OutgoingResponse	Server	The context that enables a service to change the HTTP header that will be sent in response to a client request

These context objects contain a number of useful properties and methods. They actually are just thin wrappers around `HttpRequestMessageProperty` and `HttpResponseMessageProperty`. WCF includes message properties that the HTTP transport channel will use to modify the HTTP interactions in the case of a client request or a server response.

> If you are plugging into the WCF extensibility model by creating objects that will plug into parts of the WCF channel stack execution, `WebOperationContext` will not be available (since `OperationContext` isn't generally available either).
>
> For those cases, you will need to use the raw HTTP message properties to perform HTTP inspection and customization. I'll show you an example of that later in this chapter.

You can retrieve these message properties via either the raw `System.ServiceModel.Channels.Message` type if you are programming at that level, or the standard `OperationContext` object (through a similar `OperationContext.Current` property). The downside of the names, in my opinion, is that they are all so similar that it can be hard to keep track of when each is available and useful (see Figure 11-1).

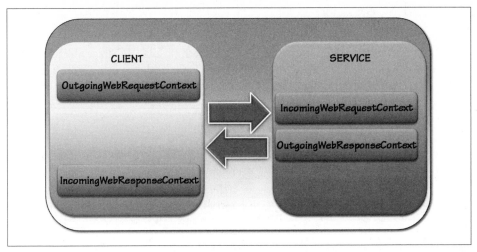

Figure 11-1. WebOperationContext

The client-side objects `OutgoingWebRequestContext` and `IncomingWebResponseContext` are available before and after an HTTP request is made. The `IncomingWebRequestContext` and `OutgoingWebResponseContext` objects are available during execution of methods inside the service only.

These objects are only for programming against HTTP headers; they don't enable you to modify message bodies. However, there is one way in which you can affect whether a body is in fact sent with a request or a response, and I'll cover that later in this chapter.

Even though these objects provide a *thin* wrapper around lower-level constructs, it doesn't mean the objects aren't useful. They are useful because they allow you to access the message properties *directly*. They provide a nice programming model on top of those lower-level objects. I'll cover the basic shape of these objects first, and then talk about different use cases.

IncomingWebRequestContext

The `IncomingWebRequestContext` object (defined in Example 11-2) is a wrapper around the incoming HTTP request from a client, so you use it inside a service to get a read-only view of the HTTP request headers.

Example 11-2. IncomingWebRequestContext

```
public class IncomingWebRequestContext
{
    public string Accept { get; }
    public long ContentLength { get; }
    public string ContentType { get; }
    public WebHeaderCollection Headers { get; }
    public string Method { get; }
    public UriTemplateMatch UriTemplateMatch { get; set; }
```

```
    public string UserAgent { get; }
}
```

By the time you can use this context, the WCF dispatching layer will have already found the correct method based on the URI and the HTTP method, but other HTTP request headers may be of interest to you. Table 11-2 lists the properties on this object and the usage of each.

Table 11-2. IncomingWebRequestContext properties

Property	Type	Description
Accept	String	Contains the value of the Accept header, which is a comma-delimited list of media types the user agent will accept
ContentLength	Long	Contains the value of the Content-Length header, which indicates the length in bytes of the incoming request body; this will be zero when the method is GET or DELETE
ContentType	String	Contains the value of the Content-Type header, which indicates the media type of the incoming request body; this will be null when the method is GET or DELETE
Method	String	Contains the HTTP method
UriTemplateMatch	UriTemplateMatch	Contains the UriTemplateMatch object obtained from the Uri TemplateTable built for this particular endpoint
UserAgent	String	Contains the User-Agent string that uniquely identifies the particular user agent making the request
Headers	WebHeaderCollection	Contains a set of name/value pairs, which contain all the HTTP header tokens and values

OutgoingWebResponseContext

When a service is processing an HTTP-based request, you may want or need to modify the outgoing HTTP headers to more fully inform down-level actors (proxies, firewalls, or user agents) about the response it is returning. Example 11-3 is shows the Outgoing WebResponseContext definition that is used to do exactly that.

Example 11-3. OutgoingWebRequestContext

```
public class OutgoingWebResponseContext
{
    //Properties
    public long ContentLength { get; set; }
    public string ContentType { get; set; }
    public string ETag { get; set; }
    public WebHeaderCollection Headers { get; }
    public DateTime LastModified { get; set; }
    public string Location { get; set; }
    public HttpStatusCode StatusCode { get; set; }
    public string StatusDescription { get; set; }
    public bool SuppressEntityBody { get; set; }
```

```
//Methods
public void SetStatusAsCreated(Uri locationUri);
public void SetStatusAsNotFound();
public void SetStatusAsNotFound(string description);
```

}

Note that `OutgoingWebResponseContext` is the only one of the four web context objects that has methods. These methods are like the objects themselves, just syntax sugar for common modifications a service might want to make to the headers in the HTTP response. Table 11-3 lists its properties and Table 11-4 lists its methods.

Table 11-3. OutgoingWebResponseContext properties

Property	Type	Description
ContentLength	Long	Specifies the length (in bytes) of the response. This will generally be set by the WCF infrastructure.
ContentType	String	Specifies the Content-Type of the response. This is filled in automatically with `application/xml` or `application/json` based on `WebMessageType`.
ETag	String	Contains a hash value that represents the resource. You can use it to implement conditional GET requests.
LastModified	DateTime	A timestamp indicating the last time the resource was modified. You can use it for conditional GET requests.
Location	String	Specifies the Location header, which should contain a URI when a new resource is created with POST.
StatusCode	HttpStatusCode	One of the enumerated values of `HttpStatusCode` to indicate the effect of the request.
StatusDescription	String	The description to go along with the status code.
SuppressEntityBody	Bool	Indicates whether or not the HTTP channel should send the entity body (if there is one); set to `true` by default. It sets the `HttpResponseMessageProperty.SuppressEntityBody` property.
Headers	WebHeaderCollection	Contains a set of name/value pairs, which contain all the HTTP header tokens and values.

Table 11-4. OutgoingWebResponseContext methods

Method	Parameter	Return	Description
SetStatusAsCreated	Uri	Void	Sets the `StatusCode` to 201 Created and sets the Location header to the value of the URI
SetStatusAsNotFound	None	Void	Sets the `StatusCode` to 404
SetStatusAsNotFound	String	Void	Sets the `StatusCode` to 404 and sets the description to the value of the parameter

OutgoingWebRequestContext

The `OutgoingWebRequestContext` object (defined in Example 11-4) is available to a client using WCF before a method call is made on the proxy/channel to an endpoint using the HTTP channel. Table 11-5 describes its properties.

Example 11-4. OutgoingWebRequestContext

```
public class OutgoingWebRequestContext
{
    public string Accept { get; set; }
    public long ContentLength { get; set; }
    public string ContentType { get; set; }
    public WebHeaderCollection Headers { get; }
    public string IfMatch { get; set; }
    public string IfModifiedSince { get; set; }
    public string IfNoneMatch { get; set; }
    public string IfUnmodifiedSince { get; set; }
    public string Method { get; set; }
    public bool SuppressEntityBody { get; set; }
    public string UserAgent { get; set; }
}
```

Table 11-5. OutgoingWebRequestContext properties

Property	Type	Description
Accept	String	Sets the value of the Accept header.
Method	String	The value of the HTTP method. This is normally set by the infrastructure automatically. It is not useful if you're using `WebHttp Behavior`.
UserAgent	String	Enables you to set the User-Agent header explicitly.
ContentType	String	The Content-Type header that is generally set by the infrastructure on the client side.
ContentLength	Long	The Content-Length header that is generally set by the infrastructure on the client side.
IfMatch	String	Used when the client is asking for a conditional request other than GET. It contains the ETag value of the resource.
IfModifiedSince	String	Used with conditional requests other than GET. It contains the value of the Last-Modified value associated with a resource.
IfNoneMatch	String	Used when the client is asking for a conditional GET. It contains the ETag value of the resource.
IfUnmodifiedSince	String	Used with conditional GET requests. It contains the value of the Last-Modified value associated with a resource.
Headers	WebHeaderCollection	Contains a set of name/value pairs, which contain all the HTTP header tokens and values.

IncomingWebResponseContext

The `IncomingWebResponseContext` property (defined in Example 11-5) is available to a WCF client after a call has been made to an HTTP service endpoint. A client can use this property to find out the status code of the response, as well as other potentially useful information. Table 11-6 lists its properties.

Example 11-5. IncomingWebResponseContext

```
public class IncomingWebResponseContext
{
    public long ContentLength { get; }
    public string ContentType { get; }
    public string ETag { get; }
    public WebHeaderCollection Headers { get; }
    public string Location { get; }
    public HttpStatusCode StatusCode { get; }
    public string StatusDescription { get; }
}
```

Table 11-6. IncomingWebResponseContext properties

Property	Type	Description
ContentLength	Long	The value of the Content-Length header, which is the length in bytes of the response representation.
ContentType	String	Specifies the media type of the response representation.
ETag	String	The ETag header is returned when the server wants the user agent to be able to do conditional GETs.
Location	String	When a new resource has been created, the Location header contains a URI to the new resource. This should be non-null when the status code is 201.
StatusCode	HttpStatusCode	Contains an enumeration value based on the known HTTP response codes.
StatusDescription	String	Contains the string associated with the status code.
Headers	WebHeaderCollection	Contains a set of name/value pairs, which contain all the HTTP header tokens and values.

Context Wrap-Up

Now that you are familiar with the basic shape of the `WebOperationContext` properties, we'll discuss a number of common RESTful scenarios in which you may decide to go further than the basic WCF infrastructure. I'll start with returning status codes other than 200 or 400 from a WCF RESTful service.

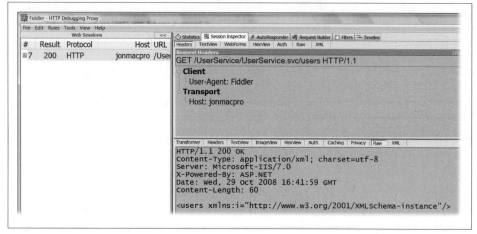

Figure 11-2. HTTP request with a "200 OK" status code

Status Codes

Earlier chapters discussed the importance of the architectural constraints of REST and how those constraints are based on the way the Web and HTTP work. One really important feature of HTTP is status codes. You can increase your use of the principles of REST by taking advantage of status codes. Since REST builds on the principles of the Web, your client will generally find specific status codes very useful.

The first line of the HTTP response header for every HTTP response includes a status code and a status description. Figure 11-2 shows the "200 OK" status code.

A status code of 200 indicates to the user agent that everything went fine when servicing the request. Other status codes can provide a user agent with more detail regarding what went right (or wrong) and can inform the user agent of what to do next. In many cases, an HTTP response has no body and the status code is really the only clue the client has to figure out what went right or wrong. Descriptions can be helpful for a human sitting at a browser; they generally aren't as helpful for programmatic interaction.

WCF will set the status code automatically if you don't set it. It will set the status code to 200 if the service method executes without exception.

The most common status code is 200 (well, at least it is the most commonly *understood* status code). HTTP status codes are classified into groups (based on number), as shown in Table 11-7.

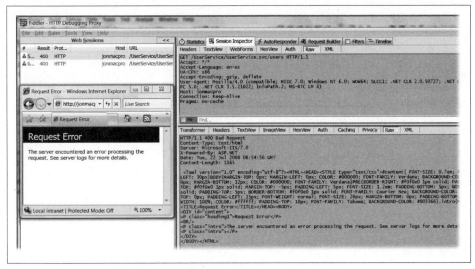

Figure 11-3. WCF's 400 error and HTML page

Table 11-7. HTTP status code classification

Status code range	Description
200–299	Status codes in this range indicate a successful request.
300–399	These status codes indicate that the client needs to request a different URI to use the requested resource successfully.
400–499	These status codes indicate that the client did something wrong, which caused an error condition on the server.
500–599	This indicates that the server had an error not caused by the client's bad request, but by some other class of exception.

WCF will use some of these additional status codes automatically.

If an exception is thrown inside the service method and it isn't caught (i.e., the exception bubbles back up to the WCF channel stack), WCF will set the status code to 400 ("Bad Request"). When this happens, it will also set the content type to text/html and return a human-readable error message (see Figure 11-3).

The error message will include the exception and the call stack if the ServiceDebugBehavior's IncludeExceptionsInFaults property is set to true. You can do this programmatically when self-hosting, as shown in Example 11-6.

Example 11-6. Setting fault details on with code

```
WebServiceHost sh = new WebServiceHost(typeof(EventLogFeed));
ServiceDebugBehavior sdb = null;
sdb = sh.Description.Behaviors.Find<ServiceDebugBehavior>();
if (sdb == null)
{
```

```
    //this should never be the case - but it *might* be so
    //better safe than sorry I say
    sdb = new ServiceDebugBehavior();
    sh.Description.Behaviors.Add(sdb);
}
sdb.IncludeExceptionDetailInFaults = true;
```

Or you can do it via a configuration file, as shown in Example 11-7.

Example 11-7. Setting fault details on with configuration

```
<system.serviceModel>
    <behaviors>
        <serviceBehaviors>
            <behavior name="faults">
                <serviceDebug includeExceptionDetailInFaults="true" />
            </behavior>
        </serviceBehaviors>
    </behaviors>
    <services>
        <service behaviorConfiguration="faults" name="ServiceName">
            <endpoint address="" binding="webHttpBinding" contract="IContract"/>
        </service>
    </services>
</system.serviceModel>
```

Unfortunately, if you are using `WebServiceHostFactory` with a simple *.svc* file, there is no way to set this property to `true` without either adding a service element (which defeats somewhat the purpose of `WebServiceHostFactory`) or creating your own `ServiceHostFactory` that sets the property on `ServiceHost` creation.

If a request comes into the WCF dispatching layer and a `UriTemplate` match isn't found (e.g., the incoming URI doesn't match any `UriTemplate` in the endpoint's `UriTemplateTable`), WCF will return a 404 response. As with the 400 status code, WCF will set the content type to "text/html" and return a preset HTML response entity (see Figure 11-4).

If the URI has a match in the `UriTemplateTable` but the request's method doesn't match any of the URI matches, WCF returns a 405 response ("Method Not Allowed").

 On the client side, WCF never sets the status code, but you should be aware that if the status code comes back as 500 (which indicates an internal server error), it will throw an exception back up the client call stack to the proxy/channel.

Other than the aforementioned cases, WCF doesn't get involved in changing the status code of a response. Let's look at a few important status codes and how to get WCF to return the correct status code based on the current context.

Figure 11-4. WCF's standard 404 response

201 — Created

The 201 status code indicates a successful request for creating a new resource. The method for resource creation will be POST if the client doesn't know the URI of the new resource, or PUT if the client does know the URI of the new resource.

Regardless of the method, two things should be set in the response when a new resource is created. The Status-Code should be set to 201, and a Location header should be added with an absolute URI that represents the newly created resource.

WCF doesn't do either of these two things to the response automatically because the WCF programming model has no high-level way to communicate the URI of a new resource. It is considered a best practice to add this functionality to methods that create a new resource.

In Chapter 3, I introduced a service that enables a user agent to create, retrieve, and modify a "user" resource. In that example, the resource creation method was based on POST instead of PUT because the user agent can't know what the correct resource URI will be for a new resource, since the unique identifier is generated on the server side. As a refresher, Example 11-8 shows this method.

Example 11-8. AddNewUser method

```
[WebInvoke(UriTemplate = "/users", Method = "POST")]
[OperationContract]
public User AddNewUser(User u)
{
    u.UserId = Guid.NewGuid().ToString();
    _users.Add(u);
```

```
    return u;
}
```

The URI of the Location header should resolve to the `GetUser` method shown in Example 11-9.

Example 11-9. GetUser method

```
[WebGet(UriTemplate = "/users/{user_id}")]
[OperationContract]
public User GetUser(string user_id)
{
    User u = FindUser(user_id);
    return u;
}
```

You use `OutgoingWebResponseContext` to modify the status code and set the location to a URI that represents this new resource. The `GET` URI for the user resource is the same URI that activates this method, plus the `UserId` property (which is a GUID). Example 11-10 shows the implementation to create this URI.

Example 11-10. Creating the URI of the new resource

```
private Uri CreateUri(User u)
{
    UriTemplate ut = new UriTemplate("/users/{user_id}");
    Uri baseUri =
      WebOperationContext.Current.IncomingRequest.UriTemplateMatch.BaseUri;
    Uri ret = ut.BindByPosition(baseUri, u.UserId);
    return ret;
}
```

Notice that the code in Example 11-10 uses a `UriTemplate` instance to generate the new URI. The URI concatenation API in the .NET Framework isn't very sophisticated. So, in Example 11-8 I'm using `UriTemplate` as an easy way to build an absolute URI for the newly created resource. For the template value, I am using the same template that is associated with `GetUser`. To be clear, I am not using the `UriTemplate` class here to do routing; I am using it to build up a URI of its component parts (this is how the `UriTemplate` is used in the WCF client-side infrastructure).

To bind the template, I can use the absolute URI of the incoming request as the base URI and the new GUID as a parameter to bind the new URI by position. The resultant new URI now contains the correct value for the Location header. Notice that to get the URI of the current request I am using `IncomingWebRequestContext` and its `UriTemplateMatch` property.

Once I have the correct absolute URI created for the Location header, I can set it and the 201 status code on the `OutgoingWebResponseContext`. This would add two lines of code to set the `StatusCode` and `Location` properties. I can instead write one line of code, since the `OutgoingWebResponseContext` has the `SetStatusAsCreated` helper method. I

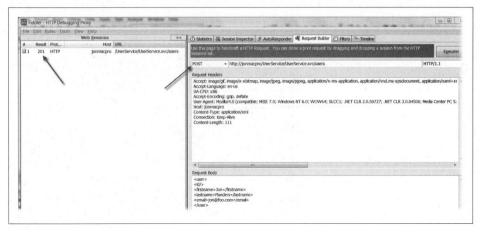

Figure 11-5. 201 status code in Fiddler

presume Microsoft added this method to help us avoid writing those same two lines of code over and over.

Example 11-11 shows the new `AddNewUser` method.

Example 11-11. New AddNewUser method

```
[WebInvoke(UriTemplate = "/users", Method = "POST")]
[OperationContract]
public User AddNewUser(User u)
{
    u.UserId = Guid.NewGuid().ToString();
    OutgoingWebResponseContext ctx = WebOperationContext.Current.OutgoingResponse;
    ctx.SetStatusAsCreated(CreateUri(u));
    _users.Add(u);
    return u;
}
```

Figure 11-5 shows the interaction at the HTTP level (using the useful Fiddler tool).

You can see the Location header in Figure 11-6.

Doing the right thing by returning a 201 and a Location header for the methods that create new resources when using WCF's Web Programming Model isn't just a simple matter of configuration, but it is a fairly simple set of steps: create the absolute URI for the new resource and call `OutgoingWebResponseContext.SetStatusAsCreated`.

404 — Not Found

The 404 status code's typical description string is "Not Found". A 404 status code indicates to a client that the resource it is requesting isn't available. Typically, this occurs when you're implementing `GET` while building a RESTful service.

Figure 11-6. Location header displayed in Fiddler

As I mentioned earlier in the chapter, WCF will set the status code to 404 if an incoming request's URI doesn't match at least one `UriTemplate` from the `UriTemplateTable` supporting the endpoint. A 405 status code is returned if at least one `UriTemplate` matches but the incoming HTTP method doesn't match the service operations associated with the `UriTemplate`.

What if the `UriTemplate` and method both match, and a request is forwarded to one of the methods, but the resource as requested doesn't actually exist? Since `UriTemplate` is simply a template, a match will be made based on the template, not based on the actual existence of a resource.

Looking back at the user service sample introduced in Chapter 3, what if a request is routed to the `GetUser` method, but the user resource that was requested doesn't exist in your system? This can happen pretty easily, since the `UriTemplate` can match without the value of `{user_id}` being an actual identifier in your list of users. What if one client does a `DELETE` on a resource, and then another client tries to do a `GET` on that same resource?

If you write your code in an unsafe way, an exception might happen whereby you can't find a particular user. If you let that exception bubble back to the WCF call stack, WCF will return a 400 ("Bad Request"), which is sort of, but not quite, correct. The 400 status code is generally reserved for when a user agent sends a request body that isn't formatted correctly via `POST` or `PUT`, although it is sort of the fallback code for a client error if no other 4*xx* status code fits.

404 is generally considered the correct status code to send back based on a request for a nonexistent resource. It is fairly simple to add this support to the `GetUser` method. You can see this code in Example 11-12.

Example 11-12. GetUser method retuning a 404 if the resource isn't found

```
[WebGet(UriTemplate = "/users/{user_id}")]
[OperationContract]
public User GetUser(string user_id)
{
    User u = FindUser(user_id);
    if (u == null)
    {
        OutgoingWebResponseContext ctx =
                            WebOperationContext.Current.OutgoingResponse;
        ctx.SetStatusAsNotFound();
        ctx.SuppressEntityBody = true;
    }
    return u;
}
```

The code in Example 11-12 first tries to find the resource in the data store. If the user isn't found, the local variable will be null, so the appropriate return code will be a 404. To send the 404, you get a reference to the `OutgoingWebResponseContext` and call the `SetStatusAsNotFound` method. For good measure, set the `SuppressEntityBody` property to `true`, since a 404 shouldn't include a response resource. If you want to add a human-readable description of why the resource wasn't found (which the client could put into a log or some other place for a human to read at some point), you can change the description on the 404 by calling the other overload of `SetStatusAsNotFound`.

Conditional GET

Web programmers and designers have long sought to make the Web more efficient. It certainly appears that the capability to build more efficient, scalable websites and services is increasing. Taking advantage of all of that work is one of the benefits of using REST for building your services.

You can make the infrastructure of the Web more scalable in a few different ways. One facility that is used extensively to increase the overall scalability of the Web is known as conditional `GET`. Conditional `GET` enables a user agent to make a `GET` request for a resource the user agent already has a copy of, and will have the server tell the user agent that the resource is exactly the same as the version already held by the user agent if the resource hasn't changed. The efficiency benefit of conditional `GET` is a reduction in bandwidth of the network between the server and the user agent, freeing up the bandwidth to be used by requests for newly created or modified resources. In addition, it saves the additional processing time to serialize the resource, just not the processing time to generate or retrieve the resource (since you need a copy of the current resource to compare it to the information sent by the user agent with the conditional `GET`).

Like most of the other "advanced" HTTP concepts, WCF doesn't support conditional `GET` automatically because the implementation of conditional `GET` is highly variable among service implementations. However, as it does for other "advanced" HTTP concepts, WCF does provide the tools to implement conditional GET. There are two approaches to accomplish this: using the time the resource was last modified, or using a special unique identifier.

LastModified

One way to implement conditional GET is to have a server return a Last-Modified header in the HTTP response for a particular resource. The Last-Modified header value will be a date/time value indicating the last time the resource was updated.

When sending an HTTP request for the same resource, the user agent presents the date/time value in a special HTTP request header: If-Modified-Since. If the resource hasn't been modified since the date/time value presented by the user agent in the If-Modified-Since header, a 304 ("Not Modified") response will be sent back to the user agent. The bandwidth reduction occurs because the server doesn't return an entity body with a 304.

In the case of a browser, this cycle occurs often because it happens every time a user refreshes the page. In a service context, this would happen when a user agent requests the same resource more than once, which can be triggered by a user if the service is being called from the context of a human-driven application, but can easily happen when the user agent is a totally automated program as well.

So, for conditional GET to work based on the Last-Modified header, your service has to know the last time the resource was modified. This seems logical, and that information might already be at your fingertips, if your resource has something like a last-modified date/time property or field, or if your resource resides in a database and it has a column with the last-modified value in it. For our service, we'll add a field to the user type specifically to support conditional GET. Of course, having this information is useful beyond conditional GET, which is why this information is often at your fingertips to begin with.

When a new user resource is created, Example 11-13 shows the code that sets the newly created property's value to the current time.

Example 11-13. Setting the LastModified property

```
[WebInvoke(UriTemplate = "/users", Method = "POST")]
[OperationContract]
public User AddNewUser(User u)
{
    u.UserId = Guid.NewGuid().ToString();
    u.LastModified = DateTimeOffset.Now;
    OutgoingWebResponseContext ctx =
                    WebOperationContext.Current.OutgoingResponse;
    ctx.SetStatusAsCreated(CreateUri(u));
    _users.Add(u);
    return u;
}
```

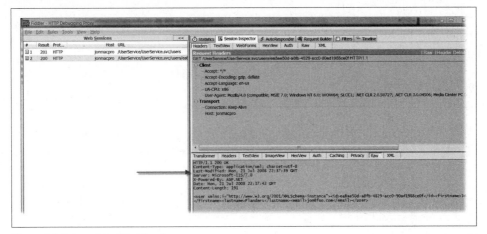

Figure 11-7. Last-Modified header

This example uses the new .NET 3.0 `DateTimeOffset` type instead of good old `DateTime`. You can consult the documentation on `DateTimeOff set` for more information, but know that `DateTimeOffset` is the best type to use when you are trying to represent a particular moment in time.

`LastModified` is the field I added to my `User` data type and is used in Example 11-11 (although I am not showing the actually property itself).

Now that the resource's modification time is available, you can use it to set the Last-Modified header. To do this, create a method named `SetLastModified` as in Example 11-14.

Example 11-14. SetLastModified

```
private void SetLastModified(User u)
{
    OutgoingWebResponseContext ctx =
        WebOperationContext.Current.OutgoingResponse;
    ctx.LastModified = u.LastModified.DateTime;
}
```

Figure 11-7 shows a request for a user resource using Fiddler, and you can see the Last-Modified header being returned to the user agent.

Next, add code at the top of the `GetUsers` method to determine whether the incoming request has an If-Modified-Since header. You can compare that value to the `User.Last Modified` field value, and if If-Modified-Since has the same value, you can return a 304. This method (named `CheckLastModified`) is shown in Example 11-15.

Example 11-15. CheckLastModified method

```
private bool CheckLastModified(User u)
{
    IncomingWebRequestContext ctx =
                WebOperationContext.Current.IncomingRequest;
    string lastModified =
        ctx.Headers[HttpRequestHeader.IfModifiedSince];
    if (lastModified != null)
    {
        DateTimeOffset dt = DateTimeOffset.Parse(lastModified);
        if (InternalDateTimeCompare(u.LastModified.UtcDateTime, dt))
        {
            SetNotModified();
            return true;
        }
    }
    return false;
}
```

This code gets the `IncomingWebRequestContext` so that you can check for the If-Modified-Since header. If that header is there, compare the value to the `LastModified` field of the `User` instance (this is done with another method I'll show you in a moment).

The `SetNotModified` method does the work on the `OutgoingWebResponseContext` to ensure the 304:

```
private void SetNotModified()
{
    OutgoingWebResponseContext ctx =
        WebOperationContext.Current.OutgoingResponse;
    ctx.SuppressEntityBody = true;
    ctx.StatusCode = HttpStatusCode.NotModified;
}
```

The `SuppressEntityBody` is set to `true` again to ensure that no response body is sent accidentally. This is a general-purpose method and could be called for any conditional GET match.

Figure 11-8 shows another request made by a user agent, which is satisfied by a 304 for the user resource.

Using conditional GET based on Last-Modified and If-Modified-Since is generally considered a good thing, but it does have one limitation. The stated problem is with the precision of the date/time value sent with Last-Modified, as it is precise down to only one second. It is somewhat plausible that a resource could change with greater precision than one second. The date comparison code illustrates this point because it can't just parse the incoming If-Modified-Since value into a `DateTimeOffset`. If it did, it would never return a 304 because it would never match `User.LastModified`, since `DateTimeOffset` and `DateTime` are more precise than to the second. Create two new `DateTime` instances based on that precision level and compare them (Example 11-16).

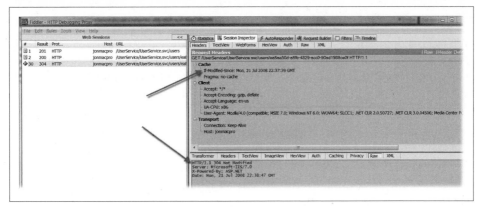

Figure 11-8. 304 conditional GET response

Example 11-16. DateTime comparison

```
private bool InternalDateTimeCompare(DateTime dt1, DateTimeOffset dt2)
{
    DateTime nd1 =
        new DateTime(dt1.Year, dt1.Month,
            dt1.Day, dt1.Hour,
            dt1.Minute, dt1.Second);
    DateTime nd2 =
        new DateTime(dt2.Year, dt2.Month,
            dt2.Day, dt2.Hour,
            dt2.Minute, dt2.Second);
    return nd1 == nd2;
}
```

This code is a little silly, but necessary.

Another possible scenario is that a convenient "last modified" value isn't available, but you could compare property or field values between a presented and current resource to determine which one was different or new. Because we are discussing GET, expecting the user agent to present the resource again when making a GET request would contradict one of the main tenets of REST (as well as the HTTP protocol itself). But what if you could put a special value that represents the current state of the resource into the HTTP response header after a GET request that could be presented again when a user agent does a conditional GET? You could then use that value when another request is made, and compare that value to the currently held special value associated with the resource. This would solve both the precision and date/time availability problems. This is why the HTTP specification was expanded in version 1.1 to include a value called ETag.

ETags

An *ETag* is a per-resource, opaque, unique value. An ETag is generally a hashed value generated by a server in response to a `GET` request for a resource that is based on some information from the resource itself. When the user agent makes another request for the same resource, the value of the ETag is presented in the If-None-Match header.

When the server receives the request, it has to generate the ETag for the resource again, and if the current ETag matches the value of the If-None-Match header, the resource hasn't changed and a 304 is returned. ETag conditional `GET` is much like Last-Modified conditional `GET`, but uses a different token for comparison.

Web servers are highly optimized to generate ETags for static content (e.g., images and HTML pages), and generally do so based on particular file attributes.

For dynamic content generation, the ETag can be slightly more complex. Unfortunately, many times the whole resource has to be generated and hashed for the comparison to work, which means you aren't saving on CPU or memory usage by using conditional `GET` in this way. You are, however, saving bandwidth, and in some cases the ETag effort is more than paid off by the resultant savings.

To make use of ETags, add an ETag return to the `GetUser` method by hashing the `User.UserId` property and the `User.LastModified` property. This uses `LastModified` again, but remember that an ETag has a greater level of precision than the Last-Modified/If-Modified-Since conditional `GET` scheme. Example 11-17 includes one potential implementation for generating an ETag.

Example 11-17. Sample ETag generation

```
string GenerateETag(User u)
{
    byte[] bytes = Encoding.UTF8.GetBytes(u.UserId +
                                   u.LastModified.ToString());
    byte[] hash = MD5.Create().ComputeHash(bytes);
    string etag = Convert.ToBase64String(hash);
    return etag;
}
```

Now add code inside the `GetUser` method that is similar to the one in the Last-Modified version (and you can use both Last-Modified and an ETag together). You can see a sample implementation in Example 11-18.

Example 11-18. Checking for ETag

```
[WebGet(UriTemplate = "/users/{user_id}")]
[OperationContract]
public User GetUser(string user_id)
{
    User u = FindUser(user_id);
    if (CheckLastModified(u))
        return null;
```

```
    string etag = GenerateETag(u);
    if (CheckETag(etag))
        return null;
    if (u == null)
    {
        OutgoingWebResponseContext ctx =
                    WebOperationContext.Current.OutgoingResponse;
        ctx.SetStatusAsNotFound();
        ctx.SuppressEntityBody = true;
    }
    SetLastModified(u);
    SetETag(etag);
    return u;
}
```

The basic steps to check for new values are to generate the ETag for the current resource, and then to check whether the ETag matches the value of the If-None-Match header. See Example 11-19.

Example 11-19. ETag comparison code

```
private bool CheckETag(string currentETag)
{
    IncomingWebRequestContext ctx =
        WebOperationContext.Current.IncomingRequest;
    string incomingEtag =
        ctx.Headers[HttpRequestHeader.IfNoneMatch];
    if (incomingEtag != null)
    {
        if (currentETag == incomingEtag)
        {
            SetNotModified();
            return true;
        }
    }
    return false;
}
```

If this method returns `true`, the request is over and the `GetUser` method returns null. Notice that again the code calls the `SetNotModified` method inside the `CheckETag` method, since setting the 304 is the same whether it uses an ETag or Last-Modified.

If the request doesn't match on a conditional `GET`, the system must return the resource. But before doing so, the `GetUser` method will set the ETag using the `OutgoingWebResponseContext` using my method named `SetETag`, which is shown in Example 11-20.

Example 11-20. Setting the ETag

```
void SetETag(string etag)
{
    OutgoingWebResponseContext ctx =
        WebOperationContext.Current.OutgoingResponse;
```

Figure 11-9. ETag HTTP response from WCF

Figure 11-10. 304 conditional GET return based on If-None-Match

```
    ctx.ETag = etag;
}
```

The interaction is exactly the same as the Last-Modified conditional GET. The HTTP response from WCF is shown in Figure 11-9, and the 304 conditional GET return based on If-None-Match is shown in Figure 11-10.

The main savings from using conditional GET are based primarily on bandwidth. In most cases of dynamic content, you will have to generate or retrieve the resource before you can do the conditional comparison.

Another HTTP/web feature that can help immensely with scalability is caching. In some cases caching can help to preserve bandwidth, and in other cases it can greatly decrease CPU load. Next, I'll discuss some of the caching options available when using WCF.

Caching

One of the biggest benefits of using a RESTful design for your services over a SOAP-based design is the ability to cache responses. SOAP responses can never safely be cached since they are all based on POST, which isn't safe to cache. No client or intermediary (such as a proxy) will cache a response to an HTTP POST request.

Because many RESTful service requests are based on GET, we can cache responses. There are many different ways to cause down-level actors to cache, but here we will focus on the caching facility built into IIS.

> For more information about general web caching semantics, see Mark Nottingham's excellent caching tutorial at *http://www.mnot.net/cache _docs/*.

Output Caching

IIS provides two levels of built-in caching for GET responses under its Output Caching feature. One level is called *kernel-mode caching*. In this mode, a resource representation is cached inside the http.sys kernel driver for HTTP. If you're using IIS, this means that if you can get your responses cached inside of the kernel, the HTTP request never even gets into user-mode code. The http.sys driver gets the HTTP request and immediately returns the cached version of the resource. The second level is *user-mode caching*. User-mode caching is at the user level instead of the kernel level because user-mode caching is more variable than kernel-mode caching (I'll show you this in a moment).

Let's look at a fairly simple scenario illustrating the benefits of caching with REST. Imagine that you have a RESTful service with WCF, and inside an operation on your service that implements GET, it takes 250 milliseconds to generate the resource representation (assuming that's the cost of going to the database and formatting the representation correctly). To show the benefits of caching in this scenario, I used Visual Studio Team System and its Web Test facility to put a small load on my service. Figure 11-11 shows the results from the first run of this test.

At this point, based on the hardware of the web server, there are 107 requests per second in a one-minute test, with 6,437 total requests made.

To turn on kernel-mode caching, access the IIS Manager and configure the WCF extension (*.svc*) to be cached. The Output Caching feature is available on all websites and virtual directories in the IIS Manager (see Figure 11-12).

Figure 11-12 shows a configuration in which kernel-mode caching is enabled and has been configured to cache GET responses for 30 seconds (you can apply a more fine-grained configuration as well—for one particular *.svc* file, for example). Figure 11-13 shows the results of running the stress test with the new caching configuration.

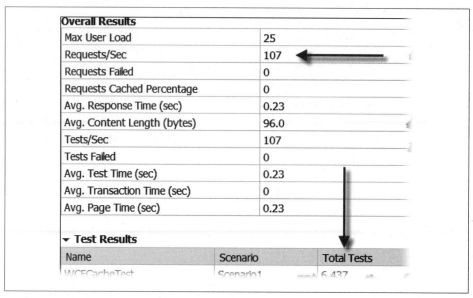

Overall Results	
Max User Load	25
Requests/Sec	107
Requests Failed	0
Requests Cached Percentage	0
Avg. Response Time (sec)	0.23
Avg. Content Length (bytes)	96.0
Tests/Sec	107
Tests Failed	0
Avg. Test Time (sec)	0.23
Avg. Transaction Time (sec)	0
Avg. Page Time (sec)	0.23

▼ Test Results		
Name	Scenario	Total Tests
WCFCacheTest	Scenario1	6,437

Figure 11-11. Stress test of GET method before caching

I sat for a long time trying to figure out what to write here. I recommend taking a deep breath and then looking over the two results again. Yes, the second result went to 1,253 requests per second from 107. I'm not really great at math, but I am pretty sure that delta is significant.

Now, to be fair, not all of your services will be able to take advantage of kernel-mode caching, which is significantly faster than user-mode caching. The limitation of kernel-mode caching is that the response cannot be variable. The same response is returned to each and every requestor regardless of any differences in the HTTP requests.

If you click the Advanced button after selecting user-mode caching in the Edit Cache Rule dialog box, you can vary the cache based on a number of factors. You can use query string variables, or HTTP headers to have multiple versions of your resource cached based on unique values in the selected query string or HTTP headers. Obviously, there is a balance between memory usage (which increases with the number of versions of a resource that are cached) and CPU (which is conserved when your code doesn't have to execute to generate a response).

There is much more to kernel- and user-mode caching. See the IIS documentation on output caching for more information. This section will hopefully be enough for you to glean this RESTful benefit, as well as set you on your way to cache as many parts of your service as make sense.

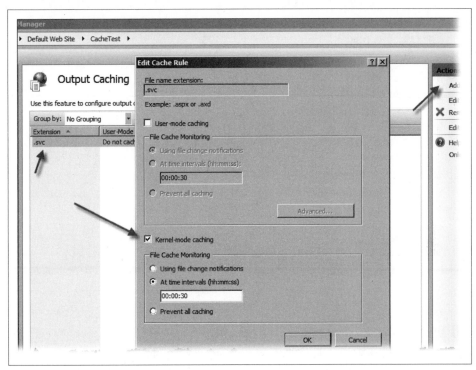

Figure 11-12. IIS caching configuration

HttpContext.Cache

Chapter 4 discussed different hosting options for your WCF RESTful service. One of the concepts we discussed was using the `AspNetCompatibilityMode` setting when hosting inside IIS. When `AspNetCompatibilityMode` is enabled, your WCF code gains access to `HttpContext` as well as `OperationContext` and `WebOperationContext`.

One pretty interesting feature available on `HttpContext` that isn't on either of the WCF context objects is the `HttpContext.Cache` property. The `HttpCache` object is a high-performance in-memory cache that you can use to store data that is used often but expensive to retrieve. Among other things, the contents of files, data from a database, and the results of expensive algorithms are all ripe for caching.

Object caching isn't as beneficial to services as output caching can be, but it is a facility that you should not overlook. This is one of the reasons I mentioned (in Chapter 4) that you might choose to host inside IIS and turn on `AspNetCompatibilityMode`. See the documentation on the `HttpContext.Cache` property for more information about using this object. The usage model for WCF with `AspNetCompatibilityMode` enabled is exactly the same as the usage model for ASP.NET applications.

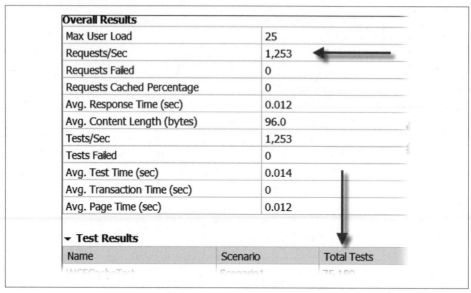

Overall Results	
Max User Load	25
Requests/Sec	1,253
Requests Failed	0
Requests Cached Percentage	0
Avg. Response Time (sec)	0.012
Avg. Content Length (bytes)	96.0
Tests/Sec	1,253
Tests Failed	0
Avg. Test Time (sec)	0.014
Avg. Transaction Time (sec)	0
Avg. Page Time (sec)	0.012

▼ Test Results

Name	Scenario	Total Tests

Figure 11-13. Stress test results with kernel-mode caching turned on

Content-Type

Another area where WCF falls slightly short in its default behavior concerns Content-Type. The default support for Content-Type is fairly static. You observed similar limitations in the way it deals with status codes.

This isn't a hugely critical use of HTTP, at least compared to conditional GET or ETags, for example, but it's nice to be complete when building a RESTful service, and setting your Content-Type correctly is a useful exercise. Your clients will likely appreciate it.

By default, WCF supports two Content-Types automatically: `application/xml` and `application/json`. If your method returns XML, the Content-Type will be set to `application/xml`. If your method returns JSON, the Content-Type will be set to `application/json`.

It's interesting to note that the feed infrastructure in WCF doesn't automatically support the correct Content-Types for RSS or Atom. Adding this support is relatively simple. Example 11-21 shows the code example from Chapter 6 with the added Content-Type.

Example 11-21. Returning correct Content-Type with feeds

```
public Rss20FeedFormatter GetRSS(string log)
{
    SyndicationFeed feed = GetFeed(log);
    Rss20FeedFormatter formatter = new Rss20FeedFormatter(feed);
    //calling the new method
    SetContentType("application/rss+xml");
```

```
    return formatter;
}
//this is the new method
void SetContentType(string contentType)
{
    OutgoingWebResponseContext ctx =
        WebOperationContext.Current.OutgoingResponse;
    ctx.ContentType = contentType;
}
public Atom10FeedFormatter GetAtom(string log)
{
    SyndicationFeed feed = GetFeed(log);
    Atom10FeedFormatter formatter = new Atom10FeedFormatter(feed);
  //calling the new method
    SetContentType("application/atom+xml");
    return formatter;
}
```

The media type string will depend on your representation format, but setting it is simple, so it is probably worth doing.

Summary

This chapter presents a hodgepodge of different things you can do with the WCF HTTP programming model. The full HTTP programming model is exposed via WebOperation Context and is available on both the client and server sides.

Using OutgoingWebResponseContext to set the status code appropriately, depending on the uniform interface of your service, is an important RESTful functionality. Another important HTTP feature is conditional GET, which you can enable by using either the LastModified or ETag headers to reduce bandwidth usage of your service.

Using the IIS kernel- or user-mode caching infrastructure is another way to leverage the fact that REST enables caching because of the usage of GET.

WCF 3.5 SP1

This book was written based on the shipping bits of WCF 3.5. Near the end of this writing, WCF 3.5 SP1 was released. This version includes some improvements and new features that are worth mentioning here. If you are already using WCF 3.5 SP1, you can still use the information in this book—everything in the main chapters will work exactly the same under SP1. In other words, SP1 doesn't change the way anything in the Web Programming Model works, it just adds a few very useful pieces of functionality.

Atom Publishing Protocol

The Atom Syndication Format (Atom) is an XML vocabulary for describing a feed of data, which can be used to publish or syndicate information out to end users through a browser or a feed reader. Although many people think of Atom being useful only for blogs or news content, it has also become a popular resource representation for RESTful endpoints that deal with other types of content. See Chapter 6 for more detailed information about Atom.

The Atom Publishing Protocol (AtomPub) is a specification for retrieving, creating, and updating resources. AtomPub builds on the constraints of REST by defining an additional set of specific constraints above the constraints of REST. The constraints are some very specific resource representations, as well as the specific uniform interface interaction with those resources.

In Appendix B, I'll show you a technology called ADO.NET Data Services, which uses AtomPub to define the interaction between user agents and endpoints. AtomPub seems to be moving up the ladder very quickly in terms of adoption as a general-purpose way to expose RESTful resources. Like REST itself, AtomPub is useful because its set of constraints (other than the resource format constraints) are really a codification of the conventions that people have used for years in designing RESTful services.

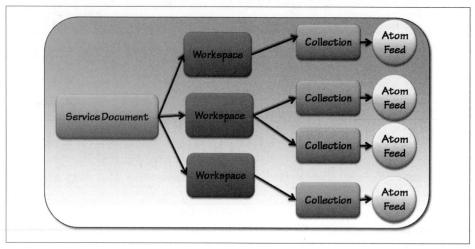

Figure A-1. AtomPub Service Document hierarchy

AtomPub defines a hierarchy of resources. First, it defines a new resource called the *Service Document*, which has the media type of `application/atomsvc+xml`. A Service Document contains workspaces, which are named groupings of collections. Collections contain *Member Resources*, each of which is represented by a feed. This part of the AtomPub specification is really about organizing a related set of feeds together in a standardized way for discovery.

AtomPub doesn't have any requirements or constraints for the URIs that represent these resources. There is no standard URI for a Service Document itself, or for any of the hierarchy that may be contained within it. The specification relies on `hrefs` attributes in certain elements in the hierarchy to allow linking between the resources. Once you have the URI of the Service Document, you can traverse its entire hierarchy (shown in Figure A-1).

 Hypermedia (linking) is an extremely important part of REST. This book hasn't covered much in terms of hypermedia because other than the feed API, WCF doesn't really have any inherent support for creating links between different resources.

In many RESTful services, hyperlinking between different resources is key because the hyperlinks represent the current state of the resources.

AtomPub also defines a document called a *Category Document*. A Category Document is a list of `atom:category` (classifications for feed entries) elements. Links to Category Documents are optional elements inside of a collection. The `atom:category` elements associated with a collection are used when adding entries into that collection.

Example A-1 shows a sample Service Document.

Example A-1. ServiceDocument resources

```xml
<?xml version="1.0" encoding="utf-8"?>
<service xml:base="http://win2008/AtomPubSample/AtomPubService.svc/"
    xmlns="http://www.w3.org/2007/app" xmlns:a10="http://www.w3.org/2005/Atom">
    <app:workspace xmlns:app="http://www.w3.org/2007/app">
        <a10:title type="text">Main</a10:title>
        <app:collection href="blog">
            <a10:title type="text">Blog</a10:title>
            <app:accept>application/atom+xml;type=entry</app:accept>
        </app:collection>
        <app:collection href="pictures">
            <a10:title type="text">Pictures</a10:title>
            <app:accept>image/png</app:accept>
            <app:accept>image/jpeg</app:accept>
            <app:accept>image/gif</app:accept>
        </app:collection>
    </app:workspace>
    <app:workspace xmlns:app="http://www.w3.org/2007/app">
        <a10:title type="text">FoodBlog</a10:title>
        <app:collection href="foodblog">
            <a10:title type="text">Food</a10:title>
            <app:categories href="foodblogcats"/>
        </app:collection>
    </app:workspace>
</service>
```

The Service Document in Example A-1 contains two workspaces. The "Main" workspace contains two Collections, one named "Blog" (with the relative URI "blog") and one named "Pictures" (with the relative URI "pictures").

The "Blog" Collection has an explicit `accept` element with a value of `application/atom` `+xml;type=entry`. The `accept` elements of a Collection indicate which media types the resource will accept as new resources. The one inside of the "Blog" Collection is actually the default, and if a Collection doesn't have an `accept` element, the user agent is to assume that `application/atom+xml;type=entry` is the only acceptable media type for new resources.

The idea of a new resource should raise a question in your mind about how AtomPub specifies the use of the uniform interface. Table A-1 lists the specified interactions for each resource based on the uniform interface.

Table A-1. AtomPub uniform interface

Resource	Uniform interface method	Description
Service Document	GET	Once the user agent knows the URI, it can retrieve the Service Document via GET
Category Document	GET	Used to retrieve the representation of the category
Collection	GET	Retrieves the representation, which will be an Atom feed
Collection	POST	Creates a new Atom entry

Resource	Uniform interface method	Description
Member	GET	Retrieves an individual member, which can be an individual Atom entry or a binary file
Member	PUT	Modifies a member
Member	DELETE	Deletes a member

AtomPub specifies that the value of the href attribute on each collection element is the URI for creating new entries into the Collection resource. Creating new entries uses POST. The default media type for new entries is application/atom+xml;type=entry, which is used explicitly in Example A-1 under the collection element with the title of "Blog". This is the typical media type for an entry in an Atom feed.

The second collection element in Example A-1 (the one with the title "Pictures") illustrates that other media types are allowed other than application/atom +xml;type=entry. This is another part of the AtomPub specification. Binary files (like images or PDFs or any other binary file type that can't be nicely embedded inside of an Atom entry inside of the content element) can be added to each collection. Instead of embedding the binary file inside of the entry/content element, AtomPub specifies that the entry resource, which is returned from using POST to create a new binary entry, will be an entry that contains a link to the binary resource.

Something that isn't in the AtomPub specification is an explicit way to create a Service Document. This is by design; the AtomPub specification leaves this and other issues up to the implementer of a particular AtomPub-based service. The specification allows you to use the uniform interface on resources in ways not explicitly covered, so if you want to implement POST on a URI for user agents to create new Service Documents, you can do so without violating the AtomPub specification.

The other new resource mentioned in the AtomPub specification is the Categories Document. This document contains a list of categories that can be applied to entries or modified in the member resources. The Atom specification defines categories, and AtomPub simply reuses those elements but adds a collection around them, so a particular collection can be associated with particular Collections. The Categories Document can either be referenced by its URI or be included in its entirety in the Collection:

```
<?xml version="1.0" encoding="utf-8"?>
<categories scheme="http://commonfoodcategories" fixed="yes"
xmlns="http://www.w3.org/2007/app" xmlns:a10="http://www.w3.org/2005/Atom">
    <a10:category term="sushi"/>
    <a10:category term="chinese"/>
    <a10:category term="deserts"/>
</categories>
```

The only new construct that AtomPub adds to the category system is the fixed attribute. If the fixed attribute is set to yes, no other categories are allowed to be used inside of a new entry resource. If the fixed attribute is missing, the value will automatically be set to no.

AtomPub in WCF 3.5 SP1

The preceding section should be enough background on AtomPub to give you the grounding for looking at the details of WCF in WCF 3.5 SP1. As you've probably already guessed, SP1 includes new types and formatters in the `System.ServiceModel.Syndication` namespace to support generating the document types from the AtomPub specification.

 If you want to learn more about AtomPub, you can view the specification at *http://bitworking.org/projects/atom/rfc5023.html*.

These new types work exactly like the types that were introduced in Chapter 6 for dealing with feeds. There is an object model that represents the underlying data that is required for creating Service and Category Documents. The WCF 3.5 SP1 formatters will automatically use the data in those objects to generate the proper AtomPub-compliant XML. Even though there is just one version of the AtomPub specification at this point, they used this layer of indirection between data and formatting to be consistent with the existing Syndication API in WCF, and also to be prepared for future revisions of the specification (should they come to exist).

The code shown in Example A-2 will generate the Service Document shown in Example A-1.

Example A-2. Generating a Service Document with WCF 3.5 SP1

```
[OperationContract]
[WebGet(UriTemplate = "/")]
[OperationContract]
[WebGet(UriTemplate = "/")]
public AtomPub10ServiceDocumentFormatter GetServiceDoc()
{
    OutgoingWebResponseContext ctx =
        WebOperationContext.Current.OutgoingResponse;
    ctx.ContentType = "application/atomsvc+xml";
    AtomPub10ServiceDocumentFormatter ret = null;
    //create the ServiceDocument type
    ServiceDocument doc =
        new ServiceDocument();
    IncomingWebRequestContext ictx =
        WebOperationContext.Current.IncomingRequest;
    //set the BaseUri to the current request URI
    doc.BaseUri =
        ictx.UriTemplateMatch.RequestUri;
    //create a Collection of resources
    List<ResourceCollectionInfo> resources =
        new List<ResourceCollectionInfo>();
    //create the Blog resource
    ResourceCollectionInfo mainBlog =
```

```
            new ResourceCollectionInfo("Blog",
                        new Uri("blog",UriKind.Relative));
    //add the Accepts for this resource
    //remember this is the default if no accepts if present
    mainBlog.Accepts.Add("application/atom+xml;type=entry");
    resources.Add(mainBlog);
    //create the Pictures resource
    ResourceCollectionInfo mainPictures =
        new ResourceCollectionInfo("Pictures",
                        new Uri("pictures", UriKind.Relative));
    //add the Accepts for this resource
    mainPictures.Accepts.Add("image/png");
    mainPictures.Accepts.Add("image/jpeg");
    mainPictures.Accepts.Add("image/gif");
    resources.Add(mainPictures);
    //create the Workspace
    Workspace main = new Workspace("Main", resources);
    //add the Workspace to the Service Document
    doc.Workspaces.Add(main);
    //create a new Collection for the next Workspace
    resources = new List<ResourceCollectionInfo>();
    ResourceCollectionInfo food =
        new ResourceCollectionInfo("Food",
                        new Uri("foodblog", UriKind.Relative));
    resources.Add(food);
    //create the link to the Categories Document
    CategoriesDocument cat =
        CategoriesDocument.Create(new Uri("foodblogcats", UriKind.Relative));
    food.Categories.Add(cat);
    //create the second Workspace
    Workspace foodBlog =
        new Workspace("FoodBlog", resources);
    //add the Workspace to the Service Document
    doc.Workspaces.Add(foodBlog);
    //get the formatter
    ret = doc.GetFormatter()
        as AtomPub10ServiceDocumentFormatter;
    return ret;
}
```

One interesting thing to note in this code is that the Service Document will be returned based on a GET request to the root URI (e.g., /). The AtomPub specification doesn't dictate any particular URI for the Service Document, so this is perfectly permissible, and works for this implementation since there is only one Service Document. It is entirely possible to have multiple Service Documents return from one endpoint, which is part of the reason that the specification doesn't dictate what the URI of a Service Document should be.

Other than the AtomPub-specific elements and attributes, this code follows the same basic pattern as the other parts of System.ServiceModel.Syndication, as does the Category Document creation (shown in Example A-3).

Example A-3. Creating categories

```
[OperationContract]
[WebGet(UriTemplate = "/foodblogcats")]
public AtomPub10CategoriesDocumentFormatter GetCats()
{
    AtomPub10CategoriesDocumentFormatter ret = null;
    //create the Collection of Categories
    Collection<SyndicationCategory> cats =
            new Collection<SyndicationCategory>();
    cats.Add(new SyndicationCategory("sushi"));
    cats.Add(new SyndicationCategory("chinese"));
    cats.Add(new SyndicationCategory("deserts"));
    //create the Categories Document
    //in this case I am specifying fixed="yes"
    //and providing the optional scheme
    CategoriesDocument cat =
        CategoriesDocument.Create(cats, true,
                        "http://commonfoodcategories");
    ret = cat.GetFormatter()
            as AtomPub10CategoriesDocumentFormatter;
    return ret;
}
```

As mentioned earlier, AtomPub is an increasingly popular way of interacting with resources, and many people are choosing it for general RESTful interaction—it isn't just
for blogs anymore.

 I already mentioned ADO.NET Data Services as one user of AtomPub.
Most of Google's RESTful APIs use AtomPub. Microsoft's Live services
are also starting to standardize on AtomPub. Live Mesh, which is a fairly
interesting service providing synchronization of files between different
machines and devices, is based on RESTful principles, and AtomPub is
its main mode of transporting data.

I should mention that, as in all of the other classes in `System.ServiceModel.Syndica
tion`, the object model is also available when you are working in a client environment.
Example A-4 illustrates this using the `ServiceDocument` type from SP1 to consume the
Service Document exposed by an ADO.NET Data Service. The Data Service happens
to be linked to an ADO.NET Entity Data Model on top of a Windows Workflow
Foundation (WF) tracking database. See Appendix B for more information about
ADO.NET Data Services.

Example A-4. Using the WCF 3.5 SP1 ServiceDocument type

```
using System;
using System.Collections.Generic;
using System.Linq;
using System.Text;
using System.ServiceModel.Syndication;
using System.Xml;
```

```
namespace WCF35SP1Client
{
    class Program
    {
        static void Main(string[] args)
        {
            string uri =
                "http://win2008/AstoriaTest/WorkflowTrackingData.svc/";
            XmlReader xr =
                XmlReader.Create(uri);
            ServiceDocument sd
                = ServiceDocument.Load(xr);
            Console.WriteLine("Retrieved Service Document");
            foreach (var ws in sd.Workspaces)
            {
                Console.WriteLine("Workspace {0} found",ws.Title.Text);
                foreach (var coll in ws.Collections )
                {
                    Console.WriteLine("Collection Name={0}, Uri={0}",
                                    coll.Title.Text,
                                    coll.Link.ToString());
                }
            }
        }
    }
}
```

This code, like its server-side counterpart, uses the same pattern as the System.Service
Model.Syndication API. Figure A-2 shows the result of running this code.

UriTemplate Changes

Chapter 2 discussed the basic rules of UriTemplate in WCF. Recall that UriTemplate is
a definition of a relative URI using static and (potentially) replaceable path segments.
The template gets associated with a method on a service type by using
WebGetAttribute or WebInvokeAttribute on each operation. All the UriTemplate definitions from a particular service are added to a UriTemplateTable. When an HTTP request
arrives, WCF tries to match the URI against the UriTemplateTable. If a match is found
(and the HTTP method matches the HTTP verb associated with the service method),
the WCF WebHttpDispatchOperationSelector selects the method associated with the
UriTemplate definition, and the WCF invocation layer invokes the method. WCF Web
Programming Model routing works by associating methods on the service instance with
a URI+HTTP verb combination.

An example of this is /staticsegment/replaceablesegment. If the URI of the HTTP
request is /staticsegment/replaceablesegment, it would match the UriTemplate, and the
value of the replaceablesegment path segment would be passed into the service method
as a parameter. The method definition would look like this.

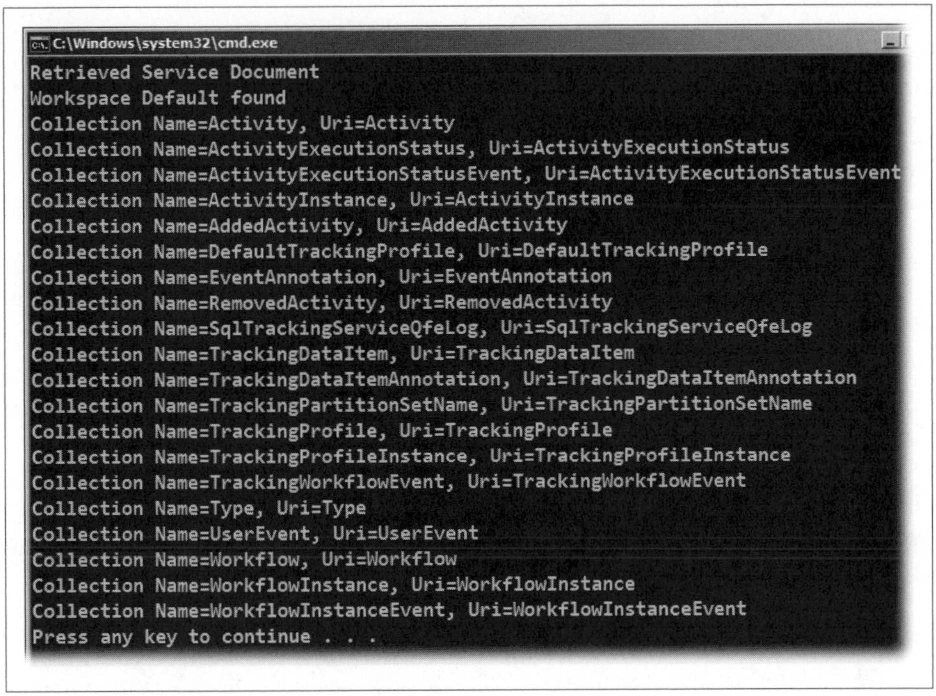

```
C:\Windows\system32\cmd.exe
Retrieved Service Document
Workspace Default found
Collection Name=Activity, Uri=Activity
Collection Name=ActivityExecutionStatus, Uri=ActivityExecutionStatus
Collection Name=ActivityExecutionStatusEvent, Uri=ActivityExecutionStatusEvent
Collection Name=ActivityInstance, Uri=ActivityInstance
Collection Name=AddedActivity, Uri=AddedActivity
Collection Name=DefaultTrackingProfile, Uri=DefaultTrackingProfile
Collection Name=EventAnnotation, Uri=EventAnnotation
Collection Name=RemovedActivity, Uri=RemovedActivity
Collection Name=SqlTrackingServiceQfeLog, Uri=SqlTrackingServiceQfeLog
Collection Name=TrackingDataItem, Uri=TrackingDataItem
Collection Name=TrackingDataItemAnnotation, Uri=TrackingDataItemAnnotation
Collection Name=TrackingPartitionSetName, Uri=TrackingPartitionSetName
Collection Name=TrackingProfile, Uri=TrackingProfile
Collection Name=TrackingProfileInstance, Uri=TrackingProfileInstance
Collection Name=TrackingWorkflowEvent, Uri=TrackingWorkflowEvent
Collection Name=Type, Uri=Type
Collection Name=UserEvent, Uri=UserEvent
Collection Name=Workflow, Uri=Workflow
Collection Name=WorkflowInstance, Uri=WorkflowInstance
Collection Name=WorkflowInstanceEvent, Uri=WorkflowInstanceEvent
Press any key to continue . . .
```

Figure A-2. AtomPub consumption with SP1

```
[OperationContract]
[WebGet(UriTemplate = "/staticsegment/replaceablesegment")]
void TemplateTest(string replaceablesegment);
```

What was missing in WCF 3.5 was the ability to split a path segment into multiple parts. Example A-5 shows some UriTemplate definitions that won't work in WCF 3.5, but will work in WCF 3.5 with SP1.

Example A-5. Multipart path segment definitions

```
[OperationContract]
[WebGet(UriTemplate = "/staticsegment/{seg1};{seg2}")]
void TemplateTest(string seg1,string seg2);
[OperationContract]
[WebGet(UriTemplate = "/staticsegment/{seg1}.json")]
void TemplateTest2(string seg1);
[OperationContract]
[WebGet(UriTemplate = "/staticsegment/{seg1}.{variableext}")]
void TemplateTest3(string seg1, string variableext);
OperationContract]
[WebGet(UriTemplate = "/staticsegment/{seg1}:{seg2}/additionalsegment")]
void TemplateTest4(string seg1,string seg2);
```

This is a nice addition to WCF 3.5 SP1. It is not quite as significant as the AtomPub functionality, but it is a very useful feature and was a blocking issue in using WCF for some people with WCF 3.5.

Attribute-Free DataContract Serialization

Another new feature in WCF 3.5 SP1 is the ability to use the DataContract serialization with Plain Old CLR Objects (POCOs). A POCO is a class that doesn't have an attached DataContractAttribute or SerializableAttribute. This feature wasn't specifically added for the Web Programming Model, but it might be a useful feature if you are building RESTful services around existing CLR types.

When WCF first shipped in WCF 3.0, it included an optional serialization layer that used the DataContractSerializer. To serialize a .NET type, the DataContract serializer had to have the DataContractAttribute or SerializableAttribute. Without these attributes, an exception would be thrown if an instance of a POCO was used in the WCF serialization infrastructure. SP1 adds the ability to use the DataContract serializer on any CLR type that has a default constructor.

 Before SP1, of course, you could use a POCO that had a default constructor with the XmlSerializer. WCF supports the use of the XmlSerializer. The new functionality described in this section uses the DataContractSerializer, not the XmlSerializer.

Example A-6 shows this new functionality by using the DataContractSerializer explicitly on a POCO named "User".

Example A-6. Using the WCF 3.5 DataContractSerializer

```
using System;
using System.Collections.Generic;
using System.Linq;
using System.Text;
using System.IO;
using System.Runtime.Serialization;

namespace _35SP1Serialization
{
    class Program
    {
        static void Main(string[] args)
        {
            User u = new User
            {
                UserId = Guid.NewGuid().ToString(),
                FirstName = "Jon",
                LastName = "Flanders",
                Email = "jon.flanders@example.org",
```

```
        LastModified = DateTimeOffset.Now
    };
    DataContractSerializer dcs =
        new DataContractSerializer(typeof(User));

    using (FileStream fs = new FileStream("user.xml", FileMode.Create))
    {

        dcs.WriteObject(fs, u);

    }

    }
}
public class User
{
    public string UserId;
    public string FirstName;
    public string LastName;
    public string Email;
    public DateTimeOffset LastModified;
}
}
```

The XML output from using the code in Example A-6 is shown in Example A-7.

Example A-7. DataContractSerializer output

```
<User xmlns="http://schemas.datacontract.org/2004/07
/_35SP1Serialization" xmlns:i="http://www.w3.org/2001/XMLSchema-instance">
    <Email>jon.flanders@gmail.com</Email>
    <FirstName>Jon</FirstName>
    <LastModified xmlns:a="http://schemas.datacontract.org/2004/07/System">
        <a:DateTime>2008-07-23T17:27:16.9832496Z</a:DateTime>
        <a:OffsetMinutes>-420</a:OffsetMinutes>
    </LastModified>
    <LastName>Flanders</LastName>
    <UserId>5d2764c9-90ce-4b1e-a45a-33b7ba46e56a</UserId>
</User>
```

This feature is useful when you are building a RESTful service around existing POCOs and you can't or don't want to annotate those types with the `DataContractAttribute`. The main downside of this feature is evident in the XML displayed in Example A-7. If you don't use `DataContractAttribute` you get the default namespace URI that is created for POCOs. In general, it is preferable to have a very specific namespace or no namespace at all. The POCO functionality doesn't allow you to customize the namespace URI or any other XML feature. Controlling the XML output is often important when building any kind of service, but especially when building RESTful services, so using the new POCO shouldn't be your first choice.

Summary

.NET 3.5 SP1 includes some very useful features for building RESTful services and clients with WCF. The new AtomPub-related types greatly simplify the creation of AtomPub-compliant service endpoints and provide the capability to consume Atom-Pub endpoints.

The new `UriTemplate` syntax places more control in our hands to create URIs that are more complex and more in tune with RESTful URI design principles.

ADO.NET Data Services

In Appendix A, I showed you the AtomPub model for creating RESTful endpoints based on the concepts of collections, feeds, and entries. I mentioned that AtomPub is quickly becoming a standard way of building services even when those services don't use the traditional data for which AtomPub was created. .NET 3.5 SP1 also includes functionality outside the core WCF functionality, and one of those pieces of functionality is called ADO.NET Data Services.

Code-named Astoria and released fairly early under that name, ADO.NET Data Services is a WCF extension framework, built on the Web Programming Model, for building AtomPub services. Specifically, it is used for building AtomPub services on top of an in-memory data model. This data model can be, and often is, backed up by a relational database, but it doesn't have to be. You can think of ADO.NET Data Services as an easy way to create a RESTful service endpoint based on AtomPub on top of a relational database model, although it has possibilities beyond that.

Building an ADO.NET Data Service

Built on top of the core Web Programming Model of WCF, ADO.NET Data Services is a framework for building RESTful services. Specifically, it is a framework for building AtomPub-based RESTful services on top of data. In some ways, ADO.NET Data Services provides a particular set of WCF programming constraints on top of AtomPub, as AtomPub provides a particular set of constraints on top of REST.

 Earlier versions of ADO.NET Data Services exposed AtomPub through both the Atom Syndication Format (XML) and JSON. The JSON support isn't in the release bits of .NET 3.5 SP1, but will continue to be released as community technical previews until some future version. See *http://www.codeplex.com/aspnet/Wiki/View.aspx?title=AJAX&referring Title=Home* for current drops of this technology.

Even if you decide to use only ADO.NET Data Services for all of your service endpoints, everything else in this book is still relevant and useful. And even if you decide not to use ADO.NET Data Services, it's interesting to look at it to see a generically extensible programming model built on top of WCF.

Programming with WCF generally starts with building a service contract definition (even if you don't start with the service contract, you'll eventually need one). With ADO.NET Data Services, the service contract has already been provided for you. The ADO.NET Data Services contract is named IRequestHandler and looks like Example B-1.

Example B-1. ADO.NET Data Services IRequestHandler contract

```
namespace System.Data.Services
{
    [ServiceContract]
    public interface IRequestHandler
    {
        [WebInvoke(UriTemplate = "*", Method = "*")]
        [OperationContract]
        Message ProcessRequestForMessage(Stream messageBody);
    }
}
```

Based on what you have seen in earlier chapters of this book, the preceding code is what would typically be referred to as a *universal contract*. All messages received at the endpoint on which this contract is registered, regardless of HTTP method, will be routed to the ProcessRequestForMessage method.

In addition, the format of the message body will be irrelevant since the parameter is one of the WCF "generic" message types: System.IO.Stream. The return value is Message, so the method is free to return a message that may be formatted as XML, JSON, or perhaps some other future format (see Chapter 7 for a discussion of returning both XML and JSON from a WCF method).

Every ADO.NET Data Services endpoint implements this contract (and only this contract). One nice feature of ADO.NET Data Services is that you don't have to implement the contract; the contract is already implemented by a generic service types: the Data Service of *T* (see Example B-2).

Example B-2. The DataService type

```
namespace System.Data.Services
{
    [ServiceBehavior(InstanceContextMode = InstanceContextMode.PerCall)]
    [AspNetCompatibilityRequirements(RequirementsMode =
                             AspNetCompatibilityRequirementsMode.Allowed)]
    public class DataService<T> : IRequestHandler
    {
        public DataService();
```

```
        protected T CurrentDataSource { get; }

        protected virtual void ApplyingExpansions(IQueryable queryable,
                        ICollection<ExpandSegmentCollection> expandPaths);
        public void AttachHost(IDataServiceHost host);
        protected virtual T CreateDataSource();
        protected virtual void HandleException(HandleExceptionArgs args);
        public void ProcessRequest();
        public Message ProcessRequestForMessage(Stream messageBody);
    }
}
```

We'll get into some of the other methods on `DataService` of *T* later in this appendix, but for now the most important thing to understand is that `DataService` implements `IRequestHandler`.

Up to this point, we've looked at two constraints that ADO.NET Data Services provides on top of WCF. First, all ADO.NET Data Service endpoints have a predetermined contract type of `IRequestHandler`, and all service types will have a predetermined base class of `DataService` of *T*.

That seems to beg the question of what *T* can be. There isn't a generic restriction on *T*, so you could specify *T* to be `System.Object`. That wouldn't do very much, so what does the ADO.NET Data Services infrastructure do with *T*? The key interface is `System.Linq.IQueryable<T>`, which is the generic type derived from `System.Linq.IQueryable`.

When objects want to provide LINQ query access on top of object data sources, they implement the `IQueryable` interface. ADO.NET Data Services doesn't look for `IQuery able` on *T*; rather, it reflects against the type of *T* and looks for public properties that return `IQueryable<T>`, and then it uses those properties to implement AtomPub on top of those entities (the properties become the names of the AtomPub Collections inside a single workspace; more on this later in this appendix). This top-level object of type *T* is generically referred to as the *data context*.

 If you haven't had a chance to look at LINQ yet, see *http://msdn.micro soft.com/en-us/library/bb308959.aspx* for more information. A general discussion of LINQ is beyond the scope of this book.

Although `IQueryable` is fast becoming a commonly used interface, it's not a common interface to implement. It's certainly useful and potentially important to know that you can just create an object with public properties that return `IQueryable<T>` and that ADO.NET Data Services will use that object as the data context. However, it's much more likely that you'll use a data context object that is generated by some tool. In the majority of cases, that tool will be the ADO.NET Entity Framework.

With some modification, you also can use LINQ to SQL classes with ADO.NET Data Services. But depending on the complexity of the model, some features may not work.

ADO.NET Data Services supports any implementation of a data context, but it is really optimized for the ADO.NET Entity Framework's `ObjectContext`. See Appendix C for a quick walkthrough of creating an ADO.NET Entity Framework data context.

So, the three constraints of ADO.NET Data Services that we have discussed so far are as follows:

- The contract is always `IRequestHandler`
- The service type is always `DataService` of *T*
- *T* is always an object that has public properties of type `IQueryable` of *T*

The next constraint relates to hosting. ADO.NET Data Services has a special `Service Host` type named `DataServiceHost` (see Chapter 4 for more details about custom `ServiceHost` types). `DataServiceHost` is pretty simple; it just derives from `WebService Host` with no additional functionality added. Of course, now that `DataServiceHost` is the required `ServiceHost`, future versions of ADO.NET Data Services can add additional functionality (which is a good reason to create a custom `ServiceHost` type for your own WCF projects). There is also a `DataServiceHostFactory` for IIS/Windows Process Activation Services (WAS) hosting (for the `Factory` attribute of the *.svc* file).

Another interesting thing about `DataServiceHost` is that when it starts up it calls a static method on the `DataService` type, which enables the `DataService` type to do some one-time initialization. This static method has to be named `InitializeService`, and it takes a single parameter, which is an interface: `IDataServiceConfiguration` (see Example B-3).

Example B-3. The IDataServiceConfiguration interface

```
namespace System.Data.Services
{
    public interface IDataServiceConfiguration
    {
        int MaxExpandCount { get; set; }
        int MaxExpandDepth { get; set; }
        bool UseVerboseErrors { get; set; }

        void RegisterKnownType(Type type);
        void SetEntitySetAccessRule(string name, EntitySetRights rights);
        void SetServiceOperationAccessRule(string name,
 ServiceOperationRights rights);
    }
}
```

We'll discuss the rest of the IDataServiceConfiguration interface later in this appendix (since some members relate to things I haven't shown you yet!), but the one member I want to cover right now is SetEntitySetAccessRule. We will cover it before going any further because, by default, ADO.NET Data Services doesn't actually expose those public IQueryable of T properties of the DataContext object into the AtomPub Service Document. By default, ADO.NET Data Services assumes that no one gets access to entities unless you specifically say so. To put it another way, before ADO.NET Data Services will expose any of your entities, you have to tell it what authorization rights users of your service endpoint receive. If you don't add an entity via SetEntitySetAccessRule, ADO.NET Data Services won't expose it.

SetEntitySetAccessRule expects a name of an entity (i.e., the name of the IQueryable of T property) and an EntitySetRights flag. Wildcards are allowed as well (* for all entities). Assuming that you have a DataContext object named UserDataContext, a useful InitializeService might look like this:

```
public class UserService : DataService<UserDataContext>
{
    public static void InitializeService(
            IDataServiceConfiguration config)
    {
        config.SetEntitySetAccessRule("user", EntitySetRights.All);
        config.SetEntitySetAccessRule("group", EntitySetRights.AllRead);
    }

}
```

In this example, all EntitySetRights are given to the user property, and all read access is given to the group property. Here are the EntitySetRights flags:

```
namespace System.Data.Services
{
    [Flags]
    public enum EntitySetRights
    {
        None = 0,
        ReadSingle = 1,
        ReadMultiple = 2,
        AllRead = 3,
        WriteAppend = 4,
        WriteUpdate = 8,
        WriteDelete = 16,
        AllWrite = 28,
        All = 31,
    }
}
```

Here is the list of constraints that ADO.NET Data Services puts on top of WCF to use its services:

- The contract is always IRequestHandler
- The service type is always DataService of T

- *T* is always an object that has public properties of type `IQueryable` of *T*
- `DataServiceHost` is always used as the `ServiceHost` for `DataService` of *T*
- Entity access rights have to be set in the `InitializeService` static method on the `DataService` of *T* type for all entities to be exposed

As I said earlier, ADO.NET Data Services provides an interesting look at customizing functionality on top of WCF. The question is: what functionality do you get when you use these constraints? The answer is that you get a full AtomPub implementation on top of your data context, plus additional query capabilities not specified by the Atom-Pub specification (but not disallowed; remember from Appendix A that AtomPub is open on issues not stated explicitly in the specification).

ADO.NET Data Services and AtomPub

As mentioned earlier in this appendix, ADO.NET Data Services looks at the data context type, reflects for properties that implement `IQueryable` of *T*, and uses those properties as the name of AtomPub Collection elements inside a single workspace when returning the Service Document. The Service Document is returned based on a GET request to the base URI of the service endpoint. Adding to the "user" example from Chapter 2, if you had a database for your user data you could use the ADO.NET Entity Framework to build an Entity Data Model (EDM) on top of that database, and then configure an ADO.NET Data Services endpoint (using self- or managed hosting). For the example in this chapter, I've also added groups and mapping between users and groups to make the data a bit more interesting.

Assuming that your `UserDataContext` is an ADO.NET Entity Framework `ObjectContext`-derived type, you can use the `DataService` type to build out an ADO.NET Data Services endpoint. First, you'll need to pick a hosting mechanism, and since ADO.NET Data Services is built on top of WCF, all the WCF hosting options are available to you (refer to Chapter 5 for more information about WCF hosting options).

This example uses managed hosting, so it requires an *.svc* file with the appropriate entries:

```
<%@ ServiceHost
  Factory="System.Data.Services.DataServiceHostFactory,
  System.Data.Services, Version=3.5.0.0, Culture=neutral,
  PublicKeyToken=b77a5c561934e089"
  Service="UserService.UserService" %>
```

Given this *.svc* file, and based on the `UserService` definition in the preceding section, you can now make an HTTP GET request to the base URI and get the AtomPub Service Document (see Figure B-1).

Recall from Appendix A that one feature of AtomPub is the hyperlink capability among different documents. Notice that each collection element has an `href` that is a relative URI for each entity collection. If you make a request to the user URI, ADO.NET Data

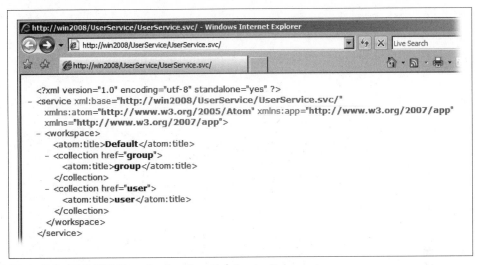

Figure B-1. ADO.NET Data Services AtomPub Service Document

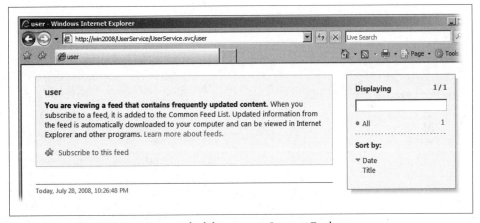

Figure B-2. ADO.NET Data Services feed document in Internet Explorer

Services will return a feed with all of the users in your data context (and since your data context is an EDM mapped to a database, it will return all the rows in your user table).

Unfortunately, Internet Explorer isn't programmed to know about the XML being returned inside the Atom content element, so (as you can see in Figure B-2) it ceases to be a useful exploration tool for ADO.NET Data Services after you get past the Service Document.

Fortunately, Fiddler comes to the rescue. The Fiddler request and response are shown in Figure B-3. Inside the Atom content element is an ADO.NET Data Services-specific schema, which shows the data of one row out of my data table (or the value of the properties of one entity, depending on how you like to think about it).

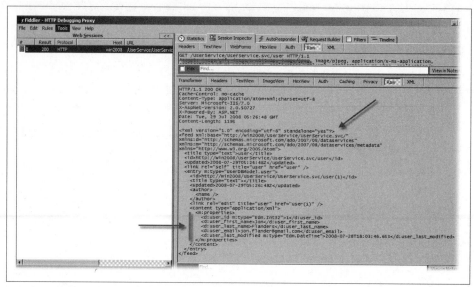

Figure B-3. ADO.NET Data Services feed in Fiddler

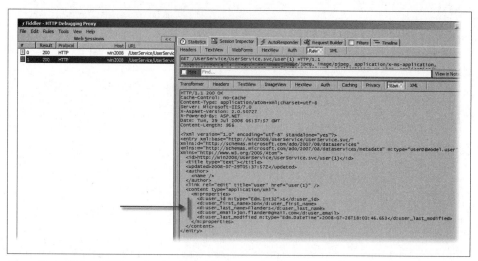

Figure B-4. ADO.NET Data Services individual entry

Notice that the entity has a link element where the `href` is `user(1)` (1 is the value of the key column of this entity). You can request that specific entity by doing a `GET` to that further URI (see Figure B-4).

ADO.NET Data Services will implement all the appropriate parts of the uniform interface based on the AtomPub specification and the access rights you set on the service during the call to `InitializeService`.

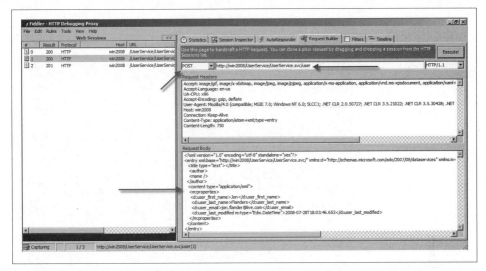

Figure B-5. POST to entity endpoint

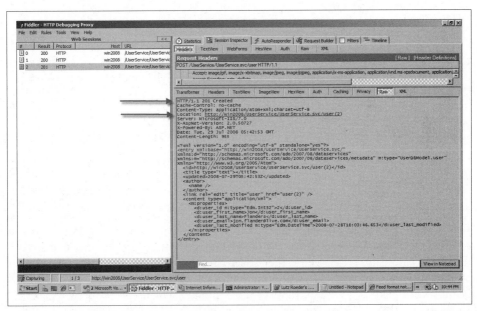

Figure B-6. ADO.NET Data Services POST response

For example, you can do an HTTP POST to the /user URI, passing in a new entry, and you'll get the expected HTTP status code of 201 with the Location header set to the URI of the newly created entity. Figure B-5 shows the POST data, and Figure B-6 shows the response from the ADO.NET Data Services endpoint.

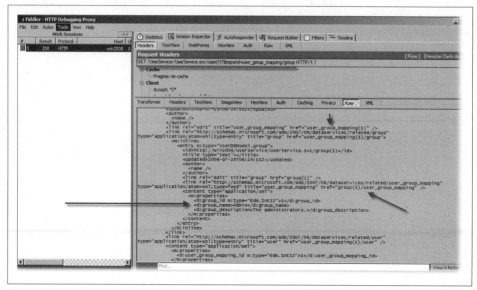

Figure B-7. Expand query option

I could continue to rehash the whole AtomPub protocol, but I already covered that in Appendix A. ADO.NET Data Services implements the AtomPub protocol in line with the specification, so the remainder of ADO.NET Data Services' basic capabilities can be inferred from AtomPub. Next, we'll look at ADO.NET Data Services features that aren't part of AtomPub.

Query Option

On top of the AtomPub functionality, ADO.NET Data Services also exposes advanced query capabilities for GET requests. Specifically, it supports additional query string options that will modify the result entity set in some way. These options correspond somewhat to the kinds of queries you might do if you were using relational data directly.

For example, if you want to see related entities when asking for a particular entity, you can use the $expand option to see the data from the mapping table for the many-to-many relationship between the user-to-group table (by using /user?$expand=user_group_mapping). Of course, this isn't as interesting as it would be if we could see the actual group names, which we can with /user?$expand=user_group_mapping/group (see Figure B-7).

Table B-1 shows the list of query options.

Table B-1. ADO.NET Data Services query string options

Option	Description	Examples
expand	Expands additional related entities	/user(1)?$expand=user_group_mapping
		/user(1)?$expand=user_group_mapping/group
orderby	Orders returned entities	/user?$orderby=user_email
		/user?$orderby=user_email desc
		/user?$orderby=user_email desc, user_last_name
top	Returns top *N* entities	/user?top=5
skip	Skips *N* entities	/user?$skip=10
		/user?$skip=10&$top=5
filter	Returns a set of entities based on a filter expression	/user?$filter=startswith(user_email,'j')
		/user?$filter=user_first_name ne 'Jon'

The `$filter` query option introduces an expression syntax, which you can see in Table B-2.

Table B-2. Expression syntax

Operator	Description	Type
eq	Equals	Logical
ne	Not equal to	Logical
gt	Greater than	Logical
gteq	Greater than or equal to	Logical
lt	Less than	Logical
lteq	Less than or equal to	Logical
not	Logical negation	Logical
or	Logical or	Logical
add	Addition	Math
sub	Subtraction	Math
mul	Multiplication	Math
div	Division	Math
mod	Modulo	Math
( )	Precedence	Grouping

Tables B-3, B-4, and B-5 show the different functions you can use within the expression syntax. Some are pretty self-explanatory, but I've added a description for each one.

Table B-3. String functions

Function	Description
`bool contains(string p0, string p1)`	Returns `true` if p0 contains p1
`bool endswith(string p0, string p1)`	Returns `true` if p0 ends with p1
`bool startswith(string p0, string p1)`	Returns `true` if p0 starts with p1
`int length(string p0)`	Returns the length of the string
`int indexof(string arg)`	Returns the index of the specified string
`string insert(string p0, int pos, string p1)`	Inserts p1 into p0 at the index of pos
`string remove(string p0, int pos)`	Removes characters from pos in p0
`string remove(string p0, int pos, int length)`	Removes the specified number of characters from p0 starting at the specified position
`string replace(string p0, string find, string replace)`	Finds the second parameter in p0 and replaces it with the third parameter
`string substring(string p0, int pos)`	Returns the substring from p0 from pos
`string substring(string p0, int pos, int length)`	Returns the substring up to `length` from p0 from pos
`string tolower(string p0)`	Converts the string to lowercase
`string toupper(string p0)`	Converts the string to uppercase

Table B-4. Date functions

Function	Description
`int day(DateTime p0)`	Gets the day of the week value from p0
`int hour(DateTime p0)`	Gets the hour value from p0
`int minute(DateTime p0)`	Gets the minute value from p0
`int month(DateTime p0)`	Gets the month value from p0
`int second(DateTime p0)`	Gets the second value from p0
`int year(DateTime p0)`	Gets the year value from p0

Table B-5. Numeric functions

Function	Description
`double round(double p0)`	Rounds p0
`decimal round(decimal p0)`	Rounds p0
`double floor(double p0)`	Gets the floor of p0
`decimal floor(decimal p0)`	Gets the floor of p0
`double ceiling(double p0)`	Gets the ceiling of p0
`decimal ceiling(decimal p0)`	Gets the ceiling of p0

Custom Service Operations

Another feature of ADO.NET is the capability to add additional methods to each endpoint. ADO.NET refers to these as *custom service operations*. Even though the `IRequestHandler` contract is predetermined as the contract for each endpoint, ADO.NET Data Services allows you to add additional "operations" to the `DataService` derived type. You can use this mechanism to add "helper" methods that simplify query functions you anticipate will be common.

In this example, imagine that a commonly performed query is to get the list of users that are in the Admin group. Certainly, you could do that with a query string expression, but a LINQ to Entities query could do this as well, and you can greatly simplify the URI for getting all the admins by adding a custom operation:

```
[WebGet()]
public IQueryable<user> admins()
{
    var result = from gm in this.CurrentDataSource.user_group_mapping
                 where gm.@group.group_name == "Admin"
                 select gm.user;
    return result;
}
```

You should also notice that this method includes `WebGetAttribute`, but not `OperationContractAttribute`. Since `ServiceContractAttribute` has already been applied to the `IRequestHandler` contract type, we can't use `OperationContractAttribute` here. ADO.NET Data Services is looking at this method and using `WebGetAttribute` itself to determine which messages to route to this method. For this to work, we have to add an additional line of code to the `InitializeService` method:

```
config.SetServiceOperationAccessRule("admins", ServiceOperationRights.AllRead);
```

Like access to the entities of the `DataContext` object, additional operations must have access rights turned on before they can be used.

An unfortunate limitation of this is that `UriTemplate` specialization can't be used; only the method name will be taken into account when routing messages to these special "operations." `WebInvokeAttribute` is supported, however, although without `UriTemplate` support. In this case, the URI would be `/admins`, since I named the method in the way I'd like the resource URI to look.

Also, note that in this case I am returning `IQueryable` of *T* as the return value of my method. ADO.NET Data Services also supports additional operations that return `IEnumerable` of *T*. An `IQueryable` return value will support the full set of additional query operators on top of the return set, where `IEnumerable` will not.

Intercepting

If you want to validate requests as they come into the ADO.NET Data Services endpoint (instead of returning specialized pieces of data), you can add methods to the `DataService`-derived class that will be called when particular entities are queried or changed.

You add `QueryInterceptorAttribute` to a method on your class that you want called when a particular entity is queried. You can add `ChangeInterceptorAttribute` to a method you want called whenever an entity is changed (created, updated, or deleted). Here is the code you can add to your `DataService`-derived type:

```
[ChangeInterceptor("user")]
public void OnChangeUser(user u, UpdateOperations operation)
{

}
[QueryInterceptor("user")]
public Expression<Func<user, bool>> InterceptQuery()
{
    return u => !String.IsNullOrEmpty(u.user_email);
}
```

Client Library

Another interesting piece of functionality ADO.NET Data Services offers is a client programming model. Having a client programming model in itself may not seem so interesting, but what makes it interesting is that it has a tool that will generate a proxy from metadata to wrap using ADO.NET Data Services from .NET code. Note that the metadata and the tool are not interoperable with any other languages or platforms; they are for .NET 3.5 SP1 and later only.

The metadata is exposed from a special URI. If you hit the URI of your ADO.NET Data Service with `/$metadata`, the service returns a special metadata document (see Figure B-8).

There isn't much point in going into detail on this XML because you generally don't ever request this URI directly; it is requested and processed by the *datasvcgen.exe* tool.

Datasvcgen.exe generates a code file that contains a set of classes you can use to interact with the ADO.NET Data Service:

```
datasvcgen.exe /out:proxy.cs /uri: http://win2008/UserService/UserService.svc
```

After the tool runs, the *proxy.cs* file contains entity types for all the different collections from the service, as well as a class that derives from `System.Data.Services.Client.Data ServiceContext`. This class is like the proxy that allows easy interaction with the service endpoint. Here is the code that uses this class to create a new user entity.

Figure B-8. ADO.NET Data Services metadata

```
Uri uri =
    new Uri("http://win2008/UserService/UserService.svc/");
UserDBEntities db = new UserDBEntities(uri);
user u = new user();
u.user_email = "jon.flander@gmail.com";
u.user_first_name = "Jon";
u.user_last_name = "Flanders";
u.user_last_modified = DateTime.Now;
db.AddTouser(u);
db.SaveChanges();
```

The `UserDBEntities` class is the main proxy and it contains a helper method to interact with the service endpoint. Distinct versions of the entity classes are also generated on the client side; the preceding code sample uses the user type.

Summary

ADO.NET Data Services is a rich framework for exposing data as an AtomPub-based RESTful endpoint. It works against any data model, but it works with the ADO.NET Entity Framework without any modification.

It enables you to expose entities from your data model as collections in an AtomPub service, and, through authorization restrictions, to determine which parts of the AtomPub RESTful model each entity will expose.

It builds on the AtomPub model with a sophisticated set of query operators for GET requests, and has a rich extensibility model for creating new URIs on top of the base URIs of the service. It also has hooks to enable you to get involved in query processing and data updating.

ADO.NET Data Services adds a client programming model that generates a .NET-callable class to simplify the interaction between your client code and the service endpoint.

ADO.NET Entity Framework Walkthrough

If you've read Appendix B and are interested in building an ADO.NET Entity Framework Entity Data Model (EDM) on top of a database for use with ADO.NET Data Services, this appendix provides a quick walkthrough of those steps.

Creating the Data Model

The first step is to add a new item to your Visual Studio 2008 SP1 project. The Add New Item dialog box contains a template for an ADO.NET Data Model (see Figure C-1). Select this template to start the ADO.NET Entity Data Model Wizard (see Figure C-2).

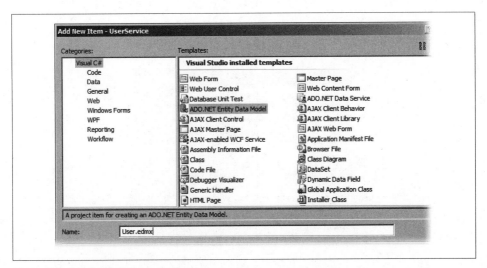

Figure C-1. ADO.NET EDM template

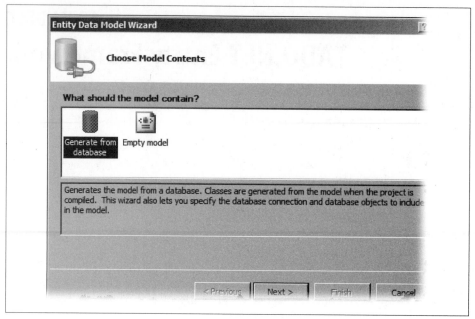

Figure C-2. Page 1 of the Entity Data Model Wizard

The first page of the wizard asks whether you want to generate an EDM on top of a relational database or create an empty EDM that can be manually modeled and mapped to a data source. Select Generate from Database. On the next page, specify the connection string for the EDM generation, and whether you want the connection string saved into the project's configuration file (see Figure C-3).

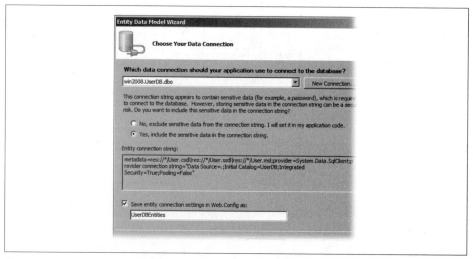

Figure C-3. Entity Data Model Wizard connection string picker

After you select the connection string, the wizard moves on to a type picker page, where you can select the entities from the database you want the wizard to use when generating the model (see Figure C-4).

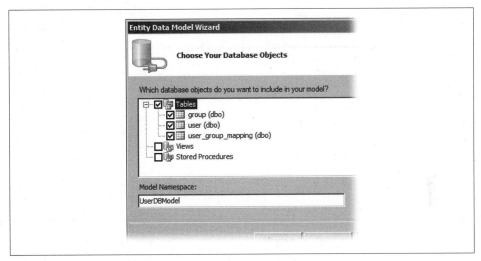

Figure C-4. Entity Data Model Wizard database object picker

In this case, I've selected all the tables I have in this database, and since I don't have any views or stored procedures, I can select Finish. After you click Finish, the wizard generates an *.edmx* file, which is a file that has the ADO.NET EDM designer associated with it. You can see this in Figure C-5.

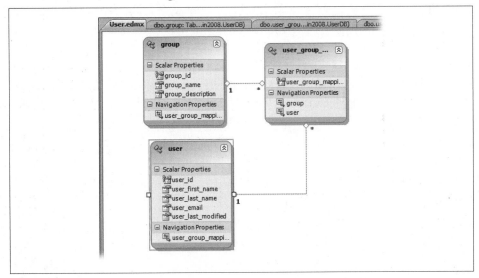

Figure C-5. EDM designer

The *.edmx* file contains three pieces of XML relating to the EDM model. It contains the storage model, the conceptual model, and the mapping of the conceptual model to the storage model (see Figure C-6).

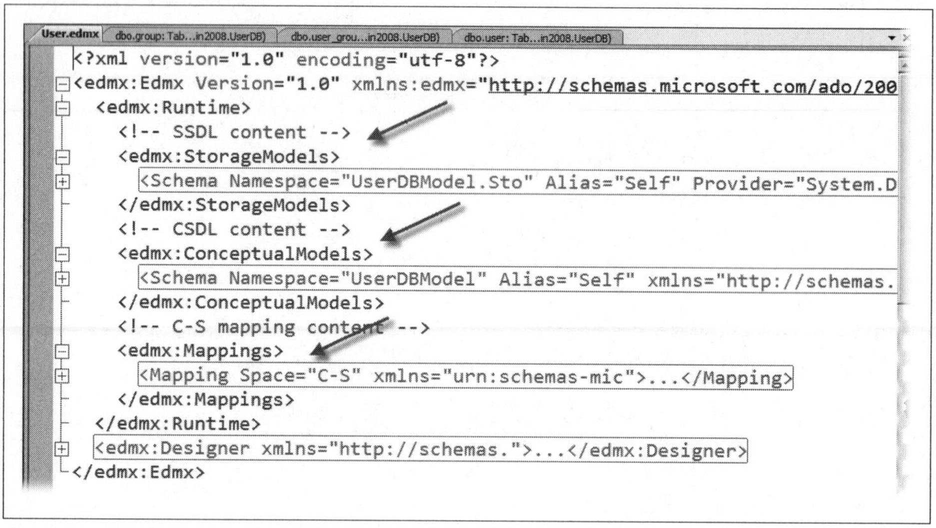

Figure C-6. The .edmx XML view

For more information on the details of the ADO.NET Entity Data Model and Entity Framework (which is the first implementation of the EDM), see *http://msdn.microsoft .com/en-us/library/bb399572.aspx*.

Once the *.edmx* file has been created, the ADO.NET `ObjectContext`-derived class will be available to your project. Now you can create an ADO.NET Data Service from the Add New Item dialog box (see Figure C-7).

When you add this template to your project, it creates the *.svc* file that references the correct service type and uses the `DataServiceHostFactory` class as its factory. This class must be modified before it can work, however, since the template leaves open the data context type (the generic *T*). The code will look like Example C-1 when generated.

Example C-1. DataService generated code

```
using System;
using System.Data.Services;
using System.Collections.Generic;
using System.Linq;
using System.ServiceModel.Web;

public class UserService : DataService< /* TODO: put your data source
 class name here */ >
{
    // This method is called only once to initialize service-wide policies.
    public static void InitializeService(IDataServiceConfiguration config)
```

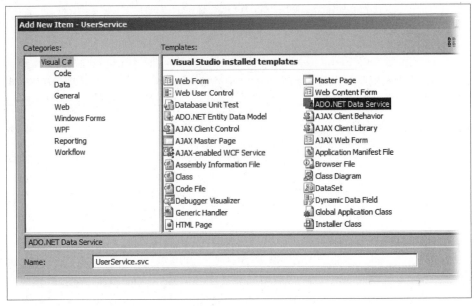

Figure C-7. ADO.NET Data Services template

```
    {
        // TODO: set rules to indicate which entity sets and service operations are
        //visible, updatable, etc.
        // For testing purposes use "*" to indicate all entity sets/service
        //operations.
        // "*" should NOT be used in production systems.

        // Example for entity sets (this example uses "AllRead" which allows reads
        //but not writes)
        // config.SetEntitySetAccessRule("MyEntityset", EntitySetRights.AllRead);

        // Example for service operations
        // config.SetServiceOperationAccessRule("MyServiceOperation",
        //      ServiceOperationRights.All);
    }

    // Query interceptors, change interceptors and service operations go here
}
```

To make the *.svc* file work, set the `DataContext` object on the `DataService` of *T*. Next, call `IDataServiceConfiguration.SetEntitySetAccessRule` to authorize at least one entity. See Example C-2.

Example C-2. DataService derived type

```
public class UserService : DataService<UserDataContext>
{
    public static void InitializeService(
                IDataServiceConfiguration config)
    {
```

```
        config.SetEntitySetAccessRule("*", EntitySetRights.All);
    }
}
```

You can also remove all the comments for clarity. In this case, I used the * wildcard to get all access rights to all entities, which the comments I deleted warned against doing. I did this for development testing; you should stick with the comments and enable specific access rights on specific entities. At this point, the ADO.NET Data Service should work.

Index

We'd like to hear your suggestions for improving our indexes. Send email to *index@oreilly.com*.

About the Author

Although **Jon Flanders** spent the first few years of his professional life as an attorney, he quickly found chasing bits more interesting than chasing ambulances. After working with ASP and COM, he made the move to .NET. Jon is most at home spelunking and trying to figure out exactly how .NET (specifically, ASP.NET and Visual Studio .NET) works. Deducing the details and disseminating that information to other developers is his passion.

Colophon

The animal on the cover of *RESTful .NET* is an electric catfish (*Siluriformes malapteruridae*). Located mainly in tropical Africa and the Nile River, the generally nocturnal catfish can produce an electric shock of up to 350 volts, which it uses to stun or kill its enemies (the shock is not fatal to humans).

Often seen in large display tanks at aquariums, the electric catfish has thick lips and a cylinder-shaped, pinkish-brown body with several dark spots. The fish's electric organ—used to generate shocks—extends the length of its body, and, when lit, helps the fish see through its murky surroundings.

In the normal course of its waking hours, the fish acts aggressively against other fish and even against others of its own kind. Each successive shock its electric organ produces, however, weakens the fish, which then must rest in order to "recharge" its electricity, thus rendering it temporarily vulnerable to predators. The fish is also vulnerable for another reason: its body has no scales or bony plates, making the fish relatively defenseless against hot aquarium tanks or sharp rocks.

The cover image is from *Dover's Animals*. The cover font is Adobe ITC Garamond. The text font is Linotype Birka; the heading font is Adobe Myriad Condensed; and the code font is LucasFont's TheSansMonoCondensed.

Related Titles from O'Reilly

.NET and C#

ADO.NET Cookbook

ADO.NET 3.5 Cookbook,
  2nd Edition

ASP.NET 2.0 Cookbook,
  2nd Edition

ASP.NET 2.0: A Developer's
  Notebook

Building an ASP.NET Web 2.0 Portal

C# 3.0 in a Nutshell, *3rd Edition*

C# Cookbook, *2nd Edition*

C# Design Patterns

C# in a Nutshell, *2nd Edition*

C# Language Pocket Reference

Exchange Server 2007
  Administration: The Definitive
  Guide

Head First C#

Learning ASP.NET 2.0 with AJAX

Learning C# 2005, *2nd Edition*

Learning WCF

MCSE Core Elective Exams in a
  Nutshell

.NET and XML

.NET Gotchas

Programming Atlas

Programming ASP.NET, *3rd Edition*

Programming ASP.NET AJAX

Programming C#, *4th Edition*

Programming MapPoint in .NET

Programming .NET 3.5

Programming .NET Components,
  2nd Edition

Programming .NET Security

Programming .NET Web Services

Programming Visual Basic 2005

Programming WCF Services

Programming WPF, *2nd Edition*

Programming Windows Presentation
  Foundation

Programming the .NET Compact
  Framework

Visual Basic 2005: A Developer's
  Notebook

Visual Basic 2005 Cookbook

Visual Basic 2005 in a Nutshell,
  3rd Edition

Visual Basic 2005 Jumpstart

Visual C# 2005: A Developer's
  Notebook

Visual Studio Hacks

Windows Developer Power Tools

XAML in a Nutshell

O'REILLY®

The O'Reilly Advantage

Stay Current and Save Money